MILITARY UNIFORMS
VISUAL ENCYCLOPEDIA

MILITARY UNIFORMS
VISUAL ENCYCLOPEDIA

amber
BOOKS

This edition first published in 2011

Published by
Amber Books Ltd
Bradley's Close
74–77 White Lion Street
London N1 9PF
United Kingdom
www.amberbooks.co.uk

ISBN: 978-1-908273-02-4

Project Editor: Sarah Uttridge
Design: Zoë Mellors

Printed in China

CONTENTS

INTRODUCTION

Uniforms as we understand them today – standardized items of dress issued to formations or armies – are actually quite a recent phenomenon. Roman, Greek, Byzantine and other ancient armies certainly had homogenous aspects to their appearance, including the use of specific colours to signal unit membership, but such were not general policy.

During the medieval period, some formations, such as knights loyal to a particular lord or the Janissaries of the Ottoman army, would strike a common form of dress, but such was often more to do with tribal or social loyalties rather than militarized clothing. Individual improvization in clothing and kit was common.

The Birth of Uniforms

Military uniforms proper are largely the creation of the 17th century, as the birth of the regimental system (initially in France) brought with it the issue of dress regulations. It took until the establishment of standing armies for this system to become permanent, and from the 18th century it became typical for soldiers to wear common, regulated uniforms, but with unit, formation and branch allegiance denoted in facing colours. Naval uniforms also put down roots from the 18th century, although until the mid 1800s many navies only dictated officer dress.

Until the late 19th century, and even beyond, the uniforms of land armies paid few concessions to the principles of camouflage and concealment we so value today. Bright colours, ostentatious headgear, and all manner of braids, tassels and plumes declared open pride and tradition. (The plainer uniforms of the American Civil War provided a notable exception.) The 20th century would change the situation dramatically.

Modern Uniforms

By the 1890s, breech-loading weapons (both artillery and firearms) had made the battlefield an increasingly lethal place. Steadily, uniforms began to lose their dramatic colours, becoming plainer to serve purposes of utility and rudimentary camouflage – increasingly, to be visible was to be dead. World War I cemented the changes, and by the end of the conflict most troops were dressed in plain olive-drab or grey uniforms, with their equipment carried in utilitarian webbing systems. The advent of air power also established an entirely new pattern of service dress. World War II brought change as well as continuity. Camouflage designed specifically to break up the silhouette of the wearer was introduced, and numerous specialist uniforms emerged for different technological roles, from paratroopers to bomber pilots. Following the war, advanced technologies steadily transformed uniforms and personal load-carrying equipment, in modern armies at least (this book will show plenty of exceptions). From the 1960s in particular, advanced materials, refined camouflages and ergonomic webbing systems gave soldiers a level of comfort and practicality never before attained. Future improvements under development at the time of writing include computers embedded directly in the uniforms, camouflages that change colour with the terrain, and active systems to control the wearer's temperature. Uniforms are likely to become even more integrated with the way soldiers fight and survive on the battlefield.

Above: A marine from the 1st Battalion 6th Marine Regiment directs his patrol through a street in Fallujah, Iraq.

18TH CENTURY

Military uniforms are a relatively recent phenomenon. Although soldiers have always had a recognizably militaristic appearance, and have shared common pieces of dress and equipment, it was largely only from the 17th century that military uniforms were centrally regulated.

The standardization of uniforms at first took the form of specific pieces of regimental or arm-of-service dress, such as a red coat for the English 2nd Regiment of Foot, issued from 1686. Over the next two centuries, the regulations became more comprehensive, until everything from footwear to load-carrying systems were specified.

Left: John Trumbull's famous painting *The Death of General Mercer at the Battle of Princeton* shows typical infantry and cavalry uniforms at the end of the 18th century, including those of the famous British 'redcoats'.

European Officers and NCOs

Officers of the 18th century dressed with a high degree of flourish and flamboyance, with little in the way of true battlefield practicality. Their uniforms, however, were visible declarations of both authority and martial tradition, and set them apart from the general ranks of men.

General Officer ▶
Austrian Army

Austrian officers of general rank and above had considerable liberty in their uniforms until 1751, when a white half-length coat was introduced. The officer here is wearing a parade uniform that includes sashes indicating social rank, a gold-edged tricorne hat and field officer's boots.

SPECIFICATIONS	
Country:	Austria
Date:	c. 1780
Unit:	Austrian Army
Rank:	General
Theatre:	Europe
Location:	Unknown

Field Marshal ▶
Austrian Army

This Austrian Army cavalry field marshal wears a classic red-lined parade coat with the rank indicated by the gold ribbon stripes on the jacket and cuffs. Regulatory distinctions between parade dress and field dress were not made in the Austrian Army until 1798.

SPECIFICATIONS	
Country:	Austria
Date:	c. 1780
Unit:	Austrian Army
Rank:	Field marshal
Theatre:	Europe
Location:	Unknown

c. 1780

1795

1790s

◀ Officer
Parham Yeomanry

The Parham Yeomanry was a cavalry force raised in October 1795. The officer's uniform here is distinguished by a green jacket with white facings, white cavalry breeches, and a matching green and white plume on the headdress. Note also the shabrack (saddlecloth), typical of British light cavalry.

SPECIFICATIONS	
Country:	Britain
Date:	1795
Unit:	Parham Yeomanry
Rank:	Officer
Theatre:	Europe
Location:	England

Grenadier Sergeant ▶
79th Highlanders

This grenadier sergeant of the 79th Highlanders wears a green kilt plus a red jacket with matching green facings. The white hackle on the headdress indicated the role of grenadier. Tartan pantaloons, known as 'trews', were seen in some Highland regiments from the 1790s.

SPECIFICATIONS	
Country:	Britain
Date:	1790s
Unit:	79th Highlanders
Rank:	Grenadier sergeant
Theatre:	Europe
Location:	Scotland

Soldiers of the Seven Years' War 1756–63

The Seven Years' War brought about some general changes in the uniforms of Europe's great armies. In terms of field uniform, there was an increasing emphasis on lightness, although many items still remained impractical.

◀ General Officer
French Army

This Prussian general wears a flamboyant dark blue velvet jacket over a red tunic. He also has knee-high cavalry boots, complete with spurs. Hung on loops on his left hip is the classic officer's rapier/smallsword, worn more for display than for combat use.

SPECIFICATIONS	
Country:	Saxony
Date:	c. 1756
Unit:	French Army
Rank:	General
Theatre:	Europe
Location:	Unknown

Officer ▶
La Reine Cavalry

The colour scheme of the famous La Reine ('The Queen') cavalry consisted of a red coat with blue facings, worn over a light yellow waistcoat and breeches. Note also the white buttons – French cavalry buttons were either yellow or white, depending on the regiment.

SPECIFICATIONS	
Country:	France
Date:	c. 1756
Unit:	La Reine Cavalry Regiment
Rank:	Officer
Theatre:	North America
Location:	Nova Scotia

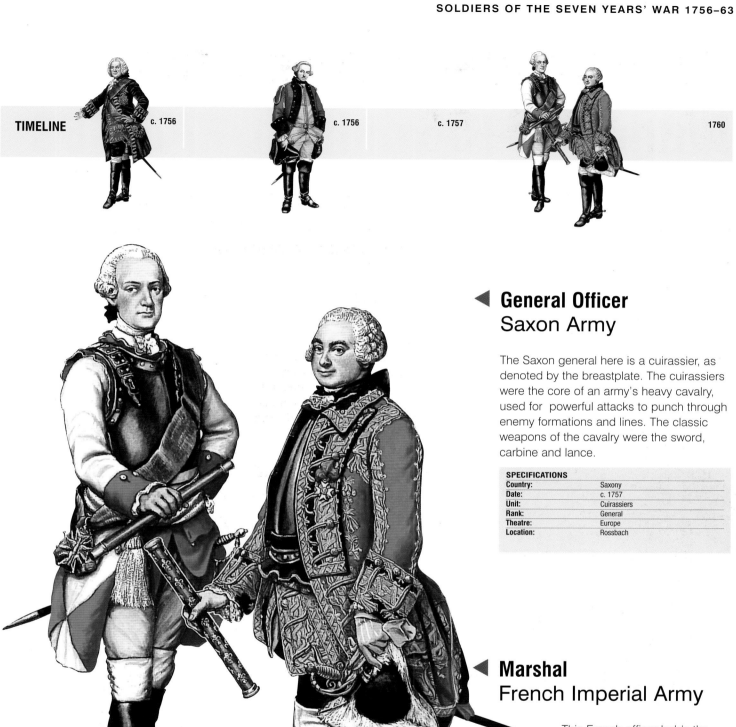

◄ General Officer
Saxon Army

The Saxon general here is a cuirassier, as denoted by the breastplate. The cuirassiers were the core of an army's heavy cavalry, used for powerful attacks to punch through enemy formations and lines. The classic weapons of the cavalry were the sword, carbine and lance.

SPECIFICATIONS	
Country:	Saxony
Date:	c. 1757
Unit:	Cuirassiers
Rank:	General
Theatre:	Europe
Location:	Rossbach

◄ Marshal
French Imperial Army

This French officer holds the highest symbol of authority in the French Army. The Marshal of France baton was covered in dark blue velvet fabric, accented by gold fleur de lys. By the 1770s, the Marshal of France rank was indicated by silver crossed batons, surrounded by silver stars, set on gold epaulettes.

SPECIFICATIONS	
Country:	France
Date:	1760
Unit:	French Army
Rank:	Marshal of France
Theatre:	Europe
Location:	Unknown

French Naval Infantry: American Revolution 1775–83

Although the American Revolutionary War was principally a war between Britain and its colony, it brought in many other combatants, including France, Spain and various Native American nations. The French Navy clashed with its British counterpart off the American coast in some major engagements.

Ville de Paris

The *Ville de Paris* was a French ship of the line completed in 1764. Armed with 90 guns, including 30 36-pdrs, she served with distinction during the American Revolutionary War in flagship roles, but sank during a storm in 1782.

Charleville Musket

The Charleville musket was a standardized French musket produced during the 18th century. It was a smoothbore weapon with a calibre of 17.5mm (0.69in), and had an accurate range (depending on the user and the way the gun was loaded) of 50–100m (164–328ft). All the furniture on the naval model was produced in brass.

Officer
Corps Royale de l'infanterie de la Marine

This officer in the French marines has the dark blue uniform adopted by the French Navy during the second half of the 18th century. Other items of standard naval dress include the white stockings with slender black shoes and the gold-edged officer's hat. He holds a naval cutlass at the ready.

SPECIFICATIONS	
Country:	France
Date:	1780
Unit:	French Naval Infantry
Rank:	Officer
Theatre:	North America
Location:	Unknown

WARS OF REVOLUTION 1789–1914

The late 18th and 19th centuries were a time of great upheaval, with major wars fought on most continents, including the Napoleonic Wars in Europe and the American Civil War in the United States.

At the beginning of the 19th century, soldiers went to war with flintlock muskets and bayonets, but by the end of the century they were equipped with bolt-action breech-loading rifles and machine guns. Similar transformations affected artillery, naval warfare and communications.

Left: Union forces go on the attack during the American Civil War (1861–65). Uniforms were now losing much of the ostentation of the previous century, not least because of the huge scale of industrial-era armies.

French Army of the Revolutionary Wars 1792–1802

The French Revolution of 1789 ushered in a new age of military service in France. The *levée en masse* ('mass levy') of the 1790s conscripted hundreds of thousands of French citizens into the armed services.

◀ Infantryman
Les bleus

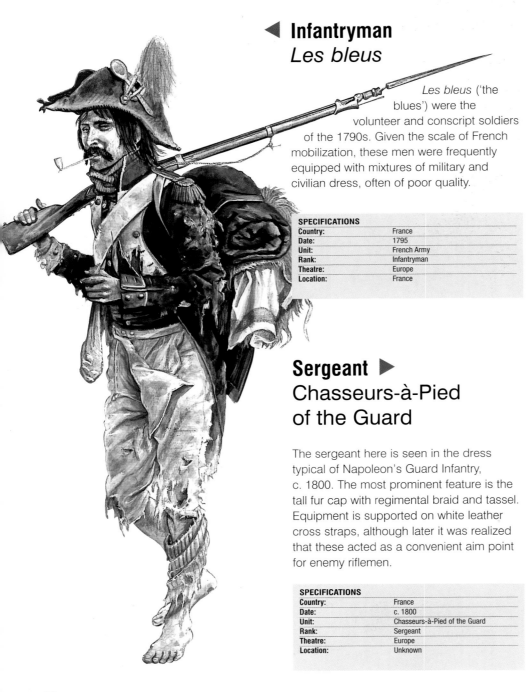

Les bleus ('the blues') were the volunteer and conscript soldiers of the 1790s. Given the scale of French mobilization, these men were frequently equipped with mixtures of military and civilian dress, often of poor quality.

SPECIFICATIONS	
Country:	France
Date:	1795
Unit:	French Army
Rank:	Infantryman
Theatre:	Europe
Location:	France

Sergeant ▶
Chasseurs-à-Pied of the Guard

The sergeant here is seen in the dress typical of Napoleon's Guard Infantry, c. 1800. The most prominent feature is the tall fur cap with regimental braid and tassel. Equipment is supported on white leather cross straps, although later it was realized that these acted as a convenient aim point for enemy riflemen.

SPECIFICATIONS	
Country:	France
Date:	c. 1800
Unit:	Chasseurs-à-Pied of the Guard
Rank:	Sergeant
Theatre:	Europe
Location:	Unknown

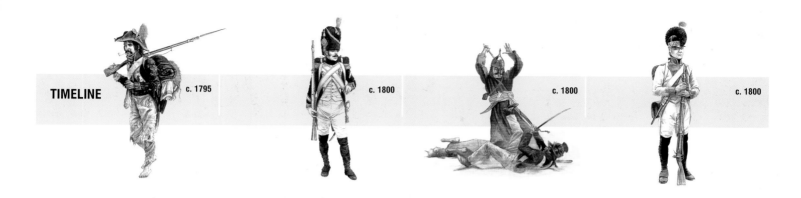

| TIMELINE | c. 1795 | | c. 1800 | | c. 1800 | | c. 1800 |

Infantryman ▶
Les blancs infantry

The regular French Army infantry were known as *les blancs* ('the whites'), after the white uniform adopted in 1786. This infantryman wears the 'Tarleton' type helmet, the tip of the plume accenting the regimental facing colours.

SPECIFICATIONS

Country:	France
Date:	c. 1800
Unit:	French Army
Rank:	Infantryman
Theatre:	Europe
Location:	France

French Grenadier ▼
9e Demi-Brigade de Bataille

A French grenadier finds himself in a sticky situation facing a Mameluke warrior. He wears the uniform typical of French soldiers at the turn of the 19th century, and he is defending himself with the AN XI pattern curved sabre.

SPECIFICATIONS

Country:	France
Date:	c. 1800
Unit:	9e Demi-Brigade de Bataille
Rank:	Grenadier
Theatre:	Europe
Location:	Spain

European Infantry 1795–1813

By the Napoleonic Wars, musket-armed infantry and artillery had largely replaced the cavalry as the arm of decision on the battlefield. Infantry uniforms made some nods towards practicality, but were still largely more concerned with form over function, and were often poorly suited to long campaigns.

◀ Trooper
Warwickshire Yeomanry

The Warwickshire Yeomanry was raised in 1794, and throughout its history operated both as cavalry and as dismounted infantry. The trooper here is evidently a mounted soldier, and is armed with a 1796-pattern light cavalry sabre.

SPECIFICATIONS	
Country:	Britain
Date:	c. 1798
Unit:	Warwickshire Yeomanry
Rank:	Trooper
Theatre:	Europe
Location:	Britain

Fusilier ▶
Line Infantry

This French fusilier wears the pre-1806 uniform, indicated by the bicorne hat that was largely replaced by a shako by 1807. The bicorne bore a tricolour cockade, although plumes and pompoms of various types and colours were also used by specific companies and battalions.

SPECIFICATIONS	
Country:	France
Date:	c. 1805
Unit:	French Infantry
Rank:	Fusilier
Theatre:	Europe
Location:	Unknown

TIMELINE

c. 1798

c. 1805

c. 1805

c. 1808

◀ **Private**
Royal Corsican Rangers

The Royal Corsican Rangers were formed under British leadership from Corsican secessionists in 1798. They served in Egypt against Napoleon before being temporarily disbanded in 1802; the force was reformed in 1803 as an official British Army unit.

SPECIFICATIONS	
Country:	Corsica
Date:	c. 1805
Unit:	Royal Corsican Rangers
Rank:	Private
Theatre:	Europe
Location:	Italy

Private ▶
Royal York Rangers

This private of the Royal York Rangers is seen firing his carbine. The black leather cartridge pouch, which typically carried about 36 cartridges, hangs on his right hip. For a headdress he wears the plumed infantry shako.

SPECIFICATIONS	
Country:	Britain
Date:	c. 1808
Unit:	Royal York Rangers
Rank:	Infantryman
Theatre:	Americas
Location:	Caribbean

European Infantry 1795–1813

The first half of the 19th century saw military uniforms retain a high degree of ostentatious display, especially among the cavalry and officers. There could be a major distinction, however, between the peacock-like image of the parade dress and the realities of campaign uniforms.

◀ Gunner
Royal Artillery

While the Royal Horse Artillery, formed in 1793, tended to have a cavalry-like appearance, the Foot Artillery dressed more in the manner of line infantry. The short artilleryman's jacket was dark blue with red collar, cuffs and shoulder straps, and was worn with a black shako.

SPECIFICATIONS	
Country:	Britain
Date:	c. 1808
Unit:	Royal Artillery
Rank:	Gunner
Theatre:	Europe
Location:	Spain

Trooper ▶
King's German Legion

The King's German Legion was a mixed-arms force formed from German soldiers displaced by Napoleonic invasion in 1803. This cavalry trooper wears the pelisse and barrel sash typical of the hussars, and is armed with a short carbine.

SPECIFICATIONS	
Country:	Hanover
Date:	1811
Unit:	King's German Legion
Rank:	Trooper
Theatre:	Europe
Location:	Spain

c. 1808   1811   1812   1812

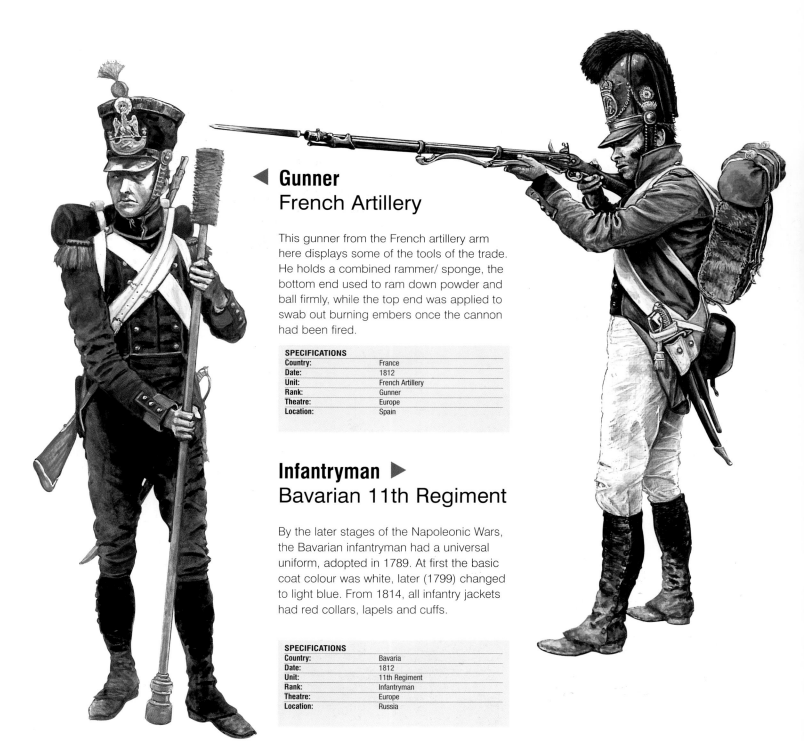

◀ Gunner
French Artillery

This gunner from the French artillery arm here displays some of the tools of the trade. He holds a combined rammer/ sponge, the bottom end used to ram down powder and ball firmly, while the top end was applied to swab out burning embers once the cannon had been fired.

SPECIFICATIONS	
Country:	France
Date:	1812
Unit:	French Artillery
Rank:	Gunner
Theatre:	Europe
Location:	Spain

Infantryman ▶
Bavarian 11th Regiment

By the later stages of the Napoleonic Wars, the Bavarian infantryman had a universal uniform, adopted in 1789. At first the basic coat colour was white, later (1799) changed to light blue. From 1814, all infantry jackets had red collars, lapels and cuffs.

SPECIFICATIONS	
Country:	Bavaria
Date:	1812
Unit:	11th Regiment
Rank:	Infantryman
Theatre:	Europe
Location:	Russia

European Cavalry 1810–12

Cavalry were the most aesthetically impressive force on the European battlefields, despite the fact that artillery and musketry were steadily eroding their authority in winning engagements.

Lancer, 2nd Chevau-légers Lanciers
Imperial Guard

This lancer displays his primary weapon – a lance several metres long – while a light pattern cavalry sabre hangs down at the rear. The headdress is the tall Polish-style *czapka*, which on campaign was typically protected by an oilskin cover, as seen here.

SPECIFICATIONS	
Country:	France
Date:	c. 1810
Unit:	2nd Chevau-légers Lanciers
Rank:	Lancer
Theatre:	Europe
Location:	Unknown

Officer ▶
13th Light Dragoons

Prior to 1830, the 13th Dragoons (as with all British light dragoon regiments) had blue double-breasted jackets. The 13th contrasted with similar regiments, however, by having gold lacing instead of silver. This officer carries a 1796 light cavalry sabre.

SPECIFICATIONS	
Country:	Britain
Date:	1810
Unit:	13th Light Dragoons
Rank:	Officer
Theatre:	Europe
Location:	Spain

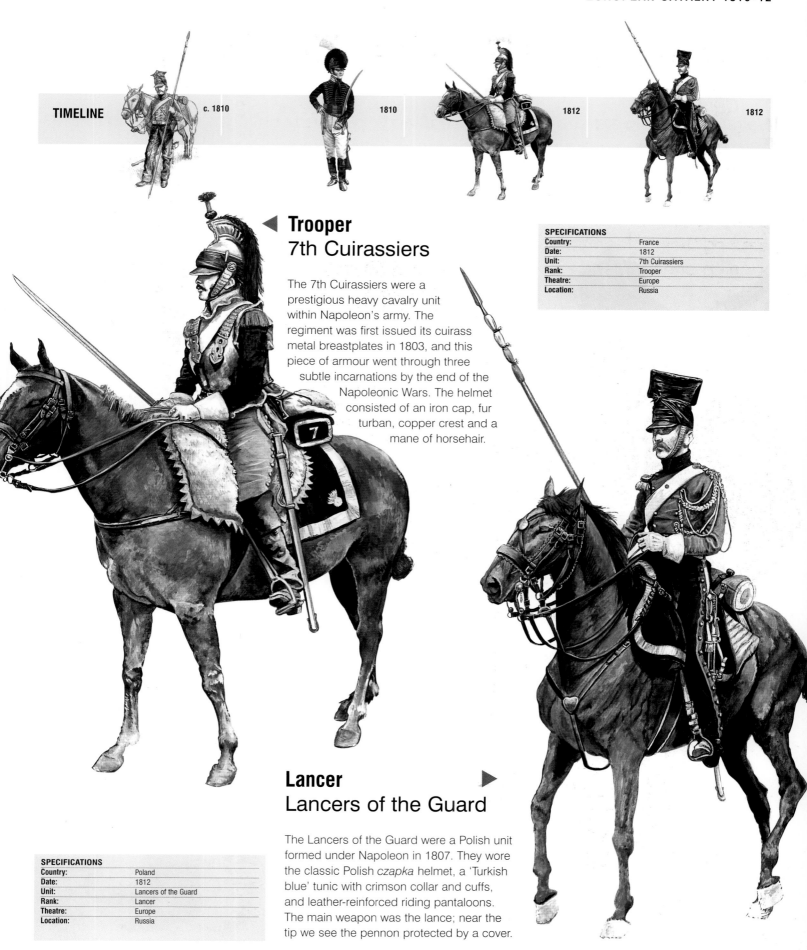

c. 1810

1810

1812

1812

Trooper
7th Cuirassiers

The 7th Cuirassiers were a prestigious heavy cavalry unit within Napoleon's army. The regiment was first issued its cuirass metal breastplates in 1803, and this piece of armour went through three subtle incarnations by the end of the Napoleonic Wars. The helmet consisted of an iron cap, fur turban, copper crest and a mane of horsehair.

SPECIFICATIONS	
Country:	France
Date:	1812
Unit:	7th Cuirassiers
Rank:	Trooper
Theatre:	Europe
Location:	Russia

Lancer
Lancers of the Guard

The Lancers of the Guard were a Polish unit formed under Napoleon in 1807. They wore the classic Polish *czapka* helmet, a 'Turkish blue' tunic with crimson collar and cuffs, and leather-reinforced riding pantaloons. The main weapon was the lance; near the tip we see the pennon protected by a cover.

SPECIFICATIONS	
Country:	Poland
Date:	1812
Unit:	Lancers of the Guard
Rank:	Lancer
Theatre:	Europe
Location:	Russia

Naval Personnel 1802–13

Naval uniforms were subject to less regularity than army uniforms until well into the 19th century, although similar approaches to styles and colour schemes often produced a standardized appearance among the world's navies.

◀ Marine
Royal Marines

This marine's classic red British Army tunic includes Royal Marine blue facings, and he wears a full-brimmed 'round hat' that stood about 15cm (6in) from the crown of the head. He is taking aim with his Sea Service Pattern version of the army's Land Pattern musket.

SPECIFICATIONS	
Country:	Britain
Date:	c. 1805
Unit:	Royal Marines
Rank:	Marine
Theatre:	Unknown
Location:	Unknown

Post-Captain ▶
Royal Navy

Royal Navy uniform was highly influential on many foreign styles of naval dress. The post-captain here wears the basic blue and white colour scheme established by George II in 1748. His tunic features the heavy epaulettes introduced in 1795.

SPECIFICATIONS	
Country:	Britain
Date:	1805
Unit:	Royal Navy
Rank:	Post-Captain
Theatre:	Mediterranean
Location:	Unknown

TIMELINE

c. 1805   1805   1805   1805

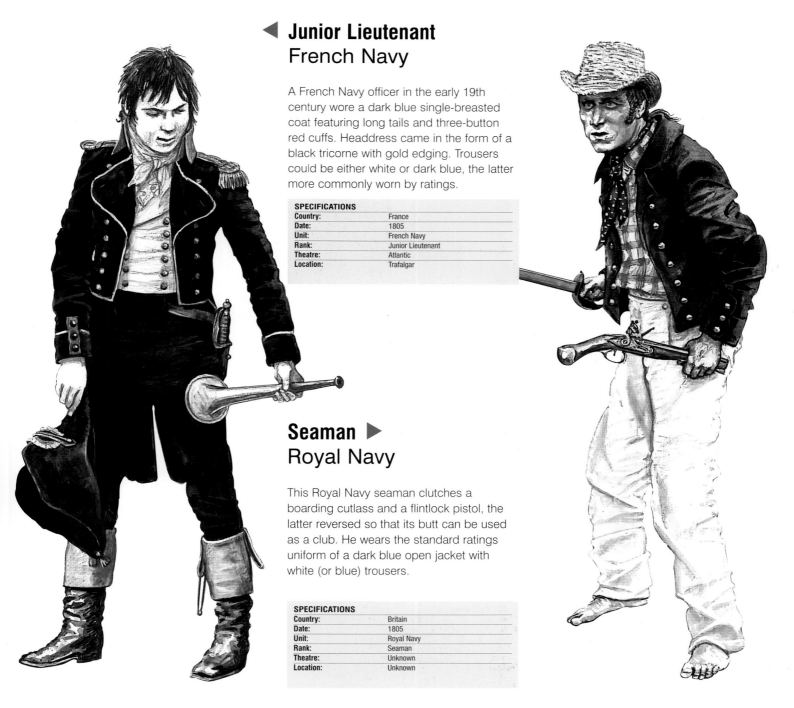

◀ Junior Lieutenant
French Navy

A French Navy officer in the early 19th century wore a dark blue single-breasted coat featuring long tails and three-button red cuffs. Headdress came in the form of a black tricorne with gold edging. Trousers could be either white or dark blue, the latter more commonly worn by ratings.

SPECIFICATIONS	
Country:	France
Date:	1805
Unit:	French Navy
Rank:	Junior Lieutenant
Theatre:	Atlantic
Location:	Trafalgar

Seaman ▶
Royal Navy

This Royal Navy seaman clutches a boarding cutlass and a flintlock pistol, the latter reversed so that its butt can be used as a club. He wears the standard ratings uniform of a dark blue open jacket with white (or blue) trousers.

SPECIFICATIONS	
Country:	Britain
Date:	1805
Unit:	Royal Navy
Rank:	Seaman
Theatre:	Unknown
Location:	Unknown

Peninsular Campaign Infantry 1808–14

The Peninsular War between 1808 and 1814 made the Iberian Peninsula one of the bloodiest theatres in the Napoleonic Wars. The fighting there ground down the French Army in particular, contributing to its final defeat in 1815.

◀ Private
95th Rifles

The green uniform of the 95th Rifles was a crude early attempt at camouflage, reflecting the regiment's role as sharpshooters and skirmishers. This soldier stands with his Baker rifle, which could deliver accurate fire to distances of 150m (492ft) and beyond.

SPECIFICATIONS	
Country:	Britain
Date:	1808
Unit:	95th Rifles
Rank:	Private
Theatre:	Iberian Peninsula
Location:	Spain

Corporal ▶
Grenadier Company, 1st Battalion, 45th Regiment of Foot (Nottinghamshire)

This British infantry corporal – his rank clearly indicated on his sleeve – carries the typical equipment of a British redcoat in the Peninsular War. Underneath the rolled blanket would be a black lacquered knapsack that held the soldier's personal belongings and kit.

SPECIFICATIONS	
Country:	Britain
Date:	1809
Unit:	45th Regiment of Foot
Rank:	Corporal
Theatre:	Iberian Peninsula
Location:	Spain

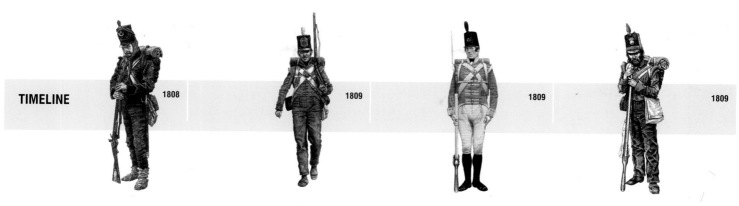

TIMELINE   1808   1809   1809   1809

◀ Private
52nd Foot (Oxfordshire Light Infantry)

The British light infantry in the Peninsular War largely dressed in the same manner as their line infantry breathren, with regimental distinctions. This private clearly displays the embroidered red coat and 'stove-pipe' shako, which features the green plume of the light infantry.

SPECIFICATIONS	
Country:	Britain
Date:	1809
Unit:	52nd Foot
Rank:	Private
Theatre:	Iberian Peninsula
Location:	Portugal

Infantryman ▶
British Army

This line infantryman illustrates the state to which a previously impressive uniform could deteriorate when on campaign. The bag hung over the left hip is a British Army ration bag, typically made out of canvas or rough linen, and containing three days' rations.

SPECIFICATIONS	
Country:	Britain
Date:	1809
Unit:	British Army
Rank:	Private
Theatre:	Iberian Peninsula
Location:	Unknown

Peninsular Campaign Infantry 1808–14

The Peninsular War pitted Spain, Portugal and the United Kingdom against the talents of Napoleon's army. The French, however, also had to contend with the actions of local partisans, who prosecuted a brutal guerrilla war.

◀ Rifleman
5th Cazadores

The 5th Cazadores was a Portuguese Army unit, raised in late 1808 and seeing subsequent heavy service in the Peninsular War. While many Portuguese units had blue uniforms, the Cazadores wore green, with red regimental collars and cuffs.

SPECIFICATIONS	
Country:	Portugal
Date:	1810
Unit:	5th Cazadores
Rank:	Rifleman
Theatre:	Iberian Peninsula
Location:	Portugal

Carabinier ▶
1st Neapolitan Light Infantry

The uniforms worn by the infantry of the Italian states during the Napoleonic Wars varied considerably, with tunics ranging from green and French blue (some regiments were equipped with French kit) through to white (from 1806). This distressed carabinier adopts the French style.

SPECIFICATIONS	
Country:	Italy
Date:	1811
Unit:	1st Neapolitan Light Infantry
Rank:	Carabinier
Theatre:	Iberian Peninsula
Location:	Unknown

TIMELINE

1810

1811

1811

1811

Sergeant
9th (East Norfolk) Regiment

A British Army line infantryman makes a fearsome charge with a sergeant's pike. He wears the short-tailed 1797 jacket with white breeches and the distinctive stove-pipe felt shako hat. During the Napoleonic wars, British line infantry sergeants were issued with half-pikes.

SPECIFICATIONS	
Country:	Britain
Date:	1811
Unit:	9th (East Norfolk) Regiment
Rank:	Sergeant
Theatre:	Iberian Peninsula
Location:	Spain

Sergeant ▶
88th Regiment of Foot (Connaught Rangers)

The 88th Regiment of Foot was formed in Ireland in September 1793. It came to take the nickname 'the Devil's Own', and fought with distinction during the Peninsular War, leading the charge at Fuentes de Oñoro in 1811. This sergeant is armed with the standard issue half-pike and an infantry sabre.

SPECIFICATIONS	
Country:	Ireland
Date:	1811
Unit:	88th Regiment of Foot
Rank:	Sergeant
Theatre:	Iberian Peninsula
Location:	Fuentes de Onoro, Spain

Peninsular Campaign Infantry 1808–14

The British Army fought some of its hardest battles of the Napoleonic era during the Peninsular War. The battle of Albuera on 16 May 1811, for example, cost British forces up to 7000 dead or wounded, while the siege of Badajoz in 1812 killed nearly 5000 British troops.

Private
5th (Northumberland) Regiment

This private of the 5th Northumberland Regiment is seen ascending an assault ladder during the storming of Badajoz on 6 April 1812. His unwieldy Land Pattern musket is fitted with a crude plug bayonet, the bayonet literally plugging into the muzzle of gun; using the bayonet therefore rendered the gun unable to fire.

SPECIFICATIONS	
Country:	Britain
Date:	6 April 1812
Unit:	5th (Northumberland) Regiment
Rank:	Private
Theatre:	Iberian Peninsular
Location:	Badajoz, Spain

Lieutenant ▶
82nd Regiment of Foot (Prince of Wales Volunteers)

The 82nd Regiment of Foot was founded in 1793, and it served in the Peninsular War between 1810 and 1812. The officer here wears the red officer's jacket with the standard infantry sash of matching colour around his waist. The deeply curved sabre is similar to the type used by hussar cavalry.

SPECIFICATIONS	
Country:	Britain
Date:	1812
Unit:	82nd Regiment of Foot
Rank:	Lieutenant
Theatre:	Iberian Peninsula
Location:	Spain

1812   1812   1812   1812

◀ Chosen Man
85th Light Infantry

The appointment of 'chosen man' was essentially that of a private but with extra pay and duties, equivalent to what became the rank of lance-corporal. The position is indicated by the single chevron on the tunic sleeve.

SPECIFICATIONS	
Country:	Britain
Date:	1812
Unit:	85th Light Infantry
Rank:	Chosen Man
Theatre:	Iberian Peninsula
Location:	Spain

Officer ▶
Royal Engineers

Engineers as a part of British forces date back to the medieval era, although the Corps of Engineers was established in 1717. This field officer has a bicorne hat of the type also worn by artillery officers (the engineers had their origins in the artillery).

SPECIFICATIONS	
Country:	Britain
Date:	1812
Unit:	Royal Engineers
Rank:	Officer
Theatre:	Iberian Peninsula
Location:	Spain

Cavalry and Specialists, Peninsular War 1808–14

The rough terrains and fortresses of the Peninsular War regularly necessitated the skills of engineers, artillerymen and other specialist personnel, while the cavalry served to provide over-the-hill reconnaissance and fast attack capabilities.

◀ Officer
Royal Artillery

The Royal Artillery officer here wears the regiment's short blue patrol tunic with dark facings, white breeches, a bicorne hat and cavalry boots. The Royal Artillery uniform traditionally had gold or yellow lacing. Field artillery became the major battle-winning force of the 19th century.

SPECIFICATIONS	
Country:	Britain
Date:	1809
Unit:	Royal Artillery
Rank:	Officer
Theatre:	Iberian Peninsula
Location:	Spain

Officer ▶
15th Hussars

Hussar cavalry at this period of British Army history wore blue dolmans and pelisses featuring yellow or white looping (both colours are present on parts of this particular uniform). The white-over-red hat plume is another hussar distinction.

SPECIFICATIONS	
Country:	Britain
Date:	1809
Unit:	15th Hussars
Rank:	Officer
Theatre:	Iberian Peninsula
Location:	Spain

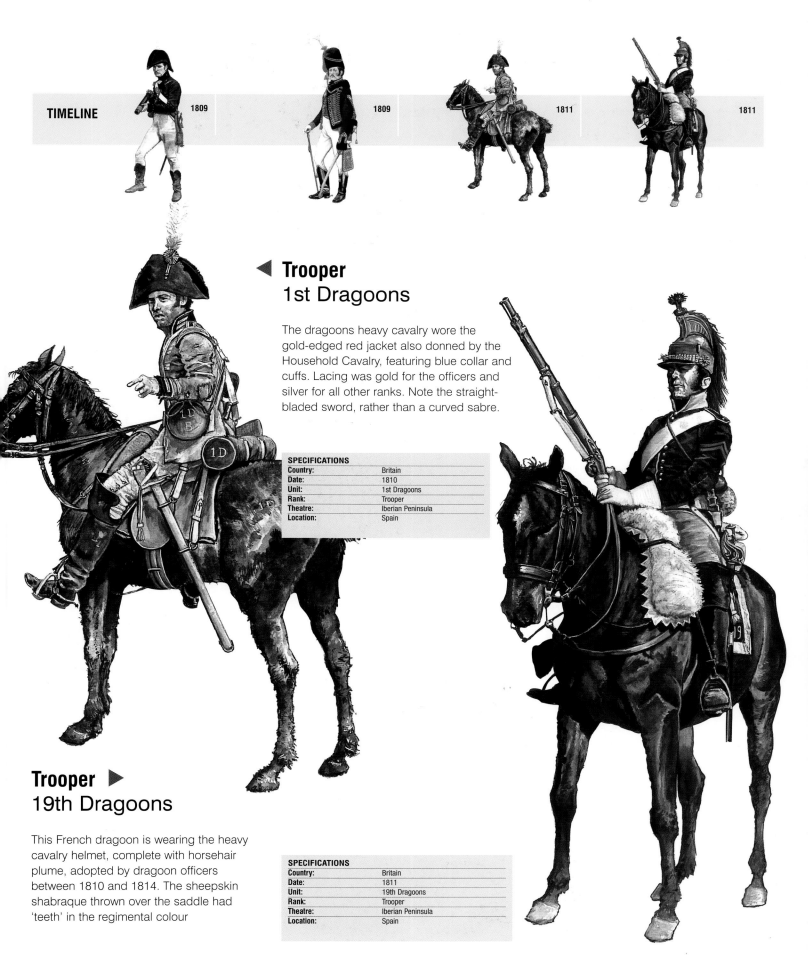

1809   1809   1811   1811

◀ Trooper
1st Dragoons

The dragoons heavy cavalry wore the gold-edged red jacket also donned by the Household Cavalry, featuring blue collar and cuffs. Lacing was gold for the officers and silver for all other ranks. Note the straight-bladed sword, rather than a curved sabre.

SPECIFICATIONS	
Country:	Britain
Date:	1810
Unit:	1st Dragoons
Rank:	Trooper
Theatre:	Iberian Peninsula
Location:	Spain

Trooper ▶
19th Dragoons

This French dragoon is wearing the heavy cavalry helmet, complete with horsehair plume, adopted by dragoon officers between 1810 and 1814. The sheepskin shabraque thrown over the saddle had 'teeth' in the regimental colour

SPECIFICATIONS	
Country:	Britain
Date:	1811
Unit:	19th Dragoons
Rank:	Trooper
Theatre:	Iberian Peninsula
Location:	Spain

British Infantryman in the Napoleonic Wars

The British infantryman's existence during the Napoleonic Wars was typically severe. In addition to brutal combat, the infantry soldier had to endure food shortages, wild terrain and harsh climates. The conflict saw British commanders make use of both line infantry and light infantry, the latter suited more to skirmishing, harassing, rearguard and reconnaissance actions.

The British Land Pattern musket, popularly known as the 'Brown Bess', served the British Army for an astonishing period of time – from the 1720s until the late 1830s. It was produced in a wide range of variants, including Long Land Pattern, Sea Service Pattern, India Pattern and a Cavalry Carbine, with barrel lengths ranging from 66cm (26in) to 117cm (46in).

The Baker rifle was slower to load than the standard-issue smoothbore musket, but its performance over range was far superior. In the hands of a competent marksman, it could put a 15.9mm (0.625in) lead ball into a human-sized target at several hundred metres. Lethal shots of up to 730m (2395ft) were recorded during the Peninsular War.

Private
51st Regiment of Foot

His membership of the 51st Regiment of Foot indicated on his water bottle, this soldier is seen advancing alongside an assault ladder team at the storming of Badajoz in April 1812. Other battles at which the regiment distinguished itself during the Peninsular War included Lugo, Corunna, Fuentes d'Onoro, Salamanca and Vittoria. This soldier has fitted his musket with a socket bayonet, which began service with the British Army at the beginning of the 18th century. The scabbard for the blade can be seen on the man's left hip, while the cartridge pouch sits on his lower back, the flap open and the cartridges ready for use.

SPECIFICATIONS	
Country:	Britain
Date:	1812
Unit:	51st Regiment of Foot
Rank:	Private
Theatre:	Iberian Peninsula
Location:	Badajoz, Spain

Sharpshooter
King's German Legion

Here a sharpshooter from the 1st Light Battalion, King's German Legion (KGL) spends time cleaning his rifle. Such procedures were vital, as the primary disadvantage of the rifle was that the rifling fouled up quickly during repeated firing, slowing down the loading speed as the bore effectively became tighter. Yet in terms of performance, the rifle was clearly superior, able to hit human-sized targets at ranges in excess of 200m (656ft).

SPECIFICATIONS	
Country:	Britain
Date:	1813
Unit:	King's German Legion
Rank:	Sharpshooter
Theatre:	Iberian Peninsula
Location:	Spain

French Infantry 1813–15

By 1813 the French Army was a veteran force, having fought in campaigns ranging from North Africa to the steppes of Russia. Yet losses in these very campaigns meant that the infantry and other arms no longer had the power or efficiency of the earlier *Grande Armée*.

◀ Sergeant-Major
5th Regiment, Tirailleurs of the Imperial Guard

The French word *tirailleur* essentially means 'skirmisher', and two regiments of these troops fought at Waterloo. The tirailleur uniform was based around a short-skirted blue coatee, which featured a red standing collar and matching cuffs. Equipment here includes a backup with a bedroll on top.

SPECIFICATIONS	
Country:	France
Date:	1813
Unit:	Tirailleurs of the Imperial Guard
Rank:	Sergeant-Major
Theatre:	Europe
Location:	Germany

Infantryman ▶
Marie-Louise Campaign Dress

Marie-Louises referred to the huge numbers of young French men drafted into the French Army to make up for the losses of the Russian campaign of 1812. Uniforms for these men were extremely basic, kit items being stripped down to the bare essentials for survival and fighting.

SPECIFICATIONS	
Country:	France
Date:	1814
Unit:	Infantry
Rank:	Infantryman
Theatre:	Europe
Location:	France

TIMELINE

1813

1814

1814

1814

Infantryman
12th Light Infantry

Here a light infantryman of the French Army raises his hat to signal the charge. Like many of his British Army counterparts at the time, he has been issued with a socket bayonet. The cross belts on the chest feature the infantry bugle horn insignia.

SPECIFICATIONS	
Country:	France
Date:	1814
Unit:	12th Light Infantry
Rank:	Infantryman
Theatre:	Europe
Location:	France

Sapper ▶
French Army

Looking partly like a medieval knight, this French Army sapper has donned a visored iron helmet and cuirassier body armour to protect himself from enemy fire. Engineers were, along with officers, good targets of opportunity for enemy riflemen.

SPECIFICATIONS	
Country:	France
Date:	1814
Unit:	French Army
Rank:	Sapper
Theatre:	Europe
Location:	France

Artillery and Transport Troops 1813–15

The Napoleonic Wars saw the ongoing development of horse-mobile field artillery, as well as heavier guns. Artillery, in addition to the thousands of infantry in the field, had huge logistical demands to be satisfied.

◀ Corporal
Artillerie de Marine

The Artillerie de Marine was the gunnery branch of the Troupes de Marine, and was formed into a single regiment in 1814. This corporal – his rank is denoted on sleeve and cuff – has a socket-type bayonet on his musket. The water container on the left hip consists of a glass bottle encased in a wicker container.

SPECIFICATIONS	
Country:	France
Date:	1814
Unit:	Artillerie de Marine
Rank:	Corporal
Theatre:	Europe
Location:	France

Officer ▶
Royal Horse Artillery

The Royal Horse Artillery was a flamboyant regiment in terms of dress, its officers appearing more as hussars than as infantry. The blue jacket had red collar and cuffs and gold loopings, with a looped dolman draped over the shoulders.

SPECIFICATIONS	
Country:	Britain
Date:	c. 1814
Unit:	Royal Horse Artillery
Rank:	Officer
Theatre:	Europe
Location:	Unknown

◀ Gunner
Royal Artillery

A gunner of the Royal Artillery helps set up an artillery piece. The Royal Artillery was less ostentatious in appearance when compared to the Royal Horse Artillery, the uniform largely resembling that donned by the line infantry.

SPECIFICATIONS

Country:	Britain
Date:	c. 1814
Unit:	Royal Artillery
Rank:	Gunner
Theatre:	Europe
Location:	Unknown

Officer ▶
Royal Wagon Train

The Royal Wagon Train was established in 1799, from what was formerly the Corps of Wagoners. It was responsible for supplying field formations, and it served primarily in the Peninsular and Waterloo campaigns. This officer has jacket ornamentation similar to that of the horse artillery.

SPECIFICATIONS

Country:	Britain
Date:	1815
Unit:	Royal Wagon Train
Rank:	Officer
Theatre:	Europe
Location:	Waterloo

European Campaigns 1813–14

The last two years of Napoleon's military campaigns brought a series of major battles to Europe, included Lützen (1813), Bautzen (1813), Kulm (1813), Leipzig (1813), Lâon (1814) and Toulouse (1814), costing thousands of infantry lives.

◀ Private
US Infantry

The US Army was tangentially involved in the Napoleonic Wars through clashes with the British in North America. By 1813, the standard uniform consisted of a single-breasted blue jacket and matching trousers, although riflemen often wore all-grey uniforms. The cylindrical hat featured a cockade and plume.

SPECIFICATIONS	
Country:	United States
Date:	1813
Unit:	US Army
Rank:	Infantryman
Theatre:	North America
Location:	Unknown

Infantryman ▶
71st (Highland) Light Infantry

The 71st Highland Light Infantry served in the Peninsular War and at the battle of Waterloo – during the latter, the regiment's 1st Battalion suffered 16 officers and 171 men killed or wounded. The uniform largely followed the standard infantry pattern, with tartan distinctions.

SPECIFICATIONS	
Country:	Britain
Date:	1813
Unit:	71st (Highland) Infantry
Rank:	Infantryman
Theatre:	Iberian Peninsula
Location:	Unknown

TIMELINE 1813   1813   1814   1814

Trooper ▶
Staff Corps of Cavalry

The Staff Corps of Cavalry was effectively Britain's first standing military police force, established in 1813. Its troopers were initially identified by a red scarf tied around the shoulder of the uniform, which some see as the precursor to the military police 'red cap' and armband.

SPECIFICATIONS	
Country:	Britain
Date:	1814
Unit:	Staff Corps of Cavalry
Rank:	Trooper
Theatre:	Iberian Peninsula
Location:	Spain

Private ▶
2nd (Coldstream) Guards

This private of the Coldstream Guards wears a long field coat to protect him against the worst of the climate while on sentry duty. The Coldstream Guards adopted the famous bearskin hats after helping defeat Napoleon's troops at Waterloo in 1815.

SPECIFICATIONS	
Country:	Britain
Date:	1814
Unit:	Coldstream Guards
Rank:	Private
Theatre:	Iberian Peninsula
Location:	Spain

Regimental and Royal Colours

Colours traditionally acted as visible rallying points in the confusion of the battlefield, enabling soldiers to locate their own regimental forces and command. Yet apart from their practical purpose, they also acquired a unique ceremonial and spiritual authority, treated as near-priceless embodiments of regimental pride, never to fall into the hands of the enemy.

The regimental colours of the Scots Fusilier Guards, as seen during the late 19th century. The colours display the regiment's battle honours, set on a Union Jack flag with other regimental imagery.

Ensign
3/14th Buckinghamshire Regiment of Foot

Here we see an ensign of the 3/14th Buckinghamshire Regiment of Foot in 1815, presenting the King's Colours. The King's/Queen's Colours displayed the Union Jack (here in the upper corner, but other regiments might have a full-size national flag) with the regimental insignia in the centre. These colours were paired with the Regimental Colours, which were generally in the colour of the uniform facings and again featuring the regimental insignia. They were often embroidered with the names of famous victories or campaigns. The pike on which colours were mounted measured 2.6m (8ft 6in).

SPECIFICATIONS	
Country:	Britain
Date:	1815
Unit:	3/14th Bucks
Rank:	Ensign
Theatre:	Europe
Location:	Unknown

Battle of Waterloo 1815

The battle of Waterloo, fought in Belgium on 18 June 1815, was the thunderous climax to the Napoleonic Wars. The combined force of British, Prussian and other allied armies took victory, but by the end of the day more than 50,000 dead and wounded littered the battlefield and aid stations.

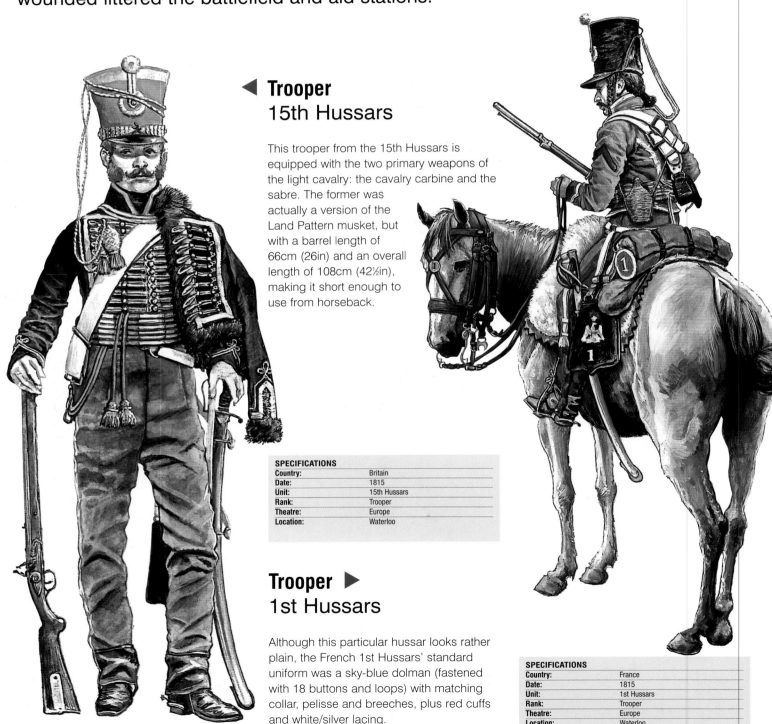

◀ Trooper
15th Hussars

This trooper from the 15th Hussars is equipped with the two primary weapons of the light cavalry: the cavalry carbine and the sabre. The former was actually a version of the Land Pattern musket, but with a barrel length of 66cm (26in) and an overall length of 108cm (42½in), making it short enough to use from horseback.

SPECIFICATIONS	
Country:	Britain
Date:	1815
Unit:	15th Hussars
Rank:	Trooper
Theatre:	Europe
Location:	Waterloo

Trooper ▶
1st Hussars

Although this particular hussar looks rather plain, the French 1st Hussars' standard uniform was a sky-blue dolman (fastened with 18 buttons and loops) with matching collar, pelisse and breeches, plus red cuffs and white/silver lacing.

SPECIFICATIONS	
Country:	France
Date:	1815
Unit:	1st Hussars
Rank:	Trooper
Theatre:	Europe
Location:	Waterloo

TIMELINE

1815

1815

1815

1815

◄ Musketeer
10th (1st Silesian) Regiment

The battle of Waterloo brought together field troops from across Europe. The musketeers from the 10th (1st Silesian) Regiment wore blue jackets with yellow regimental facings. Reflecting the realities of the European climate, this soldier's shako hat is fitted with an oilcloth cover.

SPECIFICATIONS	
Country:	Prussian Silesia
Date:	1815
Unit:	10th (1st Silesian) Regiment
Rank:	Musketeer
Theatre:	Europe
Location:	Waterloo

Private ►
92nd Regiment of Foot

This soldier of the 92nd Regiment of Foot, seen here loading his musket, clearly illustrates the regiment's highland origins. The regiment later amalgamated with the 75th Regiment of Foot in 1881 to create the famous Gordon Highlanders regiment.

SPECIFICATIONS	
Country:	Britain
Date:	1815
Unit:	92nd Regiment of Foot
Rank:	Private
Theatre:	Europe
Location:	Waterloo

American Civil War 1861–65

The American Civil War was a devastating conflict, one that cost the lives of 900,000 Americans between 1861 and 1865. The nature of the conflict was diverse, and ranged from major set-piece battles to forms of guerrilla warfare. Similarly, uniforms varied from modified civilian outfits through to standardized military dress.

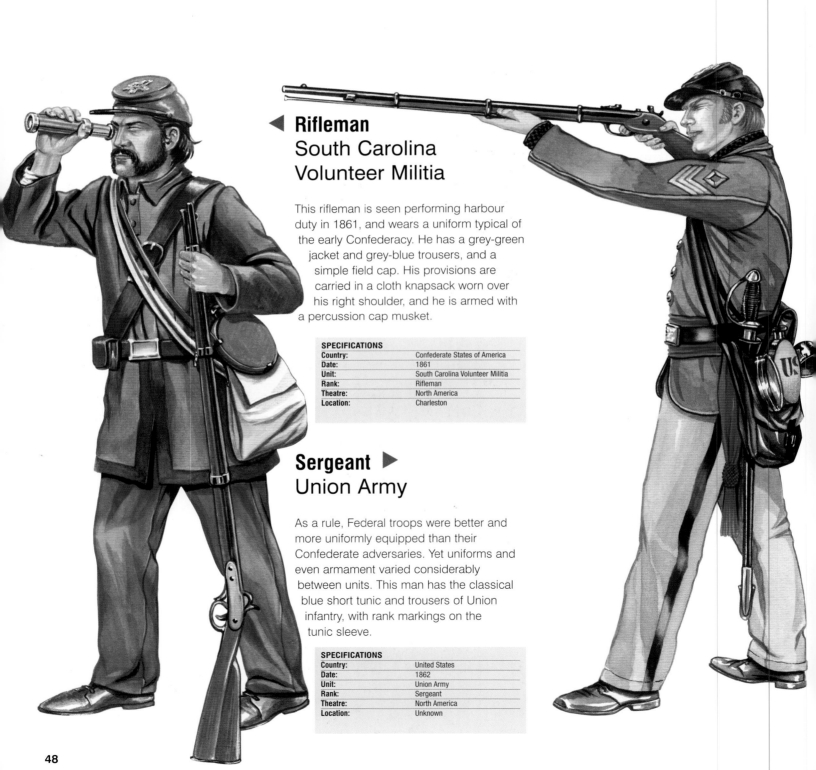

◀ Rifleman
South Carolina Volunteer Militia

This rifleman is seen performing harbour duty in 1861, and wears a uniform typical of the early Confederacy. He has a grey-green jacket and grey-blue trousers, and a simple field cap. His provisions are carried in a cloth knapsack worn over his right shoulder, and he is armed with a percussion cap musket.

SPECIFICATIONS	
Country:	Confederate States of America
Date:	1861
Unit:	South Carolina Volunteer Militia
Rank:	Rifleman
Theatre:	North America
Location:	Charleston

Sergeant ▶
Union Army

As a rule, Federal troops were better and more uniformly equipped than their Confederate adversaries. Yet uniforms and even armament varied considerably between units. This man has the classical blue short tunic and trousers of Union infantry, with rank markings on the tunic sleeve.

SPECIFICATIONS	
Country:	United States
Date:	1862
Unit:	Union Army
Rank:	Sergeant
Theatre:	North America
Location:	Unknown

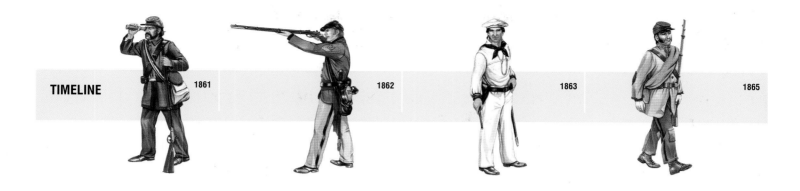

TIMELINE

1861   1862   1863   1865

◄ Petty Officer
US Navy

This petty officer wears classic navy blue/white uniform, with the woollen 'flat-hat'. The hat was typically made of dark blue wool, but during the summer months it could be fitted with a white cover to reflect sunlight. Sometimes the hat also bore the ship's name.

SPECIFICATIONS	
Country:	United States
Date:	1863
Unit:	US Navy
Rank:	Petty Officer
Theatre:	North America
Location:	Unknown

Infantryman ►
Confederate Army

Problems with uniform supply in the Confederate Army meant that soldiers wore whatever was available, and home-dyed 'butternut' jackets and trousers, as seen here, became characteristic items rather than traditional Confederate grey. The lack of standardization frequently caused confusion on the battlefield.

SPECIFICATIONS	
Country:	Confederate States of America
Date:	1865
Unit:	Confederate Army
Rank:	Infantryman
Theatre:	North America
Location:	Southern United States

Anglo-Zulu War 1879

The Anglo-Zulu War of 1879 brought a complacent British force into contact with a numerically superior Zulu Army. The disaster at Isandlwana, which cost more than 1300 British dead, taught the British commanders to respect their enemy.

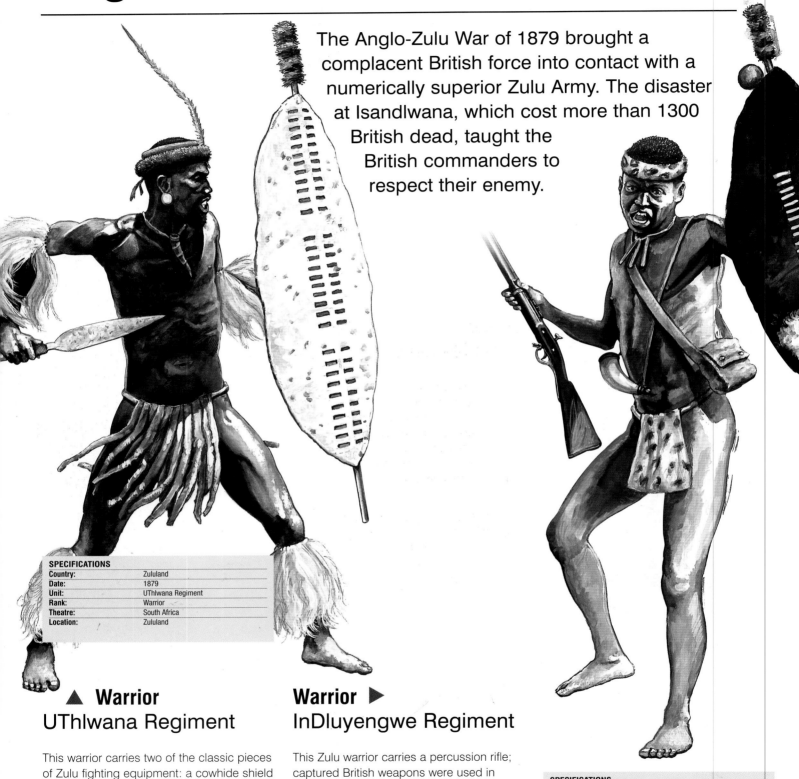

▲ Warrior
UThlwana Regiment

SPECIFICATIONS	
Country:	Zululand
Date:	1879
Unit:	UThlwana Regiment
Rank:	Warrior
Theatre:	South Africa
Location:	Zululand

This warrior carries two of the classic pieces of Zulu fighting equipment: a cowhide shield (which also displayed regimental markings) and an *iklwa* stabbing spear. The latter was used for close-quarters fighting, whereas the longer *isijula* spear was designed as a throwing weapon.

Warrior ▶
InDluyengwe Regiment

This Zulu warrior carries a percussion rifle; captured British weapons were used in increasing numbers in the Anglo-Zulu War, but not always efficiently. Note also the ball-like head of the *knobkerrie* club which is projecting from behind the top of the shield.

SPECIFICATIONS	
Country:	Zululand
Date:	1879
Unit:	InDluyengwe Regiment
Rank:	Warrior
Theatre:	South Africa
Location:	Zululand

TIMELINE 1879   1879   1879   1879

Officer
Natal Native Contingent

The NNC was an auxiliary formation manned by indigenous African troops and officered by men of European extraction. Its men were not issued with official British Army uniforms, so wore a mixture of military apparel. NCOs and officers typically wore khaki and black uniform items.

SPECIFICATIONS	
Country:	South Africa
Date:	1879
Unit:	Natal Native Contingent
Rank:	Officer
Theatre:	South Africa
Location:	Zululand

Lieutenant ▶
Royal Engineers

This figure is of Lieutenant John Chard, who won a Victoria Cross for his part in the defence of Rorke's Drift. He is armed with the weapon that made possible the defence – the Martini-Henry rifle, which packed a fearsome punch against Zulu ranks.

SPECIFICATIONS	
Country:	Britain
Date:	1879
Unit:	Royal Engineers
Rank:	Lieutenant
Theatre:	South Africa
Location:	Rorke's Drift

WORLD WAR I

World War I was effectively the beginning of industrialized warfare; firepower came to matter more than the bravery of individual soldiers, and artillery and machine guns became kings of the battlefield.

The war also began the modern era of military uniforms. Although the conflict saw some forces and formations cling on to elaborate 19th-century uniforms, particularly among the cavalry, in the main military dress became utilitarian and homogenized. At the same time, however, kit and weaponry became more advanced, and the soldier's burden remained a heavy one.

Left: British troops attempt to mount a Vickers machine-gun on a motorcycle sidecar. They wear the 1908-pattern webbing system to carry their personal equipment, which includes water bottle, entrenching tool and ammunition pouches.

Western Front 1914–15

Many regiments of 1914 went into battle wearing brightly coloured items of uniform. It was soon realized, however, that such items drew the attention of machine gunners and snipers, and they were quickly removed or obscured.

◄ Officer
French Cuirassiers

During the first year of World War I, many French cavalry units – cuirassiers, dragoons, hussars and chasseurs – wore service versions of full ceremonial dress, as seen here. However, by 1915 such units realized the hideous cost of high visibility, and began dressing more like the infantry.

SPECIFICATIONS	
Country:	France
Date:	1914
Unit:	Cuirassier
Rank:	Officer
Theatre:	Western Front
Location:	France

Private, 1st Class ►
French Army

This French infantryman's uniform includes red collar patches (the number indicating battalion or regiment), red rank markings on the sleeve (a single chevron indicated Private 1st Class) and bright red trousers; the bright colours were later removed.

SPECIFICATIONS	
Country:	France
Date:	1914
Unit:	French Army
Rank:	Private, 1st Class
Theatre:	Western Front
Location:	France

TIMELINE   1914   1914   1914   1915

◄ Sergeant
British Royal Horse Artillery

This sergeant is wearing the standard British Army uniform of tunic, trousers and puttees. The peaked service cap was also standard dress until an unacceptably high percentage of head wounds on the Western Front led to the introduction and standardization of the Mk 1 steel helmet in 1916.

SPECIFICATIONS	
Country:	Britain
Date:	1914
Unit:	Royal Horse Artillery
Rank:	Sergeant
Theatre:	Western Front
Location:	France

Officer ►
German Uhlan (Lancer) Regiment

Although the M1910 uniform – the standard uniform of German cavalry soldiers – worn by the Uhlan officer here follows the general field-grey army colour scheme, the style is much more theatrical, and includes the distinctive *czapka* helmet.

SPECIFICATIONS	
Country:	Germany
Date:	1915
Unit:	Uhlan Cavalry
Rank:	Officer
Theatre:	Western Front
Location:	Belgium

British Royal Marine 1914

As war expanded in 1914 and 1915, the British armed forces were tasked with finding uniforms not only for its regular soldiers, but also for millions of conscripts. Thus it was common for soldiers in the first years of the war to be wearing older patterns of clothing and equipment. Although a Royal Marine, the figure here illustrates the general appearance of many land forces troops in 1914.

The 7.7mm (.303in) Short-Magazine Lee-Enfield (SMLE) rifle was the standard-issue firearm of the British Army for two world wars. Its longevity was assured by its rugged design, ease of use and accuracy within ranges of 1.6km (1 mile) and sometimes beyond. At the battle of Mons in 1914, British soldiers delivered such a rate of fire from their SMLEs that the German attackers thought the fusillade came from machine guns.

The Royal Marine cap badge consists of a lion and crown atop a globe, the globe indicating the reach of the Royal Marines through the words 'Africa, Asia, Europe'. The badge is framed by the laurel wreath of victory.

Marine
Royal Marines

This soldier presents a typical view of an RM soldier in 1914. He is wearing the standard British Army khaki serge uniform instead of the blue uniform worn by pre-war RM units. His web gaiters, however, are actually Royal Navy issue. The only designations of his RM status are the 'RMLI' (Royal Marine Light Infantry) badges set on the shoulder straps and the RM badge centred on the field cap. His webbing is the 1908 pattern, featuring multiple ammunition pouches for his 7.7mm (.303in) SMLE rifle.

Country:	Britain
Date:	1914
Unit:	Royal Marines
Rank:	Marine
Theatre:	Northwest Europe
Location:	France

Western Front 1916–18

By the end of 1915, most armies had recognized the inadvisability of ceremonial dress on the battlefield. Frontline officers of all arms-of-service were toning down their tendency to dress boldly – to be visible to the enemy was to be dead.

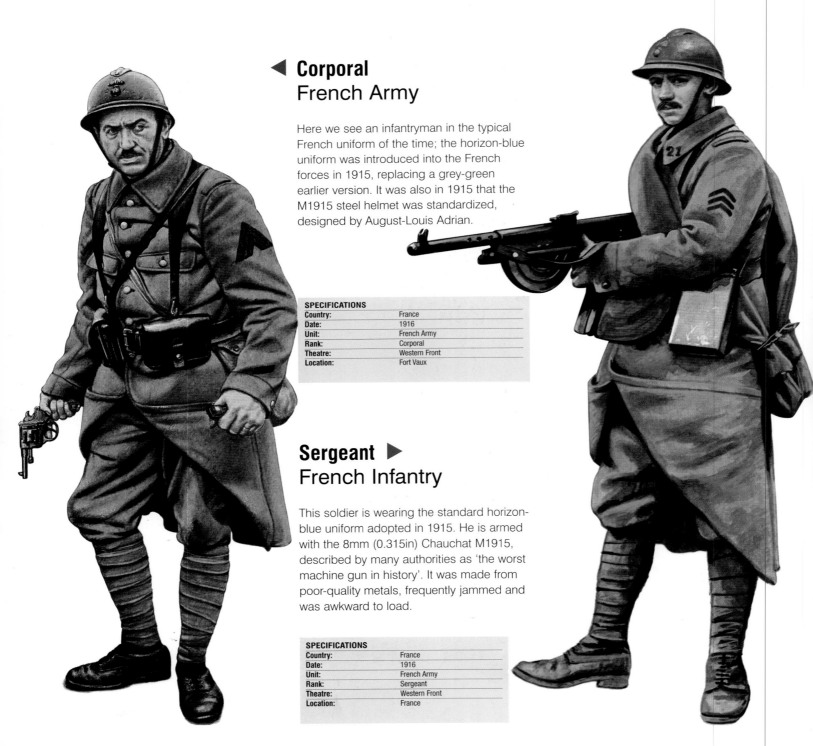

◄ Corporal
French Army

Here we see an infantryman in the typical French uniform of the time; the horizon-blue uniform was introduced into the French forces in 1915, replacing a grey-green earlier version. It was also in 1915 that the M1915 steel helmet was standardized, designed by August-Louis Adrian.

SPECIFICATIONS	
Country:	France
Date:	1916
Unit:	French Army
Rank:	Corporal
Theatre:	Western Front
Location:	Fort Vaux

Sergeant ►
French Infantry

This soldier is wearing the standard horizon-blue uniform adopted in 1915. He is armed with the 8mm (0.315in) Chauchat M1915, described by many authorities as 'the worst machine gun in history'. It was made from poor-quality metals, frequently jammed and was awkward to load.

SPECIFICATIONS	
Country:	France
Date:	1916
Unit:	French Army
Rank:	Sergeant
Theatre:	Western Front
Location:	France

TIMELINE 1916 1916 1916 1918

◀ ## 2nd Lieutenant
Artists' Rifles

This lieutenant gives an especially clear view of the 1908 pattern webbing worn by almost all British soldiers during World War I. Although he is actually wearing the officer's version (by virtue of the Webley revolver in the holster on his hip), most of the other items are in standard infantry configuration.

SPECIFICATIONS	
Country:	Britain
Date:	1916
Unit:	Artists' Rifles
Rank:	2nd Lieutenant
Theatre:	Western Front
Location:	France

Lieutenant ▶
Tank Corps

This officer of the Tank Corps is, on the whole, wearing the standard British Army service dress, though with some notable variations. Most conspicuous of these is the chain-mail face mask. This was designed to protect the face from steel splinters caused by enemy small-arms fire striking the tank.

SPECIFICATIONS	
Country:	Britain
Date:	1918
Unit:	Tank Corps
Rank:	Lieutenant
Theatre:	Western Front
Location:	France

Western Front 1916–18

The UK military introduced a khaki service dress for personnel in India in 1885, but in 1902 khaki became the standard colour of military battledress throughout the British Army (it should be noted that some soldiers arrived in France in blue serge outfits because of uniform shortages).

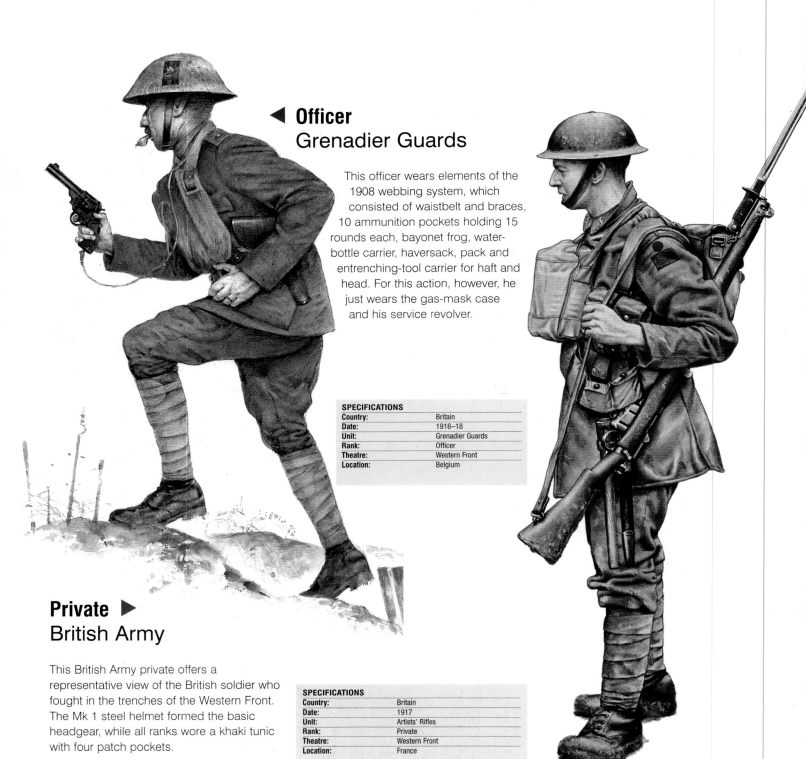

◀ Officer
Grenadier Guards

This officer wears elements of the 1908 webbing system, which consisted of waistbelt and braces, 10 ammunition pockets holding 15 rounds each, bayonet frog, water-bottle carrier, haversack, pack and entrenching-tool carrier for haft and head. For this action, however, he just wears the gas-mask case and his service revolver.

SPECIFICATIONS	
Country:	Britain
Date:	1916–18
Unit:	Grenadier Guards
Rank:	Officer
Theatre:	Western Front
Location:	Belgium

Private ▶
British Army

This British Army private offers a representative view of the British soldier who fought in the trenches of the Western Front. The Mk 1 steel helmet formed the basic headgear, while all ranks wore a khaki tunic with four patch pockets.

SPECIFICATIONS	
Country:	Britain
Date:	1917
Unit:	Artists' Rifles
Rank:	Private
Theatre:	Western Front
Location:	France

◄ Stormtrooper
German Army

The stormtroopers were a new breed of German soldier, and here we see one such soldier in 1918. Metal body armour, a mail headdress and non-standard steel helmet gave protection in trench battles, though at the expense of mobility. This soldier is armed with a Mauser Model 1914 pistol, two hand-grenades, and a sharpened spade.

SPECIFICATIONS	
Country:	Germany
Date:	1918
Unit:	German Army
Rank:	Stormtrooper
Theatre:	Western Front
Location:	France

Stormtrooper ►
German Army

This stormtrooper's M1915 uniform is typical of the German soldier in 1918. It replaced the M1910 as the standard-issue German army blouse in 1915 and initially featured exposed buttons. These were eventually covered with a fly front, as shown here.

SPECIFICATIONS	
Country:	Germany
Date:	1918
Unit:	German Army
Rank:	Stormtrooper
Theatre:	Western Front
Location:	France

The German Machine-Gunner

Although machine guns had first been developed in the late 19th century, it was during World War I that their full, horrible potential was revealed on the battlefield. The hammering of the Maxim MG08 machine gun was the last sound heard by thousands of British, French, Commonwealth and US troops as they attempted to cross the killing zone of no man's land.

A view of the MG08/15, without its bulky water jacket. The MG08/15 was Germany's poor early attempt to create a light machine gun. It was, however, too heavy for mobile assault tactics, and compared unfavourably with the British/US Lewis gun.

The spiked *Pickelhaube* helmet was introduced into German service back in the 1840s. It was still in use in the early years of World War I, but its poor protective qualities (it was made from hardened leather) and its sniper-attracting spike quickly removed it from use.

Infantryman
German Army

The German infantryman here wears German Army service dress, c. 1915, with a cloth cover over his field cap and the rather impractical calf-height jackboots. Like most machine-gun personnel, he carries a pistol as a secondary weapon, but his principal firearm is the Maxim Maschinengewhr MG08. Developed by Hiram Maxim in the late 1890s, the MG08 was a short-recoil gun that used a toggle system of breech locking. The bulky jacket around the barrel was filled with water to keep the barrel cool under sustained fire.

SPECIFICATIONS	
Country:	Germany
Date:	1916
Unit:	German Army
Rank:	Infantryman
Theatre:	Northwest Europe
Location:	France

Air War

World War I gave birth to combat aviation. At first, aircraft were generally used only for reconnaissance, but gradually the demands of controlling the airspace resulted in armed variants and combat-trained pilots.

◀ Kapitänleutnant
Zeppelin Airship

This Zeppelin *Kapitänleutnant*, commander of Zeppelin *L16*, wears a base layer of a thick woollen jumper. Over this he has a double-breasted naval jacket featuring a German cross and rank markings on the cuffs, this being worn with leather trousers and a naval cap.

SPECIFICATIONS	
Country:	Germany
Date:	1915
Unit:	Naval Airship Division
Rank:	*Kapitänleutnant*
Theatre:	North Sea
Location:	Germany

Lieutenant ▶
Escadrille N. No.3
Groupe de Chasse
No.12

Here we see Lieutenant Deullin, a distinguished French pilot of World War I, in the uniform of the *French Aviation Militaire*. The tunic is horizon-blue in colour with a stand-and-fall collar. On this collar is the insignia of a qualified aviator – a five-pointed winged star.

SPECIFICATIONS	
Country:	France
Date:	1916
Unit:	French Air Force
Rank:	Lieutenant
Theatre:	Western Front
Location:	France

1915

1916

1917

1917

◀ Captain
Royal Flying Corps

Fighter 'ace' Captain Albert Ball is seen here wearing standard British Army field dress with service cap, with the Royal Flying Corps badge in its customary position, on the left of the cap. Rank is displayed on the cuffs, and the collar features the Royal Flying Corps badge.

SPECIFICATIONS	
Country:	Britain
Date:	1917
Unit:	Royal Flying Corps
Rank:	Captain
Theatre:	Western Front
Location:	France

Pilot ▶
Royal Flying Corps

A downed British pilot wearing typical RFC flying gear. A long leather coat and silk scarf provide the main elements, while fur-lined boots and flying helmet shielded the feet and the head respectively. Long gauntlet-type gloves would also have been fur-lined for warmth.

SPECIFICATIONS	
Country:	Britain
Date:	1917
Unit:	Royal Flying Corps
Rank:	Pilot
Theatre:	Western Front
Location:	Franc

Eastern and Southern Fronts 1914–17

The war on the Eastern Front saw the extremes of military dress in evidence. Uniforms ranged from the imperial ostentation of the Austro-Hungarian cavalry through to the utilitarian approach of the Russian infantryman.

◀ Private
Austro-Hungarian Army

The uniform of the Austro-Hungarian forces was established in its basic form in 1909. During this year a new uniform in pike-grey (known as *Hechtgrau*) was introduced to all infantry units (not to cavalry regiments). The tunic was single-breasted with a stand collar (later a stand-and-fall collar), made in wool for winter and drill for summer.

SPECIFICATIONS	
Country:	Austria-Hungary
Date:	1914
Unit:	Austro-Hungarian Infantry
Rank:	Private
Theatre:	Eastern Front
Location:	Unknown

Officer ▶
Austrian Hussars

This Austrian hussar's bright blue Attila jacket and red trousers were incongruous on the modern battlefield. Before the war, hussars wore the elaborate shako helmet, but after 1914, a peaked field cap with grey cover. The tunic was often worn slung over the left shoulder like a pelisse. Note the sabre on the left hip.

SPECIFICATIONS	
Country:	Austria-Hungary
Date:	1914
Unit:	Austrian Hussars
Rank:	Officer
Theatre:	Balkans
Location:	Serbia

TIMELINE

1914

1914

1916

1917

◀ **Private**
Russian Army

The basic pattern of the World War I Russian Army uniform was established in 1907. The pattern chosen was an olive-green uniform of *Gimnastirka* shirt (for non-officer ranks) or *Kitel* tunic (for officers) with a woollen or cloth peaked cap and *Shinel* greatcoat.

SPECIFICATIONS	
Country:	Russia
Date:	1916
Unit:	Russian Army
Rank:	Private
Theatre:	Eastern Front
Location:	Western Russia

Private ▶
Württemberg Mountain Rifles

At the outset of World War I, most German infantry were clothed in field-grey uniforms. However, certain specialist units such as the Jäger and Schützen (Rifles) were issued with grey-green uniforms, as seen on this soldier, pictured during the bloody battle of Caporetto in 1917.

SPECIFICATIONS	
Country:	Germany
Date:	1917
Unit:	Württemberg Mountain Rifles
Rank:	Private
Theatre:	Italian Front
Location:	Italy

Naval Officers at Jutland

The great naval battle of Jutland (31 May–1 June 1916) was an indecisive affair, with both sides claiming victory. Photographs of the opposing commanders show a similarity in uniform, both in cut and coloration. Partly this was through the influence of the Royal Navy uniform, which had settled into an established pattern during the 19th century.

This early semi-automatic pistol was in service from 1908 until the end of World War II, and served as a sidearm to many officers of the Central Powers, including naval officers. It fired 8mm (0.315in) Roth-Steyr cartridges, which were fed from a 10-round magazine in the pistol grip. The gun was clip-loaded from the top, the clip being inserted down through an opened bolt into the magazine.

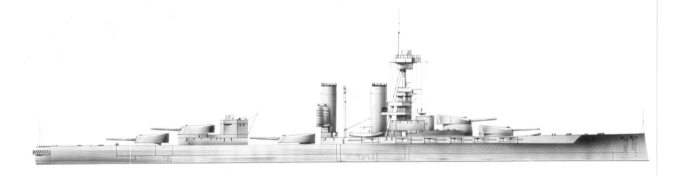

HMS *Iron Duke* was a powerful ship, the lead of her class, commissioned in 1914. Its main armament was 10 340mm (13.5in) guns, which were mounted in five two-gun turrets. The vessel's top speed was 40km/h (25mph). The *Iron Duke* fought at the battle of Jutland in 1916, but this was largely the only combat service of its career.

The officer on the right is a lieutenant in the Royal Navy, wearing a mix of his naval whites and his standard service jacket and cap. The jacket was a double-breasted 'reefer' type. Rank was kept simply to gold lace around the cuffs, the upper row always featuring a loop. The officer on the left is a *Kapitänleutnant* in the German navy. The typical dress of a German naval officer in the Great War was a blue tunic with matching trousers, a white shirt with wing collar and black tie, black shoes, and the naval peaked cap.

◄ **Kapitänleutnant**
German Navy

SPECIFICATIONS (left)	
Country:	Germany
Date:	1916
Unit:	German Navy
Rank:	Kapitänleutnant
Theatre:	North Sea
Location:	Jutland

Lieutenant ▶
Royal Navy

SPECIFICATIONS (right)	
Country:	Britain
Date:	1916
Unit:	Royal Navy
Rank:	Lieutenant
Theatre:	North Sea
Location:	Jutland

Mediterranean, Africa and Middle East 1915–25

In 1915, the war began to spread further, with fighting from the Far East to the Atlantic Ocean. Significant new theatres opened up in the Middle East and Africa.

◀ Corporal
Schutztruppe

The Schutztruppe, a small defence unit maintained by Germany in its East African colony, consisted of only 260 Germans and 2472 *askaris* (local soldiers). This corporal shows off typical Schutztruppen dress, distinct from that of German forces in northern Europe.

SPECIFICATIONS	
Country:	Germany
Date:	1914
Unit:	Schutztruppe
Rank:	Corporal
Theatre:	Africa
Location:	East Africa

Corporal ▶
Australian Infantry

This Australian soldier wears the standard service dress: a single-breasted khaki tunic in a British pattern, corduroy trousers (though khaki trousers of the same material as the tunic were also worn), puttees and brown leather shoes, plus the distinctive Australian wide-brimmed slouch hat.

SPECIFICATIONS	
Country:	Australia
Date:	1915
Unit:	Australian Army
Rank:	Corporal
Theatre:	Dardanelles
Location:	Gallipoli

TIMELINE   1914   1915   1916   1925

Private
Turkish Army

This private is seen at Gallipoli wearing the standard olive-drab uniform of the Turkish Army. For headgear, Turkish soldiers wore either the traditional fez or the cloth-covered solar topi, as shown here. Over his tunic this soldier wears a cartridge belt; the rounds are exposed under the leather flaps of the pouches.

SPECIFICATIONS	
Country:	Turkey
Date:	1916
Unit:	Turkish Army
Rank:	Private
Theatre:	Dardanelles
Location:	Gallipoli

Private ▶
French Foreign Legion

Here a Legionnaire wears a loose cotton tunic and trousers, plus the traditional kepi – the white colour of these items would reflect some of the sun's intense heat and glare. Footwear is a pair of brown shoes worn with long puttees to the knee to stop the intrusion of sand and wildlife.

SPECIFICATIONS	
Country:	France
Date:	1925
Unit:	French Foreign Legion
Rank:	Private
Theatre:	Syria
Location:	Unknown

WORLD WAR II

In September 1939, after a furious period of rearmament, Germany invaded Poland. This campaign launched a world war that would last six years and revolutionized the way that wars were fought.

Although there were many instances of static defensive warfare during World War II, the conflict was essentially one of manoeuvre and firepower, with great changes in technology. Air superiority became vital to win a campaign; submarines and aircraft carriers replaced battleships as the naval weapons of choice; and armoured vehicles formed the spearhead of armies, alongside increasingly heavily armed infantry.

Left: During World War II, uniforms were increasingly adapted to specialist roles, such as airborne deployment. Here we see US Army paratroopers preparing to make a static-line jump in full combat gear.

German Infantry and Panzer Troops 1939

Because of Germany's intensive pre-war investment in its armed forces, *Wehrmacht* soldiers at this stage of the war tend to be seen with an excellent standard of uniform and kit, at least compared to many of their enemies.

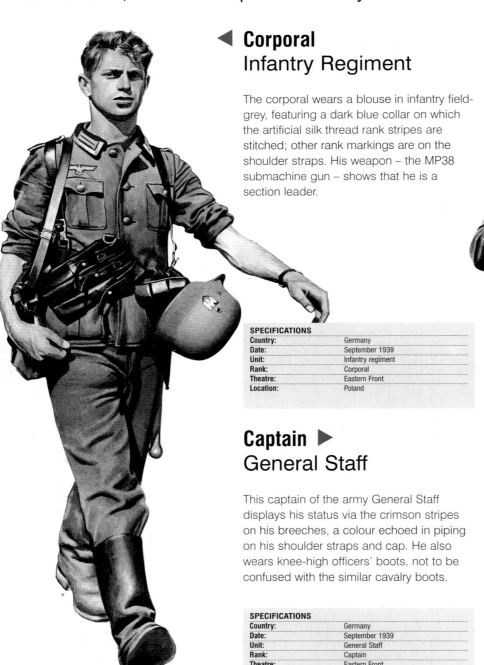

◀ Corporal
Infantry Regiment

The corporal wears a blouse in infantry field-grey, featuring a dark blue collar on which the artificial silk thread rank stripes are stitched; other rank markings are on the shoulder straps. His weapon – the MP38 submachine gun – shows that he is a section leader.

SPECIFICATIONS	
Country:	Germany
Date:	September 1939
Unit:	Infantry regiment
Rank:	Corporal
Theatre:	Eastern Front
Location:	Poland

Captain ▶
General Staff

This captain of the army General Staff displays his status via the crimson stripes on his breeches, a colour echoed in piping on his shoulder straps and cap. He also wears knee-high officers' boots, not to be confused with the similar cavalry boots.

SPECIFICATIONS	
Country:	Germany
Date:	September 1939
Unit:	General Staff
Rank:	Captain
Theatre:	Eastern Front
Location:	Poland

◄ Senior Sergeant
Anti-Aircraft Artillery

This is a senior sergeant of an anti-aircraft artillery unit. His blue-grey tunic identifies him as a member of the air force. Between 1 April and 30 September – the summer months – before the war, officers and NCOs were allowed to wear a cap with white top and white trousers and shoes.

SPECIFICATIONS	
Country:	Germany
Date:	1939
Unit:	Luftwaffe Anti-Aircraft Artillery
Rank:	Senior Sergeant
Theatre:	Germany
Location:	Unknown

Lieutenant ►
German Police

This member of the *Ordungspolizei* (order police) – Germany's regular uniformed police – has been drawn into military service in a police battalion. Such units were used to implement German martial law in the occupied territories. He wears officers' form-fitting knee-high boots.

SPECIFICATIONS	
Country:	Germany
Date:	1939
Unit:	Military Police
Rank:	Lieutenant
Theatre:	Eastern Front
Location:	Poland

German Officer 1939

The figure seen here is that of *Generaloberst* Eduard Dietl. He rose to fame and influence for his leadership during the German campaign in Norway in 1940, when he commanded the 3rd Mountain Division in the battles for and around Narvik. Although a *Wehrmacht* officer, Dietl was also a committed Nazi.

The cloth sleeve patch here depicts the edelweiss flower, the traditional symbol of German mountain troops. It was first depicted in a military context in 1907, by the Austro-Hungarian alpine soldiers, but it subsequently entered German use (*Wehrmacht* and *Waffen-SS*). It was chosen because the flower tends to grow in high-altitude, inaccessible locations.

The Iron Cross was a military decoration established in the early 19th century in the Kingdom of Prussia, and it later became a standard, and prestigious, German medal. It was awarded in two classes – 1st and 2nd – the latter being a prerequisite of receiving the former.

Colonel-General
German Army

Dietl here shows the uniform and insignia of a mountain division commander. The tunic is piped in crimson, and the breeches feature corresponding red stripes down the sides. In typical mountain soldier style, he avoids the regular German Army jackboots in preference for thick-soled mountain boots, and his calves are wrapped in thick puttees. He wears various decorations and insignia, including the army mountain guide badge (right breast pocket), plus the Knight's Cross of the Iron Cross around his neck.

SPECIFICATIONS	
Country:	Germany
Date:	1939
Unit:	German Army
Rank:	Colonel-General
Theatre:	Europe
Location:	Germany

Polish Army 1939

Polish forces were significantly outclassed by the *Wehrmacht* during the German invasion of 1939, but the campaign was not the walkover popular history likes to claim. The Polish Army still managed to inflict significant casualties.

◀ Colonel
7th Mounted Rifles

This commanding officer of the 7th *Wielkopolski* Mounted Rifles wears the standard Polish officers' khaki service dress with traditional flat-topped, square-shaped *czapka*. His regiment is identified by the colour of the cap band and the pennant-shaped collar patches.

SPECIFICATIONS	
Country:	Poland
Date:	1939
Unit:	7th Mounted Rifles
Rank:	Colonel
Theatre:	Eastern Front
Location:	Poland

Tank Crewman ▶
Armoured Corps

This soldier is wearing a uniform with many similarities to French armoured-unit clothing, and the leather crash helmet is actually of French issue. A black beret was often worn under the crash helmet or on its own when outside the vehicle, this matching the black leather coat or long, black greatcoat.

SPECIFICATIONS	
Country:	Poland
Date:	1939
Unit:	Polish Armoured Corps
Rank:	Crewman
Theatre:	Eastern Front
Location:	Poland

TIMELINE 1939 1939 1939 1939

◄ **Trooper**
Polish Cavalry

Poland entered World War II using cavalry in a traditional, mounted manner, with terrible results. The trooper here wears the cavalry's sheepskin coat (more practical on horseback than the infantry greatcoat) and he has a French M1915 Adrian steel helmet.

SPECIFICATIONS	
Country:	Poland
Date:	1939
Unit:	Polish Cavalry
Rank:	Trooper
Theatre:	Eastern Front
Location:	Poland

Private ►
Polish Army

The standard Polish Army uniform was a two-piece tunic and trousers, the former having a stand-and-fall collar. Here the collar features the dark blue infantry arm-of-service colour. Running across his waist are ammunition pouches for his rifle, a Polish copy of the German Mauser.

SPECIFICATIONS	
Country:	Poland
Date:	1939
Unit:	Polish Army
Rank:	Private
Theatre:	Eastern Front
Location:	Poland

Winter War 1939–40

The Winter War between Finland and Russia was one in which the quality of uniforms was vital against the severe Finnish winter. Those troops wearing inferior uniforms were likely to suffer from frostbite or would even freeze to death.

◄ Private
Infantry Division, Red Army

The average Russian soldier in 1939 was kitted out in designs that dated back to the beginning of the century. This private in Finland is wearing the distinctive pointed grey cloth helmet, known officially as the *shelm*. His collar patches and helmet star are in the infantry colour.

SPECIFICATIONS	
Country:	Soviet Union
Date:	1939
Unit:	Infantry Division
Rank:	Private
Theatre:	Eastern Front
Location:	Finland

Marshal Mannerheim ►
Finnish Army

Marshal Mannerheim was the head of the very small (nine divisions) but resilient Finnish Army. He wears a plain field-grey tunic and riding trousers, while around his neck is the Mannerheim Cross of the Cross of Liberty for bravery. Other decoration ribbons are placed over his left breast.

SPECIFICATIONS	
Country:	Finland
Date:	1939
Unit:	Finnish Army
Rank:	Marshal
Theatre:	Eastern Front
Location:	Finland

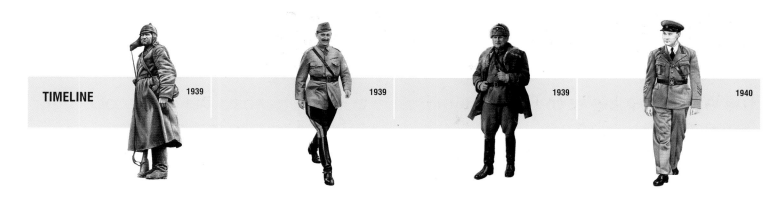

TIMELINE   1939   1939   1939   1940

◀ Captain
Finnish Army

This captain (his rank is indicated by the three brass roses on each collar patch) shows some of the classic winter uniform items of the Finnish Army, including the fur-lined winter field cap and the thick sheepskin coat. The uniform beneath is the M1936 version.

SPECIFICATIONS	
Country:	Finland
Date:	1939
Unit:	Finnish Army
Rank:	Captain
Theatre:	Eastern Front
Location:	Finland

Colonel ▶
Armoured Division, Red Army

The steel-grey uniform here, the standard-issue service dress for Soviet armoured soldiers from 1935, replaced the khaki service dress worn by the rest of the infantry. It is a simple uniform of tunic and matching trousers, a peaked service cap, and a white shirt and black tie.

SPECIFICATIONS	
Country:	Soviet Union
Date:	1940
Unit:	Armoured Division
Rank:	Colonel
Theatre:	Eastern Front
Location:	Kiev

Maritime War 1939–40

The Germany Navy at the beginning of the war was organized into three basic arms – capital ships, naval security and submarines – each one being under the command of a flag officer, or *Führer*. It was known to be a professional but rather sidelined arm-of-service.

◀ Seaman
German Navy

This seaman, who is operating in the Baltic, is wearing the standard summer whites of the German Navy just prior to the onset of war. The cap features a Nazi eagle set above a national cockade – a standard insignia for ratings – while on the tunic, the national emblem is over the right breast.

SPECIFICATIONS	
Country:	German Navy
Date:	1939
Unit:	German Navy
Rank:	Seaman
Theatre:	Germany
Location:	Baltic Sea

Petty Officer ▶
Panzerschiff

This petty officer of the German Navy is wearing the pre-war walking-out dress, which was discarded after 1941. The cap tally advertising the name of the ship – here *Panzerschiff Deutschland* – was soon to be replaced by a standardized model bearing the word *Kriegsmarine*.

SPECIFICATIONS	
Country:	Germany
Date:	1939
Unit:	Battleship *Deutschland*
Rank:	Petty Officer
Theatre:	Germany
Location:	Kiel

TIMELINE 1939 1939 1940 1940

◄ **Lieutenant**
German Navy

This rank of this heavily decorated lieutenant in the German Navy is identified at the cuff, and consists of two thick and one thin gold stripes surmounted by a gold star. The gold stars accompanied virtually all officer ranks, while the stripes and shoulder straps (when worn) denoted the specific rank.

SPECIFICATIONS	
Country:	Germany
Date:	1940
Unit:	German Navy
Rank:	Lieutenant
Theatre:	Western Europe
Location:	North Sea

Seaman ▶
German Navy

This German seaman is shown wearing the uniform for naval land warfare, and hence is dressed largely like a regular army infantryman. He has the 1935 steel helmet and infantry field equipment, including the standard army rifle, the Kar 98k.

SPECIFICATIONS	
Country:	Germany
Date:	1940
Unit:	German Navy
Rank:	Seaman
Theatre:	Scandinavia
Location:	Norway

Maritime War 1939–40

At the outset of the war, most of the combatants perceived maritime power in terms of capital ships such as battleships and cruisers. In reality, it would be submarines and carriers that came to determine the outcome of the naval war.

◄ Seaman
Northern Fleet, Red Navy

This rating is wearing the standard uniform for a Russian seaman operating in the Arctic Circle. Over a square rig outfit (dark blue jumper and black, bell-bottomed trousers; the Russians were the only navy to mix black and blue), he dons a long, blue greatcoat issued for winter use.

SPECIFICATIONS	
Country:	Soviet Union
Date:	1939
Unit:	Northern Fleet
Rank:	Seaman
Theatre:	Arctic
Location:	Archangel

Korvettenkapitän ►
Kriegsmarine

This *Korvettenkapitän* wears the standard German Navy uniform for officers, petty officers and cadets: a peaked cap with a single row of embroidered oak leaves on the peak and a reefer jacket with rank distinction lace on the cuffs.

SPECIFICATIONS	
Country:	Germany
Date:	1940
Unit:	German Navy
Rank:	Korvettenkapitän
Theatre:	Western Europe
Location:	North Sea

TIMELINE   1939   1940   1940   1941

◀ Admiral
Baltic Sea Fleet

This is Admiral Rolf Carls, the commanding admiral of the German Baltic Sea Fleet. Here he wears a peaked cap with embroidered oak leaves. Officers, warrant officers and midshipmen wore the same cap badges, together with eagle and cockade with wreath on a peaked cap.

SPECIFICATIONS	
Country:	Germany
Date:	1940
Unit:	Baltic Sea Fleet
Rank:	Admiral
Theatre:	Baltic
Location:	Norway

Able Seaman ▶
Polish Navy

This naval square rig uniform is of a conventional naval pattern: a naval-blue pullover with a broad, white-striped collar, plus matching trousers with the ankles fixed into white pull-on gaiters. The cap features the Polish eagle and also the name of the ship.

SPECIFICATIONS	
Country:	Poland
Date:	1941
Unit:	Polish Navy
Rank:	Able Seaman
Theatre:	Western Europe
Location:	Britain

Maritime War 1939–40

In 1939 the French Navy was also a great maritime power, but its fleet was suddenly perceived as a potential threat to the British when France fell to Germany the following year. Much of the French fleet was therefore destroyed by British warships at Mers-el-Kébir off the Algerian coast on 3 July 1940.

◀ Seaman
Finnish Navy

This Finnish sailor is amply dressed for the severe weather of the Baltic. His two-piece fleece-lined foul-weather suit with fur collar would give good protection against Arctic winds, rains and ice storms. Underneath, he would be wearing the standard square rig uniform of the Finnish Navy.

SPECIFICATIONS	
Country:	Finland
Date:	1939
Unit:	Finnish Navy
Rank:	Seaman
Theatre:	Baltic
Location:	Lake Lagoda

Leading Seaman ▶
French Navy

Presenting arms with his 8mm (0.315in) M92/16 rifle and M92 knife bayonet, this sailor is wearing the French Navy parade uniform. Some items of his uniform would only make an appearance in this context, such as the white laced and buckled gaiters that cover the tops of his boots.

SPECIFICATIONS	
Country:	France
Date:	1940
Unit:	French Navy
Rank:	Leading Seaman
Theatre:	Atlantic
Location:	Brest

1939   1940   1940   1940

◀ Seaman
Norwegian Navy

The seaman pictured here is wearing the standard Norwegian Navy uniform, which had been issued from 1907. This consisted of a blue jumper with a blue-jean collar featuring three white stripes, plus trousers in a matching navy blue. The jumper was worn with a white shirt underneath and a black scarf around the neck.

SPECIFICATIONS	
Country:	Norway
Date:	1940
Unit:	Norwegian Navy
Rank:	Seaman
Theatre:	Baltic
Location:	Norway

Leading Seaman ▶
Dutch Navy

This leading seaman wears the standard naval square rig along with a cap tally bearing the legend 'Royal Navy' (in translation) in Gothic lettering. He carries infantry equipment and a 6.5mm (0.25in) M1895 rifle.

SPECIFICATIONS	
Country:	The Netherlands
Date:	1940
Unit:	Dutch Navy
Rank:	Leading Seaman
Theatre:	Northwest Europe
Location:	Holland

Maritime War 1939–40

Of all the Allied navies at the start of the war, by far the most powerful was the British Royal Navy. Although the Royal Air Force has taken most of the credit for preventing the invasion of Britain in 1940, the Royal Navy was also a powerful deterrent to a German amphibious campaign.

◄ Captain
Home Fleet, Royal Navy

This captain illustrates the standard uniform worn by wartime Royal Navy officers. At the top we have a blue peaked cap with a black mohair band and a black, patent calf-leather peak and chin strap. The badge has a silver anchor at its centre, surrounded by gold laurel leaves and surmounted by a gold and silver crown on a red backing.

SPECIFICATIONS	
Country:	Britain
Date:	1940
Unit:	Home Fleet
Rank:	Captain
Theatre:	Northwest Europe
Location:	Scotland

Chief Petty Officer ►
Home Fleet, Royal Navy

In the Royal Navy the uniforms for chief petty officers were basically the same as those for officers except that the former had a special cap badge and wore rating badges on the sleeves. The everyday chief petty officer uniform is illustrated here.

SPECIFICATIONS	
Country:	Britain
Date:	1940
Unit:	Home Fleet
Rank:	Chief Petty Officer
Theatre:	Northwest Europe
Location:	Scapa Flow

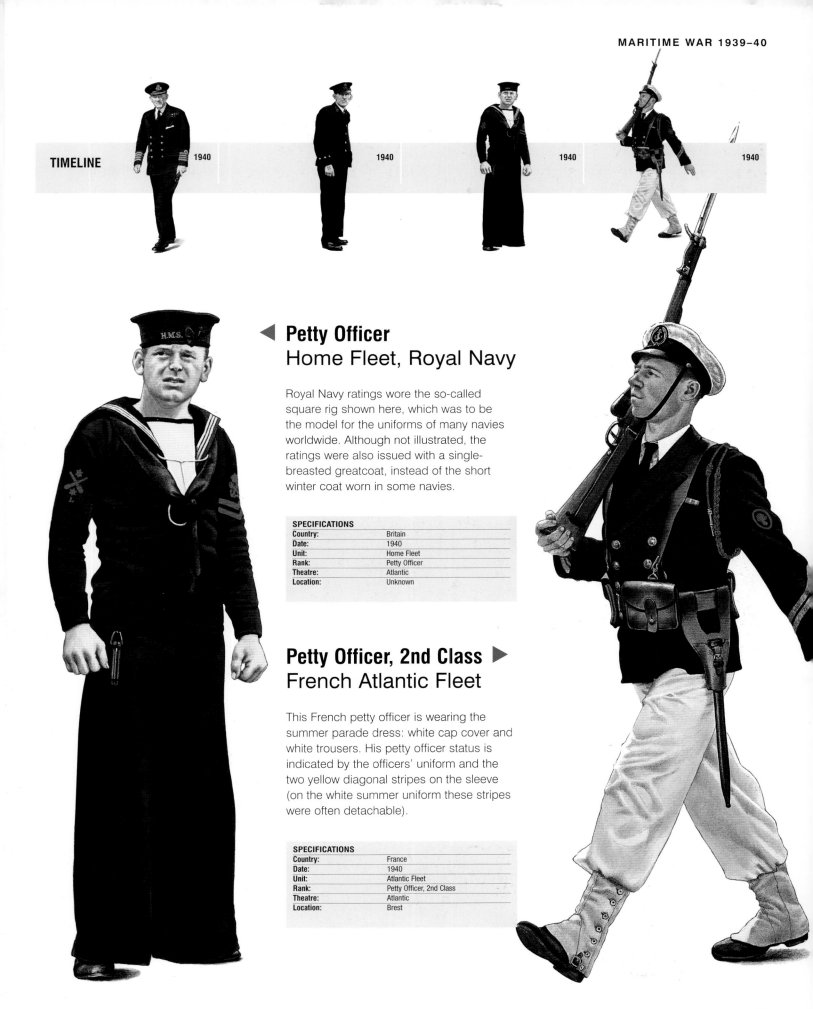

◀ Petty Officer
Home Fleet, Royal Navy

Royal Navy ratings wore the so-called square rig shown here, which was to be the model for the uniforms of many navies worldwide. Although not illustrated, the ratings were also issued with a single-breasted greatcoat, instead of the short winter coat worn in some navies.

SPECIFICATIONS	
Country:	Britain
Date:	1940
Unit:	Home Fleet
Rank:	Petty Officer
Theatre:	Atlantic
Location:	Unknown

Petty Officer, 2nd Class ▶
French Atlantic Fleet

This French petty officer is wearing the summer parade dress: white cap cover and white trousers. His petty officer status is indicated by the officers' uniform and the two yellow diagonal stripes on the sleeve (on the white summer uniform these stripes were often detachable).

SPECIFICATIONS	
Country:	France
Date:	1940
Unit:	Atlantic Fleet
Rank:	Petty Officer, 2nd Class
Theatre:	Atlantic
Location:	Brest

Scandinavia 1940

The Danish Army presented no significant resistance to the German invasion in 1940, and the occupation was on especially lenient terms. The Danes were allowed to retain widespread control over their governmental, legal and administrative affairs. Norwegian resistance, however, was much heavier, with Allied intervention.

◀ Private
Jutland Division, Danish Army

Although Denmark had a modern khaki uniform from 1923, it was in store by 1940, and soldiers were kitted out in World War I-pattern clothing. This uniform is the wool 1915-pattern in grey-blue with an M1923 helmet. Rations and personal effects are in the backpack.

SPECIFICATIONS	
Country:	Denmark
Date:	1940
Unit:	Jutland Division
Rank:	Private
Theatre:	Scandinavia
Location:	Denmark

Warrant Officer ▶
7th Infantry Regiment, Danish Army

The 1923-pattern uniform worn by the warrant officer here is entirely obscured by the heavy black 1864 greatcoat, another dated piece of uniform in Danish use. The greatcoat was double-breasted and featured a stand-and-fall collar plus turn-back cuffs with two rows of buttons.

SPECIFICATIONS	
Country:	Denmark
Date:	1940
Unit:	7th Infantry Regiment
Rank:	Warrant Officer
Theatre:	Baltic
Location:	Denmark

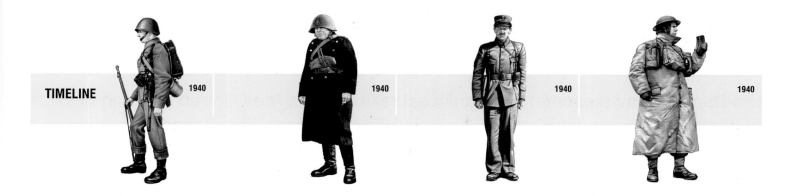

TIMELINE 1940 · 1940 · 1940 · 1940

◀ Lieutenant
Infantry Division, Norwegian Army

Like the forces of the Netherlands, the Norwegian Army adopted a new uniform of grey-green tunic and trousers from 1912 onwards. This was essentially the mode of dress for both winter and summer, although there was a winter-issue tunic with a looser fit to allow the wearing of warm underclothes.

SPECIFICATIONS	
Country:	Norway
Date:	1940
Unit:	Infantry Division
Rank:	Lieutenant
Theatre:	Scandinavia
Location:	Norway

Private ▶
49th Infantry Division

Because of his voluminous coat, this soldier could be confused with a naval rating, although he is actually an infantry private seen during the Norwegian campaign of 1940. The coat was termed the 'tropal' coat and was lined with kapok, a cotton-like substance used to pad clothes and also to stuff items like cushions.

SPECIFICATIONS	
Country:	Britain
Date:	1940
Unit:	49th Infantry Division
Rank:	Private
Theatre:	Scandinavia
Location:	Norway

French Ski Troops

In mid-April 1940, some 10,000 British and French troops, who had been assembled in British ports for possible aid to Finland, were embarked aboard landing ships. They landed at Namsos and Andalsnes in Norway, their mission being to try to take Trondheim from the Germans and to retain an Allied foothold in Scandinavia.

The M1922/26 was one of several Hotchkiss models that emerged in the interwar period. It had a standard gas operation, but the rate of fire could be reduced through a regulator in front of the trigger. It accepted three types of feed: top-mounted magazine; side-fed Hotchkiss metal strip; or the Hotchkiss metal-link belt.

The MAS Mle 1936 was a robust and sound weapon. The bolt action was especially short on account of locking taking place at the very end of the receiver, even though this did necessitate the bolt handle being angled sharply forwards for proximity to the operator's trigger hand.

Private
French Army

This *chasseur alpin*, or mountain soldier, of the 5th Demi-Brigade was one of those who were put ashore in Norway as part of the Allied Expeditionary Force. He wears the blue *chasseur* beret and waterproof cotton duck anorak; for additional protection against the cold and wet conditions, he has been issued with a sheepskin jacket, which is rolled on top of his rucksack. He carries a pistol in a holster and a 7.5mm (0.29in) MAS 36 carbine. Gaiters and skis were standard issue for French mountain troops.

SPECIFICATIONS	
Country:	France
Date:	1940
Unit:	French Army
Rank:	Private
Theatre:	Scandinavia
Location:	Norway

The Low Countries 1940

Belgium and the Netherlands were overrun in a matter of weeks in 1940, against insurmountable odds. The uniforms of these two countries were heavily influenced by the models of France and Britain.

 **Colonel**
1st Infantry Regiment, Belgian Army

Belgian military uniform in the early years of the war followed a French pattern for the private soldiers and NCOs, but adopted British-style uniforms for the officers. Here we have a British Army-type peaked service cap; the crown in the centre of the cap indicates the arm-of-service by the colour.

SPECIFICATIONS	
Country:	Belgium
Date:	1940
Unit:	1st Infantry Regiment
Rank:	Colonel
Theatre:	Northwest Europe
Location:	Belgium

Sergeant ▶
Infantry Division, Belgian Army

This NCO demonstrates the French style of other ranks' uniforms in the Belgian Army. The steel helmet is a French copy, although with a Belgian lion's head on the front. He wears a single-breasted jacket with a stand-and-fall collar, with an infantry crown on the shoulder straps.

SPECIFICATIONS	
Country:	Belgium
Date:	1940
Unit:	Infantry Division
Rank:	Sergeant
Theatre:	Northwest Europe
Location:	Belgium

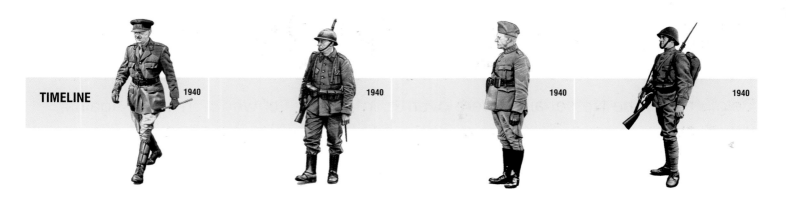

◀ Lieutenant-Colonel
Cyclist Regiment, Dutch Army

This pattern of uniform was introduced into the Dutch Army in 1912. It features a grey-green tunic and trousers, with black leather riding boots (only for officers and mounted soldiers; others wore black ankle boots) and side cap. This style of cap was introduced in 1937 instead of the traditional *kepi*.

SPECIFICATIONS	
Country:	The Netherlands
Date:	1940
Unit:	Cyclist Regiment
Rank:	Lieutenant-Colonel
Theatre:	Northwest Europe
Location:	Holland

Corporal ▶
Dutch Army

The Dutch corporal here has the 1912-pattern uniform, with his rank displayed by the chevron on his sleeve. The green piping on the collar denotes the arm-of-service. A distinctive feature is the helmet, which is similar to that worn by the Romanian Army.

SPECIFICATIONS	
Country:	The Netherlands
Date:	1940
Unit:	Dutch Army
Rank:	Corporal
Theatre:	Northwest Europe
Location:	Holland

French Forces 1940

The German campaign in Western Europe in 1940 culminated in France's catastrophic defeat. Despite being one of the largest armies in Europe, French forces were conclusively outmanoeuvred by the more nimble *Wehrmacht*.

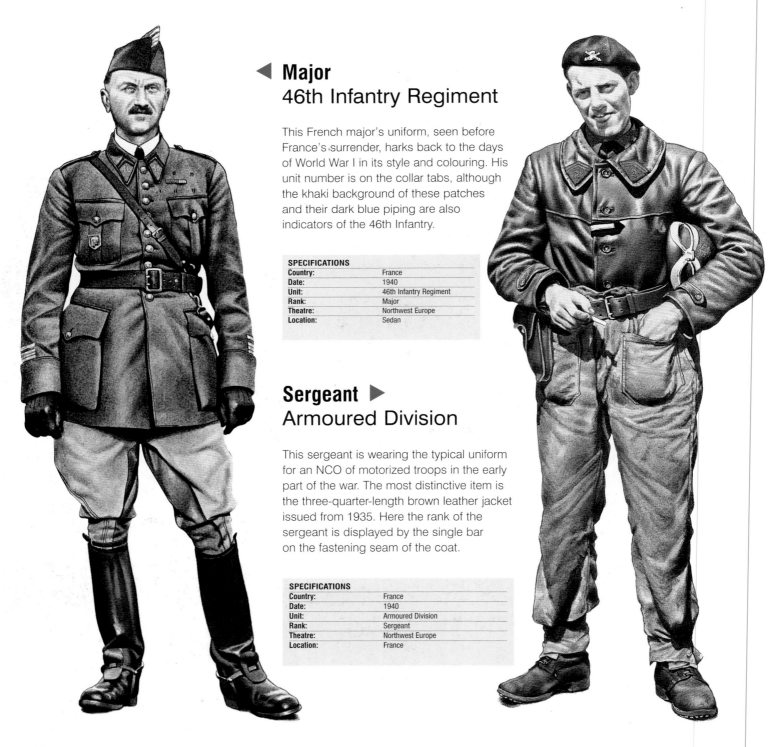

◀ Major
46th Infantry Regiment

This French major's uniform, seen before France's surrender, harks back to the days of World War I in its style and colouring. His unit number is on the collar tabs, although the khaki background of these patches and their dark blue piping are also indicators of the 46th Infantry.

SPECIFICATIONS	
Country:	France
Date:	1940
Unit:	46th Infantry Regiment
Rank:	Major
Theatre:	Northwest Europe
Location:	Sedan

Sergeant ▶
Armoured Division

This sergeant is wearing the typical uniform for an NCO of motorized troops in the early part of the war. The most distinctive item is the three-quarter-length brown leather jacket issued from 1935. Here the rank of the sergeant is displayed by the single bar on the fastening seam of the coat.

SPECIFICATIONS	
Country:	France
Date:	1940
Unit:	Armoured Division
Rank:	Sergeant
Theatre:	Northwest Europe
Location:	France

TIMELINE   1940   1940   1940   1940

◀ Private, 1st Class
182nd Artillery Regiment

In the French Army prior to 1935, the uniform was the blue World War I pattern, but 1935 saw a khaki uniform, in line with many other nations, as shown here on this artillery private. This cut is superior, however, as he is wearing walking-out dress. The khaki tunic was single-breasted with six metal buttons and a low-fall collar.

SPECIFICATIONS	
Country:	France
Date:	1940
Unit:	182nd Artillery Regiment
Rank:	Private, 1st Class
Theatre:	Northwest Europe
Location:	France

Corporal ▶
24th Infantry Regiment

This corporal has an accumulation of equipment dating from World War I to the late 1930s. Most of the load-bearing system, apart from the gas-mask case, dates to the previous conflict, while the Adrian helmet is from 1926 and the greatcoat from 1938.

SPECIFICATIONS	
Country:	France
Date:	1940
Unit:	24th Infantry Regiment
Rank:	Corporal
Theatre:	Northwest Europe
Location:	France

French Forces 1940

The years 1935 and 1936 seem pivotal for uniform design in many European armies. Styles changed as the old ways of World War I were finally left behind. Tactical changes were harder to implement, however, as the French forces discovered in 1940.

◀ Lieutenant-Colonel
French Army

The rank of this French Army lieutenant-colonel is identified by the embroidery and braid on his *kepi*, and also by the stars on the cuffs of his tunic. His footwear is in the cavalry tradition, consisting of leather boots and calf protectors, worn with pale breeches.

SPECIFICATIONS	
Country:	France
Date:	1940
Unit:	French Army
Rank:	Lieutenant-Colonel
Theatre:	Northwest Europe
Location:	France

Sergeant ▶
Polish Army

Not a Frenchman, but part of the free Polish Army based in France prior to the German invasion. He is actually wearing the most up-to-date pattern of French Army uniform, and carries a French Lebel M86/93 rifle. His rank badges and the national emblem on his helmet, however, are Polish.

SPECIFICATIONS	
Country:	France/Poland
Date:	1940
Unit:	Polish Army
Rank:	Sergeant
Theatre:	Northwest Europe
Location:	Brest

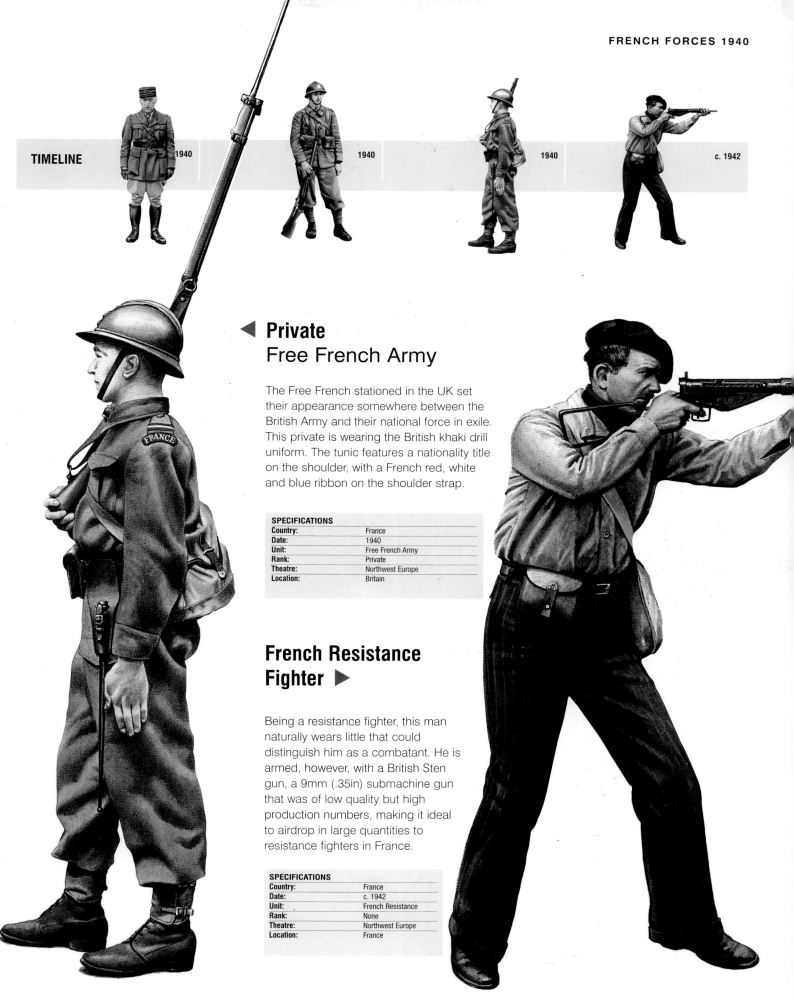

1940

1940

1940

c. 1942

◀ Private
Free French Army

The Free French stationed in the UK set their appearance somewhere between the British Army and their national force in exile. This private is wearing the British khaki drill uniform. The tunic features a nationality title on the shoulder, with a French red, white and blue ribbon on the shoulder strap.

SPECIFICATIONS	
Country:	France
Date:	1940
Unit:	Free French Army
Rank:	Private
Theatre:	Northwest Europe
Location:	Britain

French Resistance
Fighter ▶

Being a resistance fighter, this man naturally wears little that could distinguish him as a combatant. He is armed, however, with a British Sten gun, a 9mm (.35in) submachine gun that was of low quality but high production numbers, making it ideal to airdrop in large quantities to resistance fighters in France.

SPECIFICATIONS	
Country:	France
Date:	c. 1942
Unit:	French Resistance
Rank:	None
Theatre:	Northwest Europe
Location:	France

German Blitzkrieg 1939–40

Germany's strength in 1939–40 was its effective use of combined-arms tactics. The air force and army in particular could work closely together through radio communications, demonstrating a tactical movement that frequently outpaced or outmanoeuvred the enemy.

◀ Pilot
Condor Legion

The Condor Legion was a force of some 100 German aircraft (split equally between bombers and fighters) and over 16,000 personnel who fought for the Nationalist cause in the Spanish Civil War. The pilot here, pictured late in the campaign, is wearing a German aviator's cap, jacket and pantaloons, all in a dark khaki.

SPECIFICATIONS	
Country:	Germany
Date:	1939
Unit:	Condor Legion
Rank:	Pilot
Theatre:	Spain
Location:	Spain

Corporal ▶
1st Panzer Regiment

This uniform – introduced into service in 1935 – is an ideal form of dress for the cramped and hot interior of an armoured vehicle. The trousers are loose to aid movement and ventilation, and the double-breasted jacket is kept short so that buttons are not strained in a seated position.

SPECIFICATIONS	
Country:	Germany
Date:	1940
Unit:	1st Panzer Regiment
Rank:	Corporal
Theatre:	Northwest Europe
Location:	France

TIMELINE

1939

1940

1940

1940

◄ **NCO**
1st Parachute Regiment

This para wears a jump-smock typical of the summer of 1940, though field-grey seems more common than khaki. The smock, worn over the regular uniform, was removed by zip on landing (although the parachute harness had no quick-release mechanism).

SPECIFICATIONS	
Country:	Germany
Date:	1940
Unit:	1st Parachute Regiment
Rank:	NCO
Theatre:	Northwest Europe
Location:	Belgium

Private ►
SS *Polizei* Division

The SS *Polizei* Division, as the name suggests, was a *Waffen-SS* division formed from police personnel. The uniform is largely that of the regular German infantry. Rolled up on his back is a camouflage *Zeltbahn* shelter quarter.

SPECIFICATIONS	
Country:	Germany
Date:	1940
Unit:	SS Polizei Division
Rank:	Private
Theatre:	Northwest Europe
Location:	France

The German Infantryman 1940

The German infantryman in the first two years of the war had few equals. As a recruit he had usually already undergone years of paramilitary training as part of the Hitler Youth. The army instruction he subsequently received emphasized personal initiative to achieve mission goals, and the soldier generally had a good standard of kit, particularly for the conditions of the Western European theatre.

The MP40 was a version of the earlier MP38, but one configured more for the demands of wartime mass-production. It was a 9mm (.35in) Parabellum weapon firing from a single-stack 32-round box magazine. The magazine was actually the weapon's weakest part; otherwise it was an effective and dependable close-quarters weapon.

The German Army patches shown here denote private and NCO ranks; they were worn on the tunic sleeve. They are (from left to right): *Stabsgefreiter* (staff lance-corporal); *Obergefreiter* (corporal); *Gefreiter* (lance-corporal) and *Oberschutze* (private first class).

Lance-Corporal
German Army

The arm patch on this soldier – a single silver chevron on a black triangle – indicates that he is a *Gefreiter*, equivalent to a lance-corporal in the British Army. His visible kit includes the entrenching tool in its case and the cylindrical gas-mask container, although in time the latter became more useful for storing personal items than for gas masks. He is armed with an MP40 submachine gun – a development of the MP38 more suited to the mass-production needs of wartime.

SPECIFICATIONS	
Country:	Germany
Date:	1940
Unit:	German Army
Rank:	Lance-Corporal
Theatre:	Western Europe
Location:	France

British Forces 1940

By 1940, a new battledress for British Army soldiers had been established. Introduced in 1937, this consisted of khaki blouse and long trousers, both roomy in cut, with the trousers gathered at the ankle and fitted into the boots.

◀ Private
The East Yorkshire Regiment

This soldier's uniform was not typically seen on British soldiers. Over his khaki service dress he wears a large snowsuit made from padded material. The jacket is double-breasted to provide better wind resistance, while the Mk 1 steel helmet is covered in a white snow-cover for additional camouflage.

SPECIFICATIONS

Country:	Britain
Date:	1940
Unit:	East Yorkshire Regiment
Rank:	Private
Theatre:	Northwest Europe
Location:	Maginot Line

Lance-Corporal ▶
Black Watch Regiment

We see here a lance-corporal of the Scottish Black Watch Regiment, which adapted standard British Army dress to give it a local and national flavour. Instead of the standard British Army khaki-serge tunic, he wears a cutaway version known as a doublet, plus a regimental kilt.

SPECIFICATIONS

Country:	Britain
Date:	1940
Unit:	Black Watch Regiment
Rank:	Lance-corporal
Theatre:	Northwest Europe
Location:	France

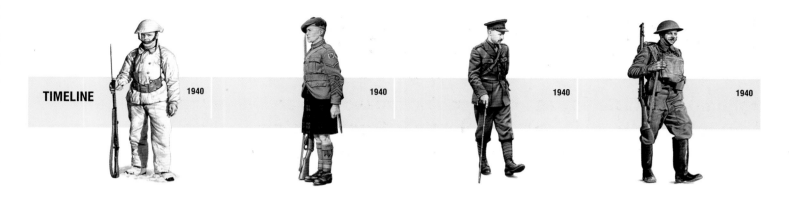

◄ Captain
Grenadier Guards

This officer figure appears to date from World War I rather than 20 years later. With the khaki service dress, British Army officers wore an open tunic with light khaki shirt and tie, matching khaki pantaloons, puttees and brown ankle boots, although long khaki trousers with brown shoes were also worn.

SPECIFICATIONS	
Country:	Britain
Date:	1940
Unit:	Grenadier Guards
Rank:	Captain
Theatre:	Northwest Europe
Location:	France

Corporal ►
Hampshire Regiment

This corporal is wearing the new battledress uniform and a Mk 1 helmet with elasticated chin strap. The single-breasted blouse is made from a rough serge material with a stand-and-fall collar and fly front, plus pleated breast patch pockets with flap and concealed buttons.

SPECIFICATIONS	
Country:	Britain
Date:	1940
Unit:	Hampshire Regiment
Rank:	Corporal
Theatre:	Northwest Europe
Location:	France

European Theatre 1940–42

Although camouflage was introduced during World War II, olive-drab, khaki and field-grey still predominated among the European infantry. The cuts of the uniforms largely depended upon the financial and material status of each state, and the distinctions between officers and other ranks.

◀ Lance-Corporal
1st Infantry Division, Czechoslovak Army

Czech soldiers in French service displayed rank on the shoulder straps, and also wore their officers' graduation badges over the right pocket. Other than these markings, the French influence runs throughout – the tunic, pantaloons and helmet are of French infantry issue.

SPECIFICATIONS	
Country:	Czechoslovakia
Date:	1940
Unit:	1st Infantry Division
Rank:	Lance-corporal
Theatre:	Northwest Europe
Location:	France

Colonel ▶
36th Infantry Regiment

Italian officer uniforms were of excellent cut and quality. In essence, the basic officer uniform was the same as that of the general ranks, yet the colour was lighter than the grey-green of lower ranks, and the twill cloth was of better quality. The colonel here is shown in his *cordellino* uniform with a vivid display of rank.

SPECIFICATIONS	
Country:	Italy
Date:	1940
Unit:	36th Infantry Regiment
Rank:	Colonel
Theatre:	Northwest Europe
Location:	Southern France

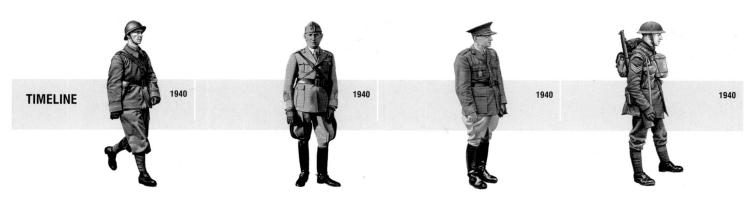

TIMELINE 1940   1940   1940   1940

◄ General Minister of Defence
Czechoslovak Army

Depicted here is the Czech Minister of Defence-in-Exile, General Sergej Ingr. The main influences on the Czech uniform were British and French. The strong Czech alliance with France meant that French tunics, helmets and trousers were common; indeed, the general's tunic is of French origin.

SPECIFICATIONS	
Country:	Czechoslovakia
Date:	1940
Unit:	Czech Army
Rank:	Minister of Defence
Theatre:	Northwest Europe
Location:	Britain

Sergeant ►
Welsh Guards, Household Division

This sergeant's khaki service dress pre-dates the 1940 British uniform, and harks back to the World War I British Army uniform, elements of which were still worn in the early years of World War II. The most anachronistic items are the long puttees and the leather jerkin overcoat.

SPECIFICATIONS	
Country:	Britain
Date:	1940
Unit:	Welsh Guards
Rank:	Sergeant
Theatre:	Northwest Europe
Location:	Pirbright, England

European Theatre 1940–42

The basic weapon of European infantry was the bolt-action rifle, although both Germany and the Soviet Union later introduced some semi-automatic weapons on a limited scale. Uniform equipment, therefore, featured ammunition pouches for rifle clips and chargers.

◀ Lance-Corporal
Home Guard, Hertfordshire Regiment

The Home Guard lance-corporal is wearing the light working version – known as 'denims' – of the British Army battledress, and on his field cap he wears the cap badge of the Hertfordshire Regiment. On his left sleeve is the Home Guard shoulder title.

SPECIFICATIONS	
Country:	Britain
Date:	1940
Unit:	Home Guard, Hertfordshire Regiment
Rank:	Lance-Corporal
Theatre:	Northwest Europe
Location:	England

Lance-Corporal ▶
Royal Military Police

Two items distinguish this man as a soldier of the Royal Military Police: the 'MP' armband and the red top to the service cap (hence the MPs' nickname of 'red caps'). His sidearm is the Webley 11.5mm (.455in) No.1 Mk 6 revolver.

SPECIFICATIONS	
Country:	Britain
Date:	1940
Unit:	Royal Military Police
Rank:	Lance-corporal
Theatre:	Northwest Europe
Location:	England

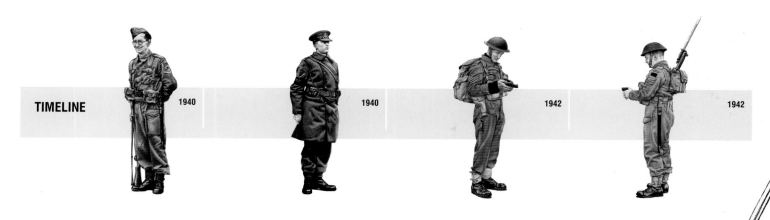

◀ ### Sergeant
No.1 Commando

A commando sergeant checks two magazines for a Sten submachine gun. He wears a khaki battledress, the trousers being fastened into light khaki anklets and over the top of the boots. These commonly worn boots, with thickly treaded rubber soles, were known as 'ammunition' boots.

SPECIFICATIONS	
Country:	Britain
Date:	1942
Unit:	No.1 Commando
Rank:	Sergeant
Theatre:	Northwest Europe
Location:	St Nazaire

Sergeant ▶
Canadian Army

Canadian Army uniform largely followed the model of the British Army, although the cloth tended to be of better quality and came in a slightly greener shade. This sergeant has fixed his Pattern 1907 bayonet to his Short-Magazine Lee-Enfield rifle.

SPECIFICATIONS	
Country:	Canada
Date:	1942
Unit:	Canadian Army
Rank:	Sergeant
Theatre:	Northwest Europe
Location:	Unknown

British Army Commando

An early morale-lifter for the British during World War II was the Royal Navy and Commando raid on the German dry dock at St Nazaire in March 1942. Although nearly 400 soldiers did not come home, including 197 killed, the raid destroyed the dock and severely restricted Germany's use of capital ships in Atlantic operations. Such was just one operation of Britain's newly-founded commando arm.

The Thompson M1928 was perhaps the best known of the US Thompson series, though it actually differed little from the earlier M1921 apart from having a reduced rate of fire and some variants coming without the foregrip. It laid the foundations for the late M1 gun, which was a simple blowback weapon designed for mass-production.

The commando name badge became a mark of the elite in the British armed forces during World War II. The term itself derived from the Afrikaans word *Kommando*, which essentially meant 'mobile infantry regiment'. The British developed specialist commando troops from June 1940; they were used for coastal raiding, small-unit assaults against difficult targets, and special operations behind enemy lines.

Commando
British Army Commandos

The commandos were an elite within the British Army, trained to perform raiding duties against targets in occupied Europe. The commando here is wearing what was known as 'light raiding order', which stripped away anything superfluous to combat. In addition to his 1937-pattern web equipment, and his M1928 Thompson submachine gun, he also carries an inflatable life belt and a toggle rope (on his left hip) for cliff climbing.

SPECIFICATIONS	
Country:	Britain
Date:	1942
Unit:	British Army Commandos
Rank:	Commando
Theatre:	Western Europe
Location:	Unknown

US Forces in Europe 1942

From 1942, US Army, Air Force and Navy units began to deploy to Britain, and they would eventually be deployed to North Africa, Italy and Northwest Europe, broadening the Allied power ranged against Germany.

◀ Captain
US Marine Corps

The uniform seen here began to be issued among the US Marines in 1929, finally settling the style of Marine Corps uniforms after about 17 years of redesign and adaptations. It consists of a single-breasted khaki-green jacket and matching pantaloons, here worn with the less common high lace-up boots.

SPECIFICATIONS	
Country:	United States
Date:	1942
Unit:	US Marine Corps
Rank:	Captain
Theatre:	Atlantic
Location:	Iceland

Corporal ▶
Military Police, US Army

A corporal of the Military Police directs personnel at a base in England in 1942. The uniform he is wearing is a standard US Army uniform of the 1940s, though here it is worn with MP additions. The basic uniform is a single-breasted khaki tunic with an open fall collar and two breast and two side patch pockets with matching trousers.

SPECIFICATIONS	
Country:	United States
Date:	1942
Unit:	Military Police
Rank:	Corporal
Theatre:	Northwest Europe
Location:	Britain

TIMELINE   1942   1942   1942   1942

◀ **Private**
29th Infantry Division

This US Army private is wearing the Class A uniform underneath his olive-drab overcoat. His trousers, of the same material, are tucked into canvas leggings and worn with russet ankle books, over which are worn rubber overboots. His headgear comprises an oversea cap with light blue piping.

SPECIFICATIONS	
Country:	United States
Date:	1942
Unit:	29th Infantry Division
Rank:	Private
Theatre:	Northwest Europe
Location:	Britain

2nd Lieutenant ▶
US Army

This 2nd lieutenant wears some of the early uniform items issued to US Army forces deployed to Europe. On his head he has the older M1918-style helmet, and his firearm is the bolt-action M1903 Springfield, rather than the more modern semi-automatic M1 Garand rifle.

SPECIFICATIONS	
Country:	United States
Date:	1942
Unit:	US Army
Rank:	2nd Lieutenant
Theatre:	Northwest Europe
Location:	Northern Ireland

Air War 1939

In 1939, the *Luftwaffe* was undoubtedly the most highly trained and technologically sophisticated air force in the world. Those ranged against it fought courageously but often with the handicap of obsolete aircraft types.

 ### Lieutenant
Fighter Squadron

This Polish airman is wearing the operational summer uniform. It is a fairly crude outfit consisting of a khaki overall (undyed) made from a stiff linen, this featuring one thigh pocket, one ankle pocket, and two slash pockets on each side at hip level. The standard blue-grey uniform of the Polish Air Force is obscured, and the only marking on the overall is a rank badge on the left sleeve.

SPECIFICATIONS	
Country:	Poland
Date:	1939
Unit:	Fighter Squadron
Rank:	Lieutenant
Theatre:	Eastern Front
Location:	Poland

Captain ▶
Bomber Brigade

This captain has the Polish Air Force uniform introduced in 1936 as a replacement for the army uniform worn by air-force personnel. Its colour was blue-grey, and consisted of a tunic and matching trousers, with a fall collar for officers and a stand-and-fall collar for other ranks, these being worn with a white shirt and black tie.

SPECIFICATIONS	
Country:	Poland
Date:	1939
Unit:	Bomber Brigade
Rank:	Captain
Theatre:	Eastern Front
Location:	Poland

◄ General
Luftwaffe

Here we see a *Luftwaffe* general in full parade dress in 1939. Essentially, this is a service uniform with all the embellishments of rank and office, although the white-striped breeches are distinctive to the general officers of the *Luftwaffe*. He also wears a sword and an aiguillette, both dropped later in the war.

SPECIFICATIONS	
Country:	Germany
Date:	1939
Unit:	Luftwaffe
Rank:	General
Theatre:	Eastern Front
Location:	Poland

Pilot ►
Red Air Force

This is a bomber pilot from the Red Air Force in 1939. His bulky appearance is on account of the fur-lined flying suit and knee-high fur-lined boots, both essential items for flying bombers at high altitudes in freezing conditions. A map case hangs over his left hip, and a pistol over his right.

SPECIFICATIONS	
Country:	Soviet Union
Date:	1939
Unit:	Red Air Force
Rank:	Pilot
Theatre:	Eastern Front
Location:	Unknown

RAF 1939–41

By the outbreak of World War II, the RAF had 1000 Fairey Battles and 1000 Bristol Blenheims. High hopes were initially attached to these aircraft, but in 1940 they were shot down in droves by enemy anti-aircraft fire and fighters.

◀ Airman
Bomber Command

This bomber pilot wears a thermally insulated jacket made from glazed sheepskin by the Irvin Parachute Company. A welcome innovation was electrically heated gloves and boots, supplied with power by a cable that ran down through the jacket sleeves and legs.

SPECIFICATIONS	
Country:	Britain
Date:	1939
Unit:	Bomber Command
Rank:	Airman
Theatre:	Northwest Europe
Location:	Britain

Sergeant ▶
11 Group

This sergeant's steel helmet alludes to the likelihood of *Luftwaffe* attack against British airfields during 1940, as RAF personnel usually wore a field service cap or, for officers, the peaked cap with a metal badge. The rest of the uniform is similar in cut to the British Army service dress, except that it is rendered in RAF blue.

SPECIFICATIONS	
Country:	Britain
Date:	1940
Unit:	11 Group
Rank:	Sergeant
Theatre:	Northwest Europe
Location:	Home Counties, England

TIMELINE 1939   1940   1940   1940

◀ Lance-Corporal
1st AA Division

This Auxiliary Territorial Service (ATS) lance-corporal is wearing a privately-bought field service cap with a khaki pattern uniform. The unit emblem on the upper sleeve is that of the 1st Anti-Aircraft Division, which was based in London in 1940–41. She also wears the Royal Artillery badge.

SPECIFICATIONS	
Country:	Britain
Date:	1940
Unit:	1st AA Division
Rank:	Lance-Corporal
Theatre:	Northwest Europe
Location:	London

Bomber Crew ▶
102 Squadron

A member of a Whitley bomber crew in France, this man wears an 'Irvin Harnsuit' over his service dress. The Harnsuit had an inflatable lifebelt and three attachment points for the parachute. In addition, he is equipped with a Type B helmet and an oxygen mask with a fitted microphone.

SPECIFICATIONS	
Country:	Britain
Date:	1940
Unit:	102 Squadron
Rank:	Bomber Crew
Theatre:	Northwest Europe
Location:	France

RAF 1939–40

In 1940, the Royal Air Force was one of Britain's greatest hopes for preventing a German cross-Channel invasion. By the autumn, it had blunted the *Luftwaffe*'s offensive and the invasion had been indefinitely postponed.

◀ Leading Aircraftwoman
WAAF

This leading aircraftwoman is wearing the women's version of the standard RAF service dress, as worn by members of the Women's Auxiliary Air Force (WAAF). On her left sleeve she has an RAF eagle above the letter 'A' (denoting 'auxiliary'), together with the flash of a wireless operator and a propeller rank indicator.

SPECIFICATIONS	
Country:	Britain
Date:	1940
Unit:	Women's Auxiliary Air Force
Rank:	Leading Aircraftwoman
Theatre:	Northwest Europe
Location:	Britain

Officer ▶
RAF

The officer here is seen in the standard RAF service dress, over which he has fitted his parachute pack. The circular quick-release mechanism for the pack rests on his stomach, while the jack and cable for his radio headset is in his right hand.

SPECIFICATIONS	
Country:	Britain
Date:	1940
Unit:	Royal Air Force
Rank:	Officer
Theatre:	Northwest Europe
Location:	Britain

TIMELINE   1940   1940   1940   1941

◄ Captain
No. 302 Squadron, Polish Air Force

Polish military personnel began to serve with the Royal Air Force from December 1939. This Polish Air Force captain holds a rank equivalent to RAF flight lieutenant, and wears RAF officers' service dress, upon which he displays the badge for No. 302 Squadron on the pocket.

SPECIFICATIONS	
Country:	Poland
Date:	1940
Unit:	No. 302 Squadron
Rank:	Captain
Theatre:	Northwest Europe
Location:	Britain

Lieutenant ►
No. 331 Squadron, Norwegian Air Force

Many Norwegians served in the RAF after Norway fell to the Germans, but they were granted a separate status from the RAF in 1941. This pilot's uniform is similar to the RAF's, but greyer in colour. It has a 'Norway' patch on the left sleeve of the tunic, and the Norwegian flag on the right.

SPECIFICATIONS	
Country:	Norway
Date:	1941
Unit:	No. 331 Squadron
Rank:	Lieutenant
Theatre:	Northwest Europe
Location:	Britain

Air War, Europe 1940

By 1940, air power had proven how decisive it could be in combined-arms operations. For Europe's air forces personnel, there was also a steep learning curve about how to survive in aerial combat.

◀ Major
1st Regiment,
Belgian Air Force

Belgian Air Force officers tended towards an English cut in the style of their uniforms. This major wears a blue-grey uniform of RAF type, though the forage cap and riding boots set him apart from that service (Belgian personnel who did serve with the RAF had a light blue shoulder flash on a dark blue or grey background to distinguish nationality).

SPECIFICATIONS	
Country:	Belgium
Date:	1940
Unit:	1st Regiment
Rank:	Major
Theatre:	Northwest Europe
Location:	Belgium

Staff Captain ▶
Czech Air Force

This staff captain is pictured here while stationed in France and has adopted French uniform. The jacket and trousers form the French Louise-Blue uniform, but the insignia and badges mark the man out as a Czech national. On the jacket, the pilot wears a French pilot's badge on the right breast pocket, with aircraft wings above.

SPECIFICATIONS	
Country:	Czechoslovakia
Date:	1940
Unit:	Czech Air Force
Rank:	Staff Captain
Theatre:	Northwest Europe
Location:	France

TIMELINE   1940   1940   1940   1940

◀ **1st Lieutenant**
Reconnaissance Unit, Danish Air Force

Danish Air Force personnel wore army uniforms for their ground dress, in this case an M1923-pattern uniform, with closed- or open-collar tunics (here the closed collar), trousers flared at the thighs, and knee-high boots. The arm-of-service is indicated by a set of flying wings on the right breast.

SPECIFICATIONS	
Country:	Denmark
Date:	1940
Unit:	Reconnaissance Unit
Rank:	1st Lieutenant
Theatre:	Northwest Europe
Location:	Denmark

Pilot ▶
Paris Air Region, French Air Force

The standard uniform of French Air Force personnel was a dark Louise-Blue tunic and trousers and either a peaked cap, a black beret (for working duties) or a steel helmet. A double-breasted greatcoat was also issued. The uniform in this case is covered by a one-piece flying overall.

SPECIFICATIONS	
Country:	France
Date:	1940
Unit:	Paris Air Region
Rank:	Pilot
Theatre:	Northwest Europe
Location:	Near Paris

Air War, Europe 1940

Many early-war European air forces were poorly equipped. For example, because of decisions made in the interwar years, the French Air Force entered the war with many obsolescent aircraft. Indeed, in May 1940, less than half of its 2200 aircraft were of modern specifications.

◄ Sergeant-Major
GAO 502
French Air Force

French Air Force senior NCOs wore the same basic uniform as officers, except that the tunic had a matching cloth belt, five buttons in front, and breast pockets with pleats. This figure is an air gunner in the *Groupe Aérienne d'Observation* (GAO) 502; he wears the Louise-Blue service dress with badges of rank on the cap and cuffs.

SPECIFICATIONS	
Country:	France
Date:	1940
Unit:	GAO 502
Rank:	Sergeant-Major
Theatre:	Northwest Europe
Location:	France

2nd Lieutenant ►
Finnish Air Force

The rank of this 2nd lieutenant is displayed on his collar patches in the form of a single rosette. The winged propeller badge on the shoulder straps also sets him apart as an officer, although the absence of a flying badge on his left breast pockets shows he doesn't yet have his 'wings'.

SPECIFICATIONS	
Country:	Finland
Date:	1940
Unit:	Finnish Air Force
Rank:	2nd Lieutenant
Theatre:	Eastern Front
Location:	Finland

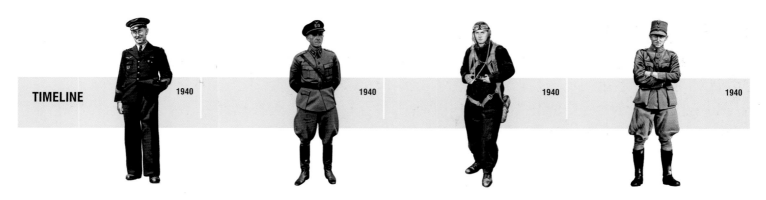

TIMELINE

1940   1940   1940   1940

◀ **Pilot**
Belgian Air Force

The Belgian Air Force was utterly outclassed
by the *Luftwaffe* during the Western
European campaign of 1940. This pilot has
a standard aviator's overall (colours could
vary), over which he wears his parachute
plus a leather flying helmet.

SPECIFICATIONS	
Country:	Belgium
Date:	1940
Unit:	Belgian Air Force
Rank:	Pilot
Theatre:	Northwest Europe
Location:	Belgium

2nd Lieutenant ▶
Fighter Squadron,
Dutch Air Force

The Dutch Air Force was classed as part of
the army and thus donned the same grey-
green tunic, pantaloons and boots. The
arm-of-service piping around the collar and
the cuffs is also blue, but of a lighter hue
than that of the infantry. Insignia and other
markings are what set the air force apart.

SPECIFICATIONS	
Country:	The Netherlands
Date:	1940
Unit:	Fighter Squadron
Rank:	2nd Lieutenant
Theatre:	Northwest Europe
Location:	Holland

Luftwaffe 1940

The *Luftwaffe* was an excellent tactical air arm, which was at its best when flying fighter missions and close air support operations. Its one major deficiency was the lack of a truly effective strategic arm.

◀ **Major**
Heinkel He 111
Luftflotte 2

During the Battle of Britain, many German airmen began to wear the one-piece canvas flying suit designed for summer use. Its canvas construction made it lighter and more breathable. Headgear in this case is the *Luftwaffe* peaked cap rather than the beige linen flight helmet.

SPECIFICATIONS	
Country:	Germany
Date:	1940
Unit:	*Luftflotte* 2
Rank:	Major
Theatre:	Northwest Europe
Location:	France

Lieutenant ▶
Jagdgeschwader 26,
III *Gruppe*

Pictured here is *Luftwaffe* 'ace' Joachim Müncheburg, a highly decorated airman of JG 26 who shot down 135 Allied aircraft before being killed in action in 1943. The decorations on display are the Iron Cross 1st and 2nd Class, and the Knight's Cross, sitting alongside pilot and wound badges.

SPECIFICATIONS	
Country:	Germany
Date:	1940
Unit:	JG 26
Rank:	Lieutenant
Theatre:	Northwest Europe
Location:	France

TIMELINE   1940   1940   1940   1940

◀ NCO
Luftwaffe

The *Luftwaffe* working dress was either the
natural-coloured cotton dress uniform or,
as can be seen here, black working
overalls. This NCO is wearing a black
twill side cap and the overalls, which
were made of cotton. Rank group is
indicated by the grey edging on the collar.

SPECIFICATIONS	
Country:	Germany
Date:	1940
Unit:	*Luftwaffe*
Rank:	NCO
Theatre:	Northwest Europe
Location:	Germany

Senior Sergeant ▶
Luftflotte 5

A senior sergeant here wears the *Luftwaffe*
NCO side cap, which has a white woven
Luftwaffe eagle and swastika badge and
the black-white-red national cockade on the
front of the cap. His tunic is the *Fliegerbluse*
(flying blouse), a garment originally intended
to be worn under flying suits.

SPECIFICATIONS	
Country:	Germany
Date:	1940
Unit:	*Luftflotte* 5
Rank:	Senior Sergeant
Theatre:	Northwest Europe
Location:	Norway

Italian Forces, North Africa 1940–42

Italy's campaign in North Africa proved to be both a tactical and strategic disaster. One of its most important consequences was that it necessitated the deployment of German forces to save their allies from outright defeat.

◀ Lieutenant
Italian Army

Italian forces had some of the best desert clothing of the war, cut for comfort and durability in the caustic African climate. This lieutenant is wearing a light khaki drill uniform, consisting of a *sahariana* jacket, shorts, long socks and suede boots. He also wears a *bustina* field cap.

SPECIFICATIONS	
Country:	Italy
Date:	1940
Unit:	Italian Army
Rank:	Lieutenant
Theatre:	Mediterranean
Location:	Sidi Azeis

Corporal ▶
Gruppi Sahariana

Gruppi Sahariana soldiers were some of the best of Italy's colonial forces. This corporal wears an Italian Army white full-dress jacket with khaki sirical trousers and a webbing belt with three long, leather pouches. The sash wrapped around his waist is an arm-of-service colour.

SPECIFICATIONS	
Country:	Libya
Date:	1942
Unit:	*Gruppi Sahariana*
Rank:	Corporal
Theatre:	Mediterranean
Location:	North Africa

◄ Captain
184th Parachute Division

The captain here is seen in a para uniform introduced in 1942. While the camouflage seems to allude to the ochre, green and mustard shades of the British Denison smock, the jacket is actually a combination of an Italian Army field tunic with the long *sahariana*.

SPECIFICATIONS	
Country:	Italy
Date:	1942
Unit:	184th Parachute Division
Rank:	Captain
Theatre:	Mediterranean
Location:	Tunisia

Sergeant ►
Polizia Africa Italiana

This sergeant of the Italian military police is wearing standard Italian Army tropical uniform, which comprises side cap (*bustina*), jacket (*sahariana*), breeches and leather leggings for motorized personnel. The standard-issue tunic had four patch pockets and a cloth belt.

SPECIFICATIONS	
Country:	Italy
Date:	1942
Unit:	*Polizia Africa Italiana*
Rank:	Sergeant
Theatre:	Mediterranean
Location:	North Africa

Italian Armoured Forces, North Africa 1941

The Italian Army suffered a chronic downscaling of its armoured resources as the war went on, mainly because Italian tanks could not compete with Allied technologies. From a total of four divisions deployed to North Africa, by 1943 the figure was reduced to one division.

The Beretta Modello 1934 was the standard Italian Army pistol between 1934 and 1945, and was often carried by tank crew. It fired the 9mm (.35in) Short cartridge, and had a seven-round detachable box magazine in the grip. Although it had some flaws in design, particularly around the reloading procedure, it was a generally reliable weapon.

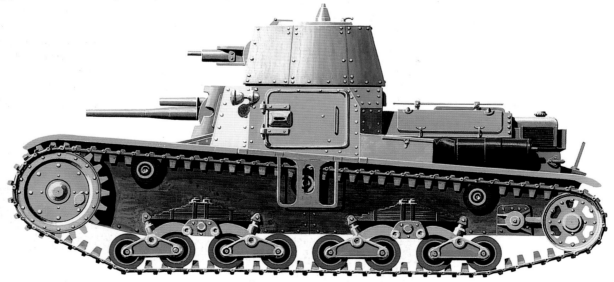

Nearly 800 M 13/40 tanks were produced in total, and they were widely used in North Africa. In combat, the M 13/40's shortcomings became very apparent: it was cramped, unreliable and caught fire easily when hit by anti-tank rounds.

Tank Crewman
Ariete Division

Here we see a soldier of the Ariete Division, one of four Italian armoured divisions that fought in North Africa: Ariete, Littorio, Centauro and Giovanni Fascisti. His uniform is that of a tank crew member, with khaki tunic and trousers covered by a three-quarter-length leather coat, and a crash helmet with neck protector. No markings are visible, but from 1940 onwards collar patches are seen, with flames on a dark blue background. The overall design of this outfit copies that of French armoured crews.

SPECIFICATIONS	
Country:	Italy
Date:	1941
Unit:	Ariete Division
Rank:	Tank Crewman
Theatre:	North Africa
Location:	Libya

Germany, North Africa 1942–43

German forces under the talented commander Erwin Rommel made some of the most spectacular advances of the war. Yet with strained logistics and locked into a war of attrition that they couldn't win, they were ultimately consigned to equally great retreats along the coast of North Africa.

◀ Major-General
15th Panzer Division

This officer, *Generalmajor* Freiherr von Esebeck, was commander of the 15th Panzer Division in North Africa. He wears a mix of the tropical uniform with a temperate-theatre peaked cap. His displayed decorations include the Knight's Cross.

SPECIFICATIONS	
Country:	Germany
Date:	1942
Unit:	15th Panzer Division
Rank:	Major-General
Theatre:	Mediterranean
Location:	North Africa

Infantryman ▶
Hermann Göring Division

The archetypal German desert uniform appeared in 1941 after a short period of trial and error. It consisted of field cap with large peak (although here the soldier has a helmet), shirt, long trousers gathered at the ankles, or shorts, woollen socks, and leather and canvas boots.

SPECIFICATIONS	
Country:	Germany
Date:	c. 1942
Unit:	Hermann Göring Division
Rank:	Infantryman
Theatre:	Mediterranean
Location:	North Africa

1942   c. 1942   1942   1943

◄ Sergeant-Major
Military Police

This military policeman in the *Africa Korps* sports a typical theatre uniform. Distinctive features, however, are the metal gorget and cuff band – the symbols of the *Feldgendarmerie* (field police). German Army regulations stated that all MPs had to wear the gorget on their chest when on duty.

SPECIFICATIONS	
Country:	Germany
Date:	1942
Unit:	Military Police
Rank:	Sergeant-Major
Theatre:	Mediterranean
Location:	North Africa

Corporal ►
Hermann Göring Division

The *Luftwaffe* had several elite ground force units under its command during World War II. This soldier is seen during one such division's operations in North Africa in 1943. He wears a khaki uniform that includes trousers with buckle ankles, hence the baggy appearance.

SPECIFICATIONS	
Country:	Germany
Date:	1943
Unit:	Hermann Göring Division
Rank:	Corporal
Theatre:	Mediterranean
Location:	Tunisia

Panzer Officer, North Africa

German forces arrived in North Africa (at Tripoli in February 1941) as what was to become the famed *Africa Korps*. The campaign in the desert, however, presented immediate problems with the issue of uniforms, forcing Germany to produce a complete range of tropical equipment and clothing in a short space of time.

The motif of the *Africa Korps* was a desert palm overset with a swastika emblem, indicating both national and regional identity. Although the swastika was at the forefront, the *Africa Korps* were one of the least ideologically motivated forces of the *Wehrmacht*, and generally fought a 'clean' war in North Africa.

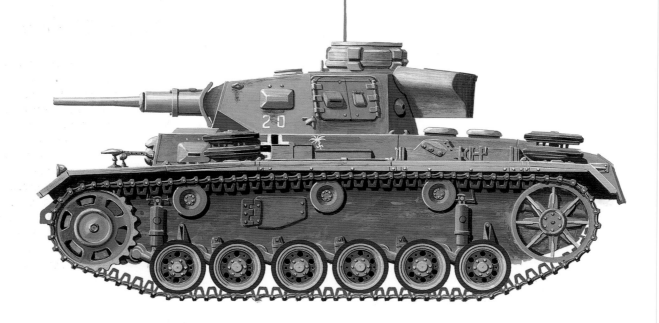

Here we see a Panzer III rendered in a desert paint scheme. Manufacture of the PzKpfw III began in 1938, and it was produced in numerous variants until August 1943. These variants included an amphibious version, a command vehicle, and an armoured recovery vehicle, as well as types sporting different firepower configurations.

Lieutenant
15th Panzer Division

This *Africa Korps* lieutenant is wearing the tropical version of the side cap, which was issued to crews of armoured fighting vehicles because it was more convenient than the field cap. He also wears the insignia from his continental uniform on his tropical blouse (note the 'Death's Head' badges on his lapels, which he has transferred from his black Panzer jacket). He displays with pride the Iron Cross 2nd Class ribbon and badge on the left breast pocket, plus the Silver Tank Assault Badge underneath. High-laced tropical field boots and shorts formed part of the basic tropical uniform.

SPECIFICATIONS	
Country:	Germany
Date:	1942
Unit:	15th Panzer Division
Rank:	Lieutenant
Theatre:	Mediterranean
Location:	Libya

Colonial Forces, North Africa 1940–43

The North African war saw the heavy involvement of colonial forces on both sides. These ranged from major foreign armies, such as British Commonwealth forces, through to small indigenous units.

◀ Corporal
6th Eritrea Battalion, Italian Colonial Army

The Italian Colonial Army formed a large part of the Italian Army's overseas contingent. The soldier here is a corporal in the 6th Eritrea Battalion, the unit identified by the green tassel on the *tarbusc* hat. The uniform was ideal for the tropics, and was established for colonial forces in 1929.

SPECIFICATIONS	
Country:	Eritrea
Date:	1940
Unit:	6th Eritrea Battalion
Rank:	Corporal
Theatre:	Africa
Location:	Ethiopia

Corporal ▶
Transjordanian Frontier Force

This Jordanian corporal wears a mixture of uniform items. Much of his webbing and equipment is of British issue; the pouches on his chest are for his Bren Gun's 30-round curved box magazines. Instead of a helmet, however, he has the practical Arab *shemagh* headdress.

SPECIFICATIONS	
Country:	Transjordan
Date:	1940
Unit:	Transjordanian Frontier Force
Rank:	Corporal
Theatre:	Middle East
Location:	Jordan

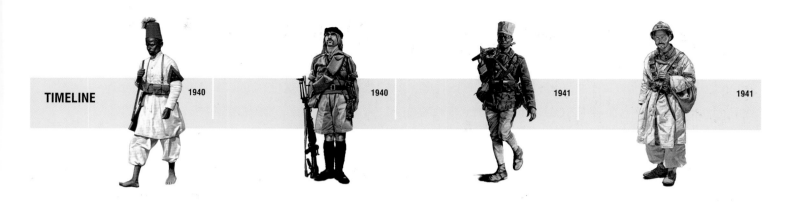

◀ Private
Free French Senegalese Rifles

In the service of the Free French in Syria, this soldier has French-issue ammunition pouches and weapon, but also some British items of kit, such as the respirator case. Unit designation is given on the collar and the cuffs of the tunic. He wears the traditional *chechia* hat, but with khaki cover.

SPECIFICATIONS	
Country:	Senegal
Date:	1941
Unit:	Free French Senegalese Rifles
Rank:	Private
Theatre:	Mediterranean
Location:	Syria

Private 1st Class ▶
Vichy French Moroccan Spahis

This Moroccan soldier is wearing typical French uniform for the desert theatre, with a standard French helmet, khaki uniform, a long *djellabah* and leather ammunition pouches. A yellow rank strip is buttoned to the front of his tunic, indicating *soldat de première classe*.

SPECIFICATIONS	
Country:	Morocco
Date:	1941
Unit:	Vichy French Moroccan Spahis
Rank:	Private 1st Class
Theatre:	Mediterranean
Location:	Syria

Colonial Forces, North Africa 1940–43

The equipment and uniforms of colonial forces in Africa varied considerably. Typically, they wore a blend of items provided by the colonial power, usually standard army kit (although often of older patterns), supplemented by local dress to distinguish their nationality.

◄ Private
Abyssinian Patriot Army

The soldier pictured here is one of the Abyssinian resistance fighters who fought alongside the Allies. There was no uniform as such – this soldier has a khaki tunic and pantaloons, worn with canvas leggings, but no boots. The rifle is the German 7.92mm (.31in) Kar 98K, and a pistol hangs from his leather belt.

SPECIFICATIONS	
Country:	Abyssinia
Date:	1941
Unit:	Abyssinian Patriot Army
Rank:	Private
Theatre:	Africa
Location:	Ethiopia

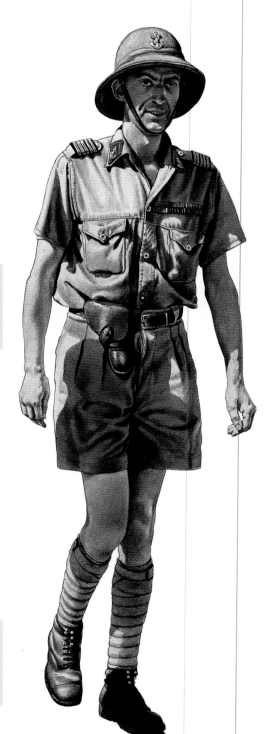

Colonel ►
Vichy French Colonial Infantry

Before World War II, French colonial officers wore a light khaki working uniform, while white undress uniform consisted of sun helmet, tunic and trousers. This officer from Madagascar wears traditional tropical dress with sun helmet. On the front of the helmet is a gilt metal anchor, the emblem of French colonial forces.

SPECIFICATIONS	
Country:	Madagascar
Date:	1942
Unit:	French Colonial Infantry
Rank:	Colonel
Theatre:	Africa
Location:	Unknown

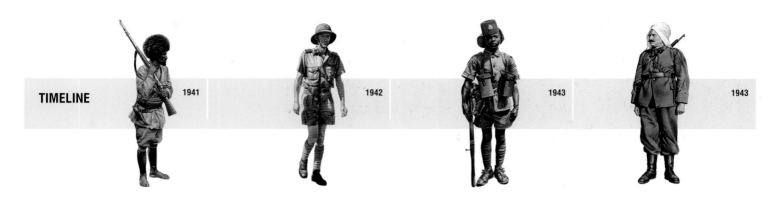

TIMELINE | 1941 | 1942 | 1943 | 1943

◀ Sergeant
Belgian Colonial Army

Belgium maintained three colonies in Africa in the first half of the 20th century, and these colonies produced a useful body of troops for service from 1940. This sergeant wears British 1939-pattern web equipment over a simple khaki uniform. The traditional fez features a neck-shield, rolled up at the back.

SPECIFICATIONS	
Country:	Belgian Congo
Date:	1943
Unit:	Belgian Colonial Army
Rank:	Sergeant
Theatre:	Africa
Location:	Unknown

Sergeant-Major ▶
Moroccan Spahis

This Moroccan sergeant-major, in French service, wears a local headdress with a green cavalry uniform. The three chevrons on his sleeve denote his rank, while the star on the collar tabs indicates that he belongs to a Moroccan formation.

SPECIFICATIONS	
Country:	Morocco
Date:	1943
Unit:	Moroccan Spahis
Rank:	Sergeant-Major
Theatre:	Mediterranean
Location:	Tunisia

Goumier, French African Troops, Italy 1944

Large numbers of French African troops were recruited to the Allied cause. These were later formed into part of the French Expeditionary Corps, which entered combat in Italy in 1943 and distinguished itself in combat.

The Berthier Mle 1916 was a variant within the Berthier rifle family, with its origins back in the 1890s. It was an improvement on the preceding Berthier Mle 1907/15, which had a limited ammunition capacity of only three rounds – the Mle 1916 took that capacity up to five rounds, which were charger-loaded into the magazine. The rifle used the distinctive French 8 x 50R (.31 x 2in) Lebel cartridge.

The Mk II was the standard British Army helmet for most soldiers between 1940 and 1945. The first incarnation of this helmet was patented by British inventor John Leopold Brodie in 1915; it also went into US service as the Helmet, Steel, Mk I.

Private
French African Troops

As the war progressed, British and US uniforms dominated within the Free French, though many troops clung to their national identity. This Moroccan goumier is no exception. His vivid overcoat is the *djellabah*, an item of clothing that also identified his tribe, and he wears a British steel helmet on top of his turban. The actual combat uniform, which is just visible, is of US pattern, as is the webbing system: the pouches at the front would take clips for the M1 Garand rifle (although it is not clear here what rifle he is carrying – possibly a French-issue Lebel or Berthier).

SPECIFICATIONS	
Country:	Morocco
Date:	1944
Unit:	French African Troops
Rank:	Private
Theatre:	Italy
Location:	Southern Italy

British Empire & Commonwealth, North Africa 1940–42

At the beginning of World War II, the British Empire had reached its greatest extent. Its forces included soldiers from around the world, and Indian, New Zealand and Australian troops were heavily committed to the North African campaign.

◀ Sergeant
8th Indian Division, Indian Army

Indian Army troops used British Army-style uniforms and kit, although with many national variations. This soldier is wearing standard British Army drill kit issued during World War II: a khaki shirt and shorts, long woollen socks, and black shoes. The webbing is mainly the old 1908 pattern.

SPECIFICATIONS	
Country:	India
Date:	1940
Unit:	8th Indian Division
Rank:	Sergeant
Theatre:	Mediterranean
Location:	North Africa

Gunner ▶
New Zealand Artillery

The only part of this New Zealand gunner distinguishing him from his British allies in the North African theatre would be the distinctive slouch hat. The NZ hat had a pointed crown indented on every quarter, with an 'NZ' badge centred and a puggaree with regimental colours worn at the base.

SPECIFICATIONS	
Country:	New Zealand
Date:	1940
Unit:	New Zealand Artillery
Rank:	Gunner
Theatre:	Mediterranean
Location:	North Africa

| TIMELINE | 1940 | 1940 | 1940 | 1940 |

◄ Private
New Zealand Army

This NZ Army private is wearing a standard khaki drill uniform of British issue, which were given to the NZ force on its arrival in Egypt. He is heavily kitted out in full British 1908-pattern webbing, rather than the 1937-pattern that most British Army soldiers would have been issued with at this point.

SPECIFICATIONS	
Country:	New Zealand
Date:	1940
Unit:	New Zealand Army
Rank:	Private
Theatre:	Mediterranean
Location:	Unknown

Private ►
Kimberley Regiment, South African Army

British Empire forces uniforms and kit were in sympathy with those of the British Army. The notable exception here is the sun helmet, khaki in colour, with a matching puggaree that featured a cloth patch with regimental or corps colours, and a metal cap badge at the front.

SPECIFICATIONS	
Country:	South Africa
Date:	1940
Unit:	Kimberley Regiment
Rank:	Private
Theatre:	Africa
Location:	South Africa

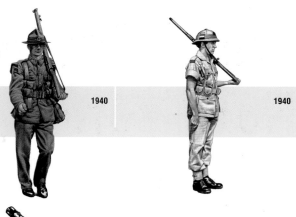

British Empire & Commonwealth, North Africa 1940–42

Although the native Australian infantry uniform was actually more suited to desert conditions because of its lighter material, British Army uniforms steadily became the norm as the North African campaign progressed.

◀ Private
6th Division,
Australian Army

The defining Australian item here is the traditional wide-brimmed felt slouch hat, with the left side fastened up by a regimental badge when worn formally. The tunic had four pockets to the front, four-button fastening and a unit insignia worn on the collar and sleeve.

SPECIFICATIONS	
Country:	Australia
Date:	1941
Unit:	6th Division
Rank:	Private
Theatre:	Mediterranean
Location:	North Africa

Private ▶
7th Division,
Australian Army

This Australian infantryman of the 7th Division wears the typical British khaki drill uniform. The webbing is the 1937 pattern, here featuring only two utility/ammunition pouches strapped to the belt, plus a scabbard for the 1897 sword bayonet.

SPECIFICATIONS	
Country:	Australia
Date:	1941
Unit:	7th Division
Rank:	Private
Theatre:	Mediterranean
Location:	North Africa

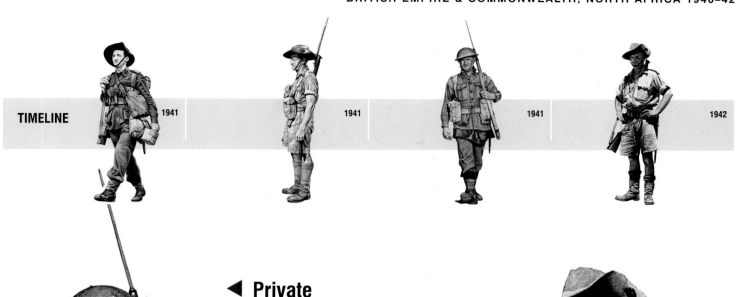

1941   1941   1941   1942

◄ Private
9th Division,
Australian Army

This soldier is one of the three Australian divisions – the 6th, 7th and 9th – deployed to North Africa in 1941. The kit and uniform are almost entirely British: Mk 1 helmet, 1937 webbing, Lee-Enfield rifle. One notable item is the leather jerkin, which provided protection against low night temperatures.

SPECIFICATIONS	
Country:	Australia
Date:	1941
Unit:	9th Division
Rank:	Private
Theatre:	Mediterranean
Location:	Tobruk

Private ►
Australian Army

The soldier here is dressed in the light uniform well-suited to warfare in North Africa. As seen in earlier illustrations, two particular items set him apart as an Australian infantryman: the felt slouch hat and the canvas anklets. The Australian Army suffered 19,351 casualties throughout the war in actions against German forces.

SPECIFICATIONS	
Country:	Australia
Date:	1942
Unit:	Australian Army
Rank:	Private
Theatre:	Mediterranean
Location:	North Africa

British Army, North Africa 1940–43

The British Army fought a three-year war in North Africa, with moments of both disaster and triumph. Its uniforms in the theatre had to meet multiple demands, from scorching daytime temperatures through to near-freezing nights.

◀ Corporal
6th Royal Tank Regiment

This soldier's shoulder straps display the colours of the 6th Royal Tank Regiment (rank is on the sleeve). He has a regimental lanyard running under the left shoulder. The hat is the black beret of the Royal Tank Regiment, although inside the tank a black fibre helmet would probably be worn.

SPECIFICATIONS	
Country:	Britain
Date:	1941
Unit:	6th Royal Tank Regiment
Rank:	Corporal
Theatre:	Mediterranean
Location:	North Africa

Captain ▶
3rd King's Own Hussars

Apart from the cap, this cavalry officer wears the standard tropical khaki service dress (although officers usually had a uniform of better tailoring than lower ranks). The rubber-soled suede 'chukka' boots were not official issue, but they were popular among officers because of their comfort.

SPECIFICATIONS	
Country:	Britain
Date:	1941
Unit:	3rd King's Own Hussars
Rank:	Captain
Theatre:	Mediterranean
Location:	North Africa

TIMELINE

1941   1941   1942   1943

◀ Sergeant
6th Royal Tank Regiment

Another soldier of a Royal Tank Regiment, wearing the distinctive cap and shoulder straps. His sidearm is the 9.7mm (.38in) Enfield No. 2 Mk I, set in a holster that was purposely designed for armoured vehicle crews.

SPECIFICATIONS	
Country:	Britain
Date:	1942
Unit:	6th Royal Tank Regiment
Rank:	Sergeant
Theatre:	Mediterranean
Location:	North Africa

Sergeant ▶
6th Battalion, Grenadier Guards

This NCO in Tunisia is wearing serge battle dress with regimental shoulder title and sergeant's chevrons. His steel helmet has a hessian cover, while around his ankles he wears 1937-pattern web anklets and ammunition boots. He is carrying a captured German MG34 machine gun.

SPECIFICATIONS	
Country:	Britain
Date:	1943
Unit:	6th Battalion, Grenadier Guards
Rank:	Sergeant
Theatre:	Mediterranean
Location:	Tunisia

US Forces, North Africa 1942

Because of the rapidity with which America entered World War II, many of its soldiers went into action in quite dated uniforms, though from 1943 the US Army began to receive uniforms of far greater sophistication than their allies' equivalents.

◀ Lieutenant-Colonel
US 1st Cavalry Division

Here an officer of the 1st Cavalry Division is wearing an older style of uniform. His shirt and breeches are part of the 'Class C' uniform, this being the standard issue for troops operating in hot climates. They are made from khaki drill, or 'chino' as it was termed in the US, and are worn with a matching belt and distinctive field boots.

SPECIFICATIONS	
Country:	United States
Date:	1942
Unit:	1st Cavalry Division
Rank:	Lieutenant-Colonel
Theatre:	Mediterranean
Location:	Morocco

Corporal ▶
Tank Battalion

The standard of uniform for US armoured crews was consistently high. The basic uniform was a one-piece olive-drab overall made from herringbone twill. This had four large utility pockets and a matching cloth belt. This corporal also wears the popular crewman's jacket.

SPECIFICATIONS	
Country:	United States
Date:	1942
Unit:	Tank Battalion
Rank:	Corporal
Theatre:	Mediterranean
Location:	Morocco

TIMELINE   1942   1942   1942   1942

◀ Officer
US Army

In combat there was often little to distinguish US officers from other ranks, to reduce the danger from snipers. This US officer wears an M1942 water-repellent jacket and standard infantry trousers, boots and helmet. His firearm is the 11.5mm (.45in) Thompson M1 submachine gun.

SPECIFICATIONS	
Country:	United States
Date:	1942
Unit:	US Army
Rank:	Officer
Theatre:	Mediterranean
Location:	North Africa

Private ▶
US Army

This US Army private is an engineer, and is using a metal detector to detect mines. For such work he is wearing a two-piece fatigue uniform rather than combat dress, plus a simple cloth fatigue cap. The elasticated anklets are typical of US infantry uniform.

SPECIFICATIONS	
Country:	United States
Date:	1942
Unit:	US Army
Rank:	Private
Theatre:	Mediterranean
Location:	North Africa

US Infantryman, North Africa 1942

Heavily burdened with equipment for the amphibious landings in Algeria, this staff sergeant wears the olive-drab uniform donned by most US Army soldiers in the Mediterranean and North European (spring and summer) theatres.

The M1 Garand was the first self-loading rifle to be adopted as a standard-issue military firearm. It fired the US 7.62mm (.30-06in) cartridge, cycling through its eight-round clip via a gas-operated mechanism. It was durable and powerful; the main drawback was that the clip had to be loaded full or not at all – single rounds could not be added to a clip from which rounds had already been fired.

These arm patches belong to various NCO and private grades, the rank stripes topped by unit insignia. They are (from left to right): sergeant 4th grade (7th Division); technician 4th grade (29th Division); corporal 5th grade (31st Division), technician 5th grade (32nd Division); and private 1st class 6th grade (90th Division).

Staff Sergeant
1st Infantry Division

On his torso this soldier has three layers. The base layer is an olive-drab wool shirt, this being covered by a lightweight field jacket, which was waterproof, sand-coloured as opposed to olive-drab, and had a zip fastening with a buttoned fly front. On this he wears his rank on the right sleeve and the national flag on the left. Although it cannot be seen easily, this soldier is also wearing a life-jacket in case his landing craft is sunk. To match his upper half, he has olive-drab trousers, the ankles being drawn in by long elasticated anklets. The steel helmet is the US M1 and he wears the M1923 cartridge belt around his waist with two cotton ammunition bandoliers around his shoulders.

SPECIFICATIONS	
Country:	United States
Date:	1942
Unit:	1st Infantry Division
Rank:	Staff Sergeant
Theatre:	Mediterranean
Location:	Oran

Air War, North Africa 1940–42

The battle for air supremacy over North Africa became critical to the outcome of the campaign. Both sides preyed on each others' supply lines, but in the end it was the Allies who gained control of the skies.

◀ Air Marshal
Italian Air Force

Air Marshal Italo Balbo is seen here in what is essentially Italian Army uniform. This is due to the fact that at this time, the air force and army shared much in the way of their uniform styles. The tunic belongs to the tropical dress, while the breeches are those that would have been used for the temperate dress.

SPECIFICATIONS	
Country:	Italy
Date:	1940
Unit:	Italian Air Force
Rank:	Air Marshal
Theatre:	Mediterranean
Location:	Unknown

Major ▶
One Group,
Italian Air Force

Despite its bulky appearance and its colouration, the flying uniform pictured here is actually a summer outfit. This one-piece overall was made of white linen and featured a distinctive cross-over breast. It is worn here with a matching padded crash helmet, also of linen.

SPECIFICATIONS	
Country:	Italy
Date:	1940
Unit:	One Group
Rank:	Major
Theatre:	Mediterranean
Location:	Libya

TIMELINE   1940   1940   1941   1941

◀ **Pilot**
112 Squadron, Royal Air Force

This pilot here is seen in North Africa in late 1941, wearing a lightweight khaki overall issued to pilots in tropical zones. His headgear is the leather flying helmet Type B, which was able to accept external communications wires. Slung low behind his knees is his Irvin parachute.

SPECIFICATIONS	
Country:	Britain
Date:	1941
Unit:	112 Squadron
Rank:	Pilot
Theatre:	Mediterranean
Location:	North Africa

Sergeant ▶
Luftwaffe

The German Stuka pilot here wears the plain *Luftwaffe* tropical uniform, consisting of a light khaki shirt with two buttoned breast pockets and matching trousers with a single pocket on the left thigh. The metal container holds a thermos flask.

SPECIFICATIONS	
Country:	Germany
Date:	1941
Unit:	Luftwaffe
Rank:	Sergeant
Theatre:	Mediterranean
Location:	Libya

Air War, North Africa 1940–42

The North African theatre placed harsh demands on the uniforms of all services, including air forces. If standard-issue dress did not meet the requirements of comfort, improvisation often resolved any problems.

◀ Flying Officer
Royal Air Force

The flying officer here is dressed in a basic khaki field uniform, over which he wears his flying gear. He is holding the jack plug to his radio microphone system – this would plug into a communications socket on the aircraft's comms panel. Hanging to his left is his parachute pack.

SPECIFICATIONS

Country:	Britain
Date:	1941
Unit:	Royal Air Force
Rank:	Flying Officer
Theatre:	Mediterranean
Location:	North Africa

Lieutenant-General ▶
X *Fliegerkorps*, *Afrika Korps*

The figure seen here is a high-ranking officer. He wears the standard *Luftwaffe* tropical uniform with the peaked service cap that accompanied the temperate uniform. The jacket was manufactured from a lightweight tan-coloured material and had four pockets.

SPECIFICATIONS

Country:	Germany
Date:	1942
Unit:	X *Fliegerkorps*
Rank:	Lieutenant-General
Theatre:	Mediterranean
Location:	Tripoli

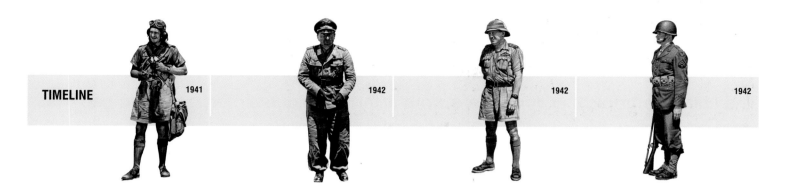

1941　1942　1942　1942

◀ Lieutenant
Royal South African Air Force

The flying officer here looks in most regards like a Commonwealth army soldier. The difference from the army lies purely in the insignia: air force wings on the left breast, with an air force badge surmounting the sun helmet and a blue arm-of-service patch on the puggaree.

SPECIFICATIONS	
Country:	South Africa
Date:	1942
Unit:	Royal South African Air Force
Rank:	Lieutenant
Theatre:	Mediterranean
Location:	North Africa

Technician, 5th Grade ▶
USAAF

As the US Army Air Forces (USAAF) were part of the army, air-force personnel also wore army uniforms. The technician shown here is wearing the Class A uniform with steel helmet, which was worn for ceremonial occasions; his weapon is the US M1903 Springfield rifle. The 'T' under the rank chevrons indicated 'Technician'.

SPECIFICATIONS	
Country:	United States
Date:	1942
Unit:	USAAF
Rank:	Technician, 5th Grade
Theatre:	Mediterranean
Location:	Morocco

Luftwaffe Officer in North Africa

The *Luftwaffe* tropical uniform, here worn with the unique air force peaked cap, was used not only in the desert, but also in Sicily, Italy, the Balkans and in the southern Soviet Union during the summer months. The light tan colour of the uniform quickly washed out and bleached into an off-white shade.

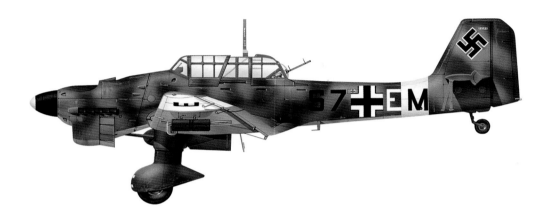

The Ju-87 Stuka dive-bomber was adapted for the North Africa theatre with modifications such as enhanced air filtration and a desert paint scheme. As experience in Europe had shown, Ju-87s were effective when they operated without an opposing air threat, but with the steady loss of German air superiority they were extremely vulnerable to enemy fighters.

Here we see the shoulder strap (top) and arm patch rank insignia for an *Oberstleutnant* (lieutenant-colonel) in the *Luftwaffe*. Within the ranks of *Luftwaffe* field officers, there was only *Oberst* (colonel) above this rank, and thereafter were the general officers.

Lieutenant-Colonel
X Fliegerkorps

No collar insignia was worn with the tropical uniform, although the shoulder straps, which served to indicate the wearer's rank and arm-of-service, were looped and buttoned to the tunic. There was no specific tropical *Luftwaffe* greatcoat, so air-force members continued to wear the blue-grey temperate model. Altogether, the air force tropical uniform was much more comfortable than the uniform worn by army personnel. Above his left breast pocket, this lieutenant-colonel wears a Front Flight Bar with pendant, which bears the number of combat missions he has flown.

SPECIFICATIONS	
Country:	Germany
Date:	1942
Unit:	X *Fliegerkorps*
Rank:	Lieutenant-Colonel
Theatre:	Mediterranean
Location:	Tunis

Sino-Japanese War 1937–39

The Sino-Japanese War is one of the 'forgotten' conflicts of World War II, at least in the West. Yet this theatre cost more than 20 million dead, the vast majority of them civilians caught between mutually ruthless opposing forces.

◀ Private, 2nd Class
Japanese Army

The Japanese Army was generally equipped in a very basic fashion for its war in China. Here we have a private 2nd class wearing a standard greatcoat that featured a detachable hood, plus a peaked cap with service colours. He is armed with a 6.5mm (0.25in) M38 Arisaka rifle.

SPECIFICATIONS	
Country:	Japan
Date:	1937
Unit:	Japanese Army
Rank:	Private, 2nd Class
Theatre:	East Asia
Location:	China

Lieutenant ▶
Japanese Army

This soldier is a Japanese artillery officer, his rank displayed via the red rank patches on the shoulders. He is wearing a rather old style of service dress, distinguished by its stand collar, although he has the standard-issue Japanese Army field cap.

SPECIFICATIONS	
Country:	Japan
Date:	1937
Unit:	Japanese Army
Rank:	Lieutenant
Theatre:	East Asia
Location:	China

TIMELINE   1937   1937   1937   1939

◄ **Superior Private**
Japanese Army

The China theatre was one of great contrasts in climate, from scorching summers to sub-zero winters. This superior private has standard-issue winter clothing, which included fur-lined double-breasted greatcoat, hat with ear protectors, mittens and felt boots.

SPECIFICATIONS	
Country:	Japan
Date:	1937
Unit:	Japanese Army
Rank:	Superior Private
Theatre:	East Asia
Location:	Eastern China

1st Lieutenant ►
Chinese Nationalist Air Force

This pilot is a 1st lieutenant, the rank indicated by the eagle and bars on the cuffs (later in the war the rank badges were moved up to the shoulder). Predominantly, the pilots and ground crew simply wore the khaki tunic and trousers of the Chinese Army.

SPECIFICATIONS	
Country:	China
Date:	1939
Unit:	Chinese Nationalist Air Force
Rank:	1st Lieutenant
Theatre:	East Asia
Location:	China

Sino-Japanese War 1941–45

The Sino-Japanese War ground on throughout World War II, drawing away tens of thousands of Japanese troops who could have served in the Pacific. Yet Chinese forces were not a unified opponent, but were split between Communist and Nationalist troops.

◄ Pilot
American Volunteer Group

This volunteer US pilot serving in China is wearing a mixture of Chinese and American kit. The zip-fronted flying jacket is American, although with a Chinese nationalist emblem on the breast. The inset patch was sewn on the back of the jacket; it gave instructions in Chinese to protect the wearer if he survived being shot down.

SPECIFICATIONS	
Country:	United States
Date:	1941
Unit:	American Volunteer Group
Rank:	Pilot
Theatre:	East Asia
Location:	China

Colonel ►
Chinese Nationalist Army

The Chinese Nationalist summer uniform was made of khaki cotton. The tunic was single-breasted with four large front and side patch pockets and a stand-and-fall collar. Rank and arm-of-service were denoted on the collar patches; in this case, the red background indicates the infantry.

SPECIFICATIONS	
Country:	China
Date:	1942
Unit:	Chinese Nationalist Army
Rank:	Colonel
Theatre:	East Asia
Location:	China

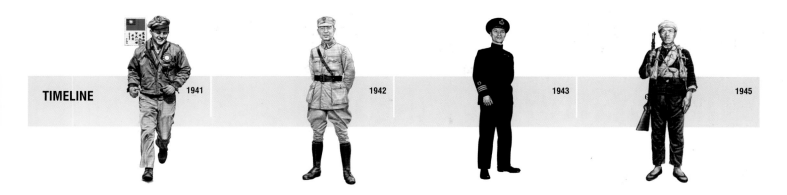

TIMELINE 1941   1942   1943   1945

◀ **Commander**
Chinese Nationalist Navy

Although this Chinese Nationalist Navy uniform remains in a recognizable maritime tradition, the tunic has a distinctly Chinese cut, having a stand collar and fly fastening at the front. The collar and the edges of the jacket are trimmed with lace, and the rank is displayed on the tunic cuff.

SPECIFICATIONS	
Country:	China
Date:	1943
Unit:	Chinese Nationalist Navy
Rank:	Commander
Theatre:	Europe
Location:	Britain

1st Lieutenant ▶
Chinese Communist Forces

Kit and uniform for the Communists was either homemade or captured from the Nationalists or the Japanese. This soldier's rifle – a 6.5mm (0.25in) 38th Year carbine – belongs to the last category, while the uniform is almost entirely traditional Chinese peasant dress with improvised 'webbing'.

SPECIFICATIONS	
Country:	China
Date:	1945
Unit:	Chinese Communist Forces
Rank:	1st Lieutenant
Theatre:	East Asia
Location:	China

Eastern Front, German Infantry and Artillery, 1941–45

The Eastern Front absorbed the bulk of German manpower, and inflicted the majority of its casualties. Uniform became a critical issue on this front, particular during the winters.

◀ Lance-Corporal
Infantry Regiment

In the German Army, NCOs wore the basic soldier's uniform – a practice that differed from many other European armies, where NCOs wore officers' uniforms – but with silver lace on the tunic collar and shoulder straps, and with rank badges on the left upper sleeves.

SPECIFICATIONS	
Country:	Germany
Date:	1941
Unit:	Infantry Regiment
Rank:	Lance-Corporal
Theatre:	Eastern Front
Location:	Belorussia

Sergeant ▶
Assault Artillery Regiment

This sergeant of an assault artillery unit wears the field-grey version of the special Panzer uniform introduced in 1940 for crews of self-propelled guns (later in the war it was also worn by Panzergrenadier divisions). Here the red piping around the collar patches indicates the artillery branch.

SPECIFICATIONS	
Country:	Germany
Date:	1942
Unit:	Assault Artillery Regiment
Rank:	Sergeant
Theatre:	Eastern Front
Location:	Smolensk

TIMELINE

1941   1942   1942   1942

◄ 2nd Lieutenant
Infantry Regiment

This infantry 2nd lieutenant in Russia is wearing the standard attire for an officer at the front (note the white piping on his shoulder straps, indicating his membership of the infantry). His headgear is the M1938 officers' side cap and his decoration is the German Cross in Gold, for leadership.

SPECIFICATIONS	
Country:	Germany
Date:	1942
Unit:	Infantry Regiment
Rank:	2nd Lieutenant
Theatre:	Eastern Front
Location:	Orel

Private ►
Das Reich Division

Pre-war, the *Waffen-SS* uniform was black, but from 1935 onwards a grey uniform began to be worn on active service. Gradually, the soldiers of the SS adopted the field-grey army uniform, although with SS rank badges and insignia. This private wears a fur-lined SS anorak and overalls.

SPECIFICATIONS	
Country:	Germany
Date:	1942
Unit:	*Waffen-SS Das Reich* Division
Rank:	Private
Theatre:	Eastern Front
Location:	Belorussia

Eastern Front, German Infantry and Artillery, 1941–45

The Germans' first winter on the Eastern Front was disastrous, as the German Army had not been issued with winter uniforms, in expectation of a short campaign. Consequently, tens of thousands of German troops succumbed to either frostbite or hypothermia, while the attempt to capture Moscow failed.

◀ Private
German Army

Learning the lessons of the winter of 1941/42, the German Army produced specialist items of uniform for the following winter. Here this private wears reversible overalls: white on one side for snow camouflage, and woodland camouflage or field-grey on the reverse.

SPECIFICATIONS	
Country:	Germany
Date:	1943
Unit:	German Army
Rank:	Private
Theatre:	Eastern Front
Location:	Russia

Private ▶
389th Infantry Division

This soldier has been drawn from a Soviet newsreel of captured Germans after the catastrophe of Stalingrad. His greatcoat is stuffed with newspaper and straw, and he has also managed to acquire a pair of straw overboots, usually issued to sentries who would have to stand for long periods.

SPECIFICATIONS	
Country:	Germany
Date:	1943
Unit:	389th Infantry Division
Rank:	Private
Theatre:	Eastern Front
Location:	Stalingrad

TIMELINE	1943	1943	1943	1944

◄ Corporal
Das Reich Division

This corporal's SS membership is stated through several items of insignia around his field-grey uniform. We have the death's-head badge dominating the peaked service-dress cap, while on the right collar of the tunic there is the double lightning flash runes of the SS.

SPECIFICATIONS	
Country:	Germany
Date:	1943
Unit:	*Das Reich* Division
Rank:	Corporal
Theatre:	Eastern Front
Location:	Kharkov

Soldier ►
German Army

The soldier here is wearing a protective suit, made from a rubber material, designed to shield him from the heat of his flamethrower unit. Here we can see the flamethrower's large main fuel tank, plus a compressed gas tank used to propel the fuel.

SPECIFICATIONS	
Country:	Germany
Date:	1944
Unit:	German Army
Rank:	Soldier
Theatre:	Eastern Front
Location:	Ukraine

SS Machine-Gun Team c. 1943

The SS machine-gun team here is equipped with the MG34, one of the finest machine guns of the 20th century. It effectively introduced the concept of the general-purpose machine gun, as it was designed to function both in assault roles using a bipod and sustained roles on a tripod (as seen here) or vehicular mounting.

The MG34 fired the 7.92 x 57mm (.31 x 2.2in) Mauser cartridge, which was fed into the gun at a cyclical rate of 800–900rpm from either a 250-round belt or a 75-round saddle drum. The gun was of excellent quality, but somewhat over-engineered for battlefield use and wartime production requirements.

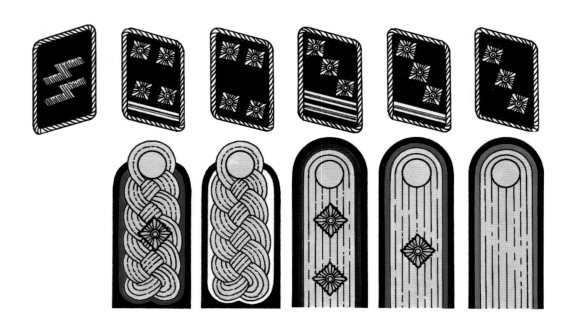

Here, on the left, we see the classic runic double lightning flash of the *Waffen-SS*. The other artworks show, in pairs, the collar patches and shoulder straps for (left to right): lieutenant-colonel (administration); major (infantry); captain (medical); lieutenant (supply) and 2nd lieutenant (mountain troops).

Soldiers
Waffen-SS

The machine-gun team here are dressed in SS camouflage jackets. The SS were the pioneers of camouflage during World War II and as far back as 1940 issued camouflage uniforms. Four types of camouflage were utilized, known as 'palm tree', 'pea', 'oak leaf' and 'plane tree' to indicate their natural patterns. The three-man team consists of a gunner, a loader and an observer. With the tripod-mounted gun they could put down sustained fire to ranges of more than 1000m (3280ft).

SPECIFICATIONS	
Country:	Germany
Date:	1943
Unit:	*Waffen-SS*
Rank:	Soldiers
Theatre:	Eastern Front
Location:	Unknown

Eastern Front, German Panzer/ Panzergrenadier 1941–43

Armoured/mechanized forces were central to the *Wehrmacht*'s tactical success on the Eastern Front. German tank crews were almost invariably superior to Soviet equivalents, although the Red Army's T-34 tank helped to correct the imbalance.

◀ Colonel-General
3rd Panzer Group

Generaloberst (Colonel-General) Hermann Hoth, the commander of the 3rd Panzer Group, is here seen in Russia in 1941. He is wearing the new pattern field cap for officers, which was introduced in 1938; this headdress displays the Nazi eagle and the red cockade of Germany.

SPECIFICATIONS	
Country:	Germany
Date:	1941
Unit:	3rd Panzer Group
Rank:	Colonel-General
Theatre:	Eastern Front
Location:	Western USSR

Lieutenant ▶
Panzer Regiment

This German Army lieutenant is wearing the special black clothing for crews of enclosed vehicles. He is also a veteran of the Spanish Civil War – in his buttonhole he wears the ribbon of the Iron Cross 2nd Class, and next to it sports the Condor Legion Tank Badge, Iron Cross 1st Class and Wound Badge.

SPECIFICATIONS	
Country:	Germany
Date:	1941
Unit:	Panzer Regiment
Rank:	Lieutenant
Theatre:	Eastern Front
Location:	Unknown

TIMELINE   1941   1941   1943   1943

Sergeant ◄
Grossdeutschland Division

This Panzergrenadier uniform is in field-grey, and the soldier belongs to an assault-gun detachment. Membership of the *Grossdeutschland* division was indicated by the letters 'GD' displayed on shoulder straps, the border of which would denote the arm-of-service within the division.

SPECIFICATIONS	
Country:	Germany
Date:	1943
Unit:	*Grossdeutschland* Division
Rank:	Sergeant
Theatre:	Eastern Front
Location:	Kursk

Major ►
Leibstandarte Division

Here we see the infamous *SS-Sturmbannführer* (major) Joachim Peiper. He wears one of the many army winter caps and special one-piece reversible winter tank overalls, which were issued in January 1943. *Waffen-SS* officers were required to wear white piping on their headdress.

SPECIFICATIONS	
Country:	Germany
Date:	1943
Unit:	*Leibstandarte* Division
Rank:	Major
Theatre:	Eastern Front
Location:	Ukraine

Private, Leibstandarte Division 1944

The *Leibstandarte* Adolf Hitler division was the first division of the *Waffen-SS*. Like many *Waffen-SS* units, they performed some heroic actions during the Eastern Front campaigns, alongside some less-than-heroic war crimes.

The MP43 was essentially history's first assault rifle, and was issued to Panzergrenadier troops of the *Leibstandarte* and other *Waffen-SS* formations on the Eastern Front. It fired the 7.92 x 33mm (.31 x 1.3in) *kurz* cartridge, of lower power than standard rifle rounds but designed for practical handling within realistic combat ranges of up to 400m (1312ft).

The *Leibstandarte* Division received Tiger tanks in late 1942. The early vehicles were prone to mechanical failure, but when they worked they were the most powerful tanks on the battlefield. The Tiger's 88mm (3.5in) gun could destroy any Allied tank, and its armour shrugged off all but the heaviest anti-tank shells.

Private
Leibstandarte Division

This tankman wears a 1944-issue camouflage two-piece uniform in a distinctive foliage pattern. This version was issued from 1944 onwards to replace the one-piece overall that was brought into service in 1941 in SS camouflage material. *Waffen-SS* units were among the first to make use of disruptive pattern material (see pp. 164–65). The patterns were carefully designed to break up the wearer's outline, with small, hard-edged splodges of colour outlined in contrasting hues. On his head this private wears the *Waffen-SS* field cap, and his shoulder straps are piped pink to indicate the Panzer arm-of-service.

SPECIFICATIONS	
Country:	Germany
Date:	1944
Unit:	*Leibstandarte* Division
Rank:	Private
Theatre:	Eastern Front
Location:	Poland

Finnish Forces 1943–44

Although their on-paper strength was far weaker than that of many other armies, the Finns proved to be extremely tough opponents, particularly adept at defending their territory in the depths of the severe Finnish winters.

◀ **Captain**
2nd Division, Finnish Army

This captain wears a dark grey Model 1936 uniform, the standard uniform of the Finnish Army; it resulted from a modernization of the old light grey uniform in that year. Subtle distinctions of cloth quality, style and insignia separated the officers from the lower ranks.

SPECIFICATIONS	
Country:	Finland
Date:	1943
Unit:	2nd Division
Rank:	Captain
Theatre:	Eastern Front
Location:	Around Leningrad

Lieutenant ▶
Finnish Army

This lieutenant of the Finnish infantry is more notable for the aberrations in his uniform than for its typicality. The most visibly anachronistic item is the large and unwieldy helmet, the German 1915-pattern. By this point in the war, the 1915-pattern helmet had been replaced by the 1935-pattern of the regular German forces.

SPECIFICATIONS	
Country:	Finland
Date:	1944
Unit:	Finnish Army
Rank:	Lieutenant
Theatre:	Eastern Front
Location:	Karelia

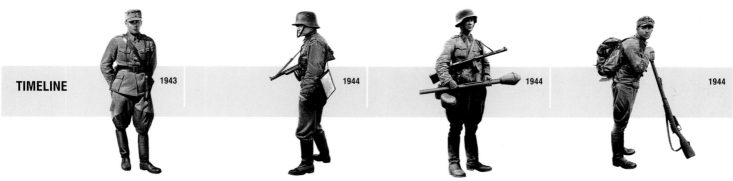

TIMELINE 1943 1944 1944 1944

◄ Sergeant
Finnish Army

This Finnish Army sergeant is armed with an indigenous Suomi KP/-31 submachine gun and a German Panzerfaust anti-tank weapon. The uniform of the Finnish Army was modernized in 1936, with a dark grey uniform replacing the old light grey version.

SPECIFICATIONS	
Country:	Finland
Date:	1944
Unit:	Finnish Army
Rank:	Sergeant
Theatre:	Eastern Front
Location:	Unknow

Private ►
IV Corps, Finnish Army

This Finnish soldier is wearing the standard field cap and lightweight tunic/shirt; he wears the latter outside his trousers, after the Russian style. By this stage of the war, the German influence over the Finnish uniform had grown stronger, which led to greater standardization of appearance.

SPECIFICATIONS	
Country:	Finland
Date:	1944
Unit:	IV Corps
Rank:	Private
Theatre:	Eastern Front
Location:	Lake Ladog

Hungarian and Romanian Forces 1941–44

Hungary and Romania both fought for the Axis during World War II, contributing much manpower on the Eastern Front. There the armies of these two countries suffered devastating losses.

◀ **Sergeant**
Hungarian Gendarmerie

This soldier represents the elite Royal Hungarian Gendarmerie. The khaki tunic and trousers are standard Hungarian Army wear. A distinctive element of the uniform is the side cap featuring a cockerel feather plume. The sergeant also wears a whistle on a green lanyard with pompoms.

SPECIFICATIONS	
Country:	Hungary
Date:	1941
Unit:	Hungarian Gendarmerie
Rank:	Sergeant
Theatre:	Eastern Front
Location:	Southern Russia

2nd Lieutenant ▶
Hungarian Infantry

Seen in 1941, before the full horrors of the Eastern Front descended upon the Hungarian Army, this lieutenant wears a double-breasted army greatcoat and a side cap displaying the national cockade and braided rank chevrons. The collar patches show the arm-of-service.

SPECIFICATIONS	
Country:	Hungary
Date:	1941
Unit:	Hungarian Infantry
Rank:	2nd Lieutenant
Theatre:	Eastern Front
Location:	Hungary

1941   1941   1942   1943

◀ **Infantryman**
Rifle Brigade, 2nd Hungarian Army

This Hungarian company bugler has the Hungarian Army pattern uniform introduced in 1922, although the helmet is recognizably of German origin; Hungarian forces wore both the 1915- and 1935-pattern of German helmet.

SPECIFICATIONS	
Country:	Hungary
Date:	1942
Unit:	2nd Hungarian Army
Rank:	Infantryman
Theatre:	Eastern Front
Location:	Unknown

2nd Lieutenant ▶
1st Armoured Division, Hungarian Army

This 2nd lieutenant wears the typical uniform of a tank crewman for 1943. It consists of a single-piece cotton khaki overall, over which he wears a leather waistcoat. The uniform is completed with a side cap that features a cockade badge in national colours.

SPECIFICATIONS	
Country:	Hungary
Date:	1943
Unit:	1st Armoured Division
Rank:	2nd Lieutenant
Theatre:	Eastern Front
Location:	Southern Russia

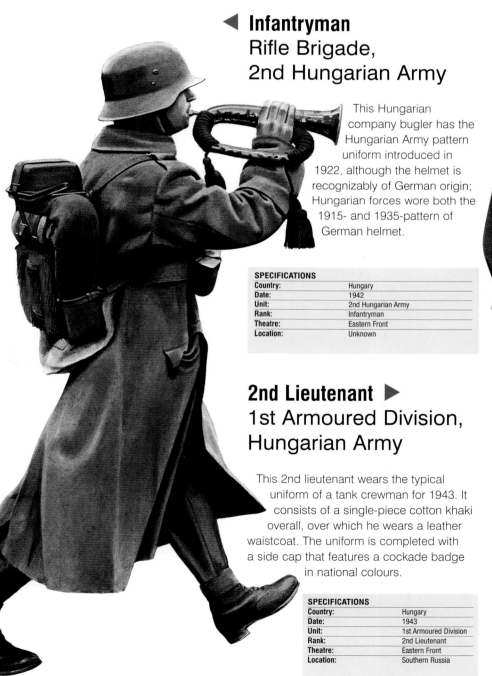

Hungarian and Romanian Forces 1941–44

As in the case of the German Army, the undoing of the Hungarian forces was its commitments on the Eastern Front. The 2nd Hungarian Army alone suffered up to 190,000 casualties during its ill-fated defence on the Soviet Don Front to the south of Voronezh, near Stalingrad, in 1943.

◀ Lieutenant
2nd Calarasci Regiment

This lieutenant is typical of the appearance of a Romanian Army officer in the post-1931 period, the date after which the uniform was based around British patterns. He wears a single-breasted khaki tunic featuring two breast pockets and two side pockets, plus, in this instance, a regimental lanyard running over his left shoulder.

SPECIFICATIONS	
Country:	Romania
Date:	1942
Unit:	2nd Calarasci Regiment
Rank:	Lieutenant
Theatre:	Eastern Front
Location:	Southern USSR

Private ▶
Infantry Division, Romanian Army

Romanian Army uniforms followed a horizon-blue colouration until 1916, from when a khaki pattern was adopted. This soldier is wearing the standard pattern for 1942 on the Eastern Front. The blanket across his chest would give adequate warmth during the summer and autumn.

SPECIFICATIONS	
Country:	Romania
Date:	1942
Unit:	Infantry Division
Rank:	Private
Theatre:	Eastern Front
Location:	Odessa

TIMELINE   1942   1942   1944   1944

◀ 2nd Lieutenant
Hungarian Infantry

The basic Hungarian uniform in summer was a khaki tunic, pantaloons or long trousers (these being worn with puttees or anklets and ankle boots respectively), a lambswool cap, and the German M1935 steel helmet, here fitted with a net for camouflage attachments. The unpadded greatcoat issued in the winter gave scant protection.

SPECIFICATIONS	
Country:	Hungary
Date:	1944
Unit:	Hungarian Infantry
Rank:	2nd Lieutenant
Theatre:	Eastern Front
Location:	Unknown

Major-General ▶
Romanian Army

This Romanian major-general wears a serge service dress and a pattern of field cap adopted later in the war. Rank and status are indicated on the collar patches, epaulettes and via the red stripes down the sides of his breeches.

SPECIFICATIONS	
Country:	Romania
Date:	1944
Unit:	Romanian Army
Rank:	Major-General
Theatre:	Eastern Front
Location:	Unknown

Other Axis Troops, Eastern Front

The *Wehrmacht* and *Waffen-SS* utilized many different nationalities on the Eastern Front. They included volunteers from the occupied territories and even Soviet collaborators, numbering in their tens of thousands.

◀ Infantryman
Spanish Blue Division

The Spanish Blue Division contributed 18,000 volunteers to Germany's campaign on the Eastern Front. Here we see a Spanish infantryman in standard German field-grey infantry uniform and kit, including an MP40 submachine gun. Badges on the right sleeve and helmet display the Spanish national colours.

SPECIFICATIONS	
Country:	Spain
Date:	1942
Unit:	Spanish Blue Division
Rank:	Infantryman
Theatre:	Eastern Front
Location:	Leningrad front

Private ▶
French Volunteer Legion

This small contingent of French troops who fought on the Eastern Front for the Germans is a little-known aspect of French wartime history. German uniforms and weapons were adopted, yet the French tricolour adorns both the coat sleeve and the helmet, and the medals are French.

SPECIFICATIONS	
Country:	France
Date:	1943
Unit:	French Volunteer Legion
Rank:	Private
Theatre:	Eastern Front
Location:	Ukraine

1942   1943   1943   1943

◄ Sergeant
Slovak Light Division

Slovakian troops fighting on the Eastern
Front continued to wear khaki uniforms of
the former Czechoslovak Army, but with
rank badges on the collar patches
instead of on the shoulder straps.
This sergeant has the special helmet
marking of the Slovak Light Division,
and his weapon is a Czech version
of the German Mauser, the VZ 24.

SPECIFICATIONS	
Country:	Czechoslovakia
Date:	1943
Unit:	Slovak Light Division
Rank:	Sergeant
Theatre:	Eastern Front
Location:	Ukraine

Captain ►
Caucasian
Cossack Cavalry

Because of their repression under Stalin,
the Cossacks provided thousands of
men for the Nazi cause. The soldier here
wears traditional Cossack clothing for
mounted troops, although his weapon
is the modern Tokarev semi-auto rifle.

SPECIFICATIONS	
Country:	Soviet Union
Date:	1943
Unit:	Caucasian Cossack Cavalry
Rank:	Captain
Theatre:	Eastern Front
Location:	Unknown

Lance-Corporal, Panzer Lehr Regiment 1944

This soldier – Lance-Corporal Freidhelm Ollenschäger – is wearing the standard uniform of an armoured crewman: loose black trousers and short double-breasted jacket. Instead of the padded beret, he has a cloth side cap.

The 9mm (.35in) Parabellum Luger P'08 was a typical sidearm of German tank crews during World War II. Some 2.5 million of these guns were produced between 1908 and 1945. It was relatively accurate and comfortable to fire, but its toggle-lock mechanism required careful cleaning to ensure reliable operation.

The Panzer IV became the core of Germany's armoured force during World War II, with nearly 9000 vehicles produced (all variants). Here we see a Panzer IV fitted with appliqué 20mm (0.79 in) steel plates to provide additional protection against enemy anti-tank fire. This Ausf H model also has a 75mm (2.95in) gun.

Lance-Corporal
Panzer Lehr Regiment

Ollenschäger's rank is displayed as a single stripe on the sleeve, while the *Wehrmacht* eagle and the death's-head badge on the collar patches indicate his arm-of-service. The standard 45mm (1.8in)-wide German Army belt would have been worn by all German Army soldiers up to officer rank. It served for all circumstances, both operational and parade, coming in black or dark brown, although lighter brown versions are seen occasionally. The highly visible aluminium belt buckle (*Koppelschloss*), painted field-grey, often bore the legend *Gott Mit Uns* ('God With Us').

SPECIFICATIONS	
Country:	Germany
Date:	1944
Unit:	Panzer Lehr Regiment
Rank:	Lance-Corporal
Theatre:	Eastern Front
Location:	Unknown

Red Army Infantry 1940–45

The Red Army was a vast force of men. Often poorly trained and equipped, they died in their millions – up to 11 million of them between 1941 and 1945 – although their blood essentially bought the defeat of Nazi Germany.

◄ Marshal of the Soviet Union
Red Army

Having risen rapidly through the military ranks, Marshal Timoshenko, pictured here, was awarded a Hero of the Soviet Union award and then rose to the status of Commander-in-Chief of the Soviet Armed Forces. Here we see him wearing the grey parade uniform of senior officers issued from 1940.

SPECIFICATIONS	
Country:	Soviet Union
Date:	1940
Unit:	Red Army
Rank:	Marshal
Theatre:	Eastern Front
Location:	Moscow

Corporal ►
Infantry Division

Over a khaki tunic and trousers, this soldier wears the standard infantry greatcoat. It was made of cheap cloth with variable production quality. Officer greatcoats often had arm-of-service piping. The weapon is the Tokarev SVT40, an early semi-auto rifle.

SPECIFICATIONS	
Country:	Soviet Union
Date:	1941
Unit:	Infantry Division
Rank:	Corporal
Theatre:	Eastern Front
Location:	Ukraine

◀ Officer
Infantry Division, Red Army

This officer is kitted out in superb winter clothing of the type issued from 1941. The jacket and trousers – known together as the *telogreika* uniform – are made from a double layer of khaki material with cotton wool stitched in strips inside to provide a warming quilted effect.

SPECIFICATIONS	
Country:	Soviet Union
Date:	1941
Unit:	Infantry Division
Rank:	Officer
Theatre:	Eastern Front
Location:	Moscow

Sergeant ▶
Polish Army in Russia

The Polish Army in Russia was composed of Polish POWs captured by Russia during its assault on Poland in 1939. This sergeant's uniform is a medley of different items, including British, Russian and Polish kit; the Polish Army in Russia initially wore what it stood up in in the prison camps.

SPECIFICATIONS	
Country:	Poland
Date:	1941
Unit:	Polish Army in Russia
Rank:	Sergeant
Theatre:	Eastern Front
Location:	Southern Russia

Red Army Infantry 1940–45

Although the Soviets coped better with the harsh Russian winters than their German adversaries, they still suffered from problems of substandard clothing – the Soviet infantry uniform was extremely basic at the best of times.

◄ Private
Red Army

This Red Army private presents a typical Soviet infantry uniform. His head is protected by an M1940 steel helmet, and the khaki breeches are tucked into knee-high puttees. He is armed with the formidable but impractical 14.5mm (.57in) PTRD 141 anti-tank rifle.

SPECIFICATIONS	
Country:	Soviet Union
Date:	1942
Unit:	Red Army
Rank:	Private
Theatre:	Eastern Front
Location:	Russia

Ski Trooper ►
Red Army

This Red Army ski trooper wears a large hooded white snow cape and overtrousers on top of his padded winter uniform, providing excellent camouflage in a snowy landscape. Across his chest he carries the redoubtable PPSh-41 submachine gun.

SPECIFICATIONS	
Country:	Soviet Union
Date:	1942
Unit:	Red Army
Rank:	Ski Trooper
Theatre:	Eastern Front
Location:	Russia

TIMELINE

1942　　　1942　　　1942　　　1943

◄ Lieutenant
Frontier Troops

Frontier Troops were essentially internal security forces, responsible (as part of the Ministry of the Interior) for policing movements in border regions. The colours on the hat and collar distinguish the arm-of-service; the rank is displayed on the tunic collar.

SPECIFICATIONS

Country:	Soviet Union
Date:	1942
Unit:	Frontier Troops
Rank:	Lieutenant
Theatre:	Eastern Front
Location:	Russia

Sniper ►
Rifle Battalion, Red Army

Here we see a female sniper deployed around Kursk in July 1943. During the war, Soviet snipers were issued with one-piece specialist camouflage overalls to wear over their standard uniforms. These featured a deep hood to obscure the head and facial features, and protect from the weather.

SPECIFICATIONS

Country:	Soviet Union
Date:	1943
Unit:	Rifle Battalion
Rank:	Sniper
Theatre:	Eastern Front
Location:	Kursk

Red Army Infantry 1940–45

The Red Army was a socially diverse entity. Because of problems in finding the manpower to fulfil military and industrial tasks, for example, the Soviet government recruited 7.75 million women, of whom 800,000 served in the armed forces.

Partisan
Partisans

Partisans had no uniform as such. This figure is wearing a mixture of civilian and military clothing – he has a civilian cap and jacket with Red Army breeches, and boots from a German source. He is armed with a PPSh-41 submachine gun and two grenades.

SPECIFICATIONS	
Country:	Soviet Union
Date:	1943
Unit:	Partisans
Rank:	Partisan
Theatre:	Eastern Front
Location:	Pripet Marshes

Private ▶
Rifle Division

This elderly Red Army private is wearing standard Soviet Army field uniform with a side cap that sports the red star. His shirt (*rubaha*) has a traditional cut and carries shoulder boards. The red piping on these boards denotes his membership of the infantry arm.

SPECIFICATIONS	
Country:	Soviet Union
Date:	1943
Unit:	Rifle Division
Rank:	Private
Theatre:	Eastern Front
Location:	Western USSR

TIMELINE   1943   1943   1943   1945

◄ Sergeant
Red Army
Medical Services

Uniforms for women who served in the Red Army were first introduced in August 1941, although they were quickly superseded by standard-issue clothing. This sergeant of the Medical Services wears a man's shirt with rank and arm-of-service badges on the shoulder straps.

SPECIFICATIONS	
Country:	Soviet Union
Date:	1943
Unit:	Red Army Medical Services
Rank:	Sergeant
Theatre:	Eastern Front
Location:	Ukraine

General ▶
Red Army

In essence, this uniform is not World War II issue, as it was produced for the celebrations and ceremonies following the defeat of Germany in May 1945. Moving away from the khaki, blues and steel-greys of earlier uniforms, the new full-dress uniform for generals and marshals was sea-green in colour.

SPECIFICATIONS	
Country:	Soviet Union
Date:	1945
Unit:	Red Army
Rank:	General
Theatre:	Eastern Front
Location:	Moscow

Russian Machine-Gunner, Stalingrad 1942

Stalingrad was arguably the turning-point of World War II in Europe. The first great defeat of the *Wehrmacht* cost the Germans the entire Sixth Army, and began their long retreat back to the Reich. The battle proved the Soviet talent for close-quarters urban warfare, the antithesis of *Blitzkrieg*.

The Degtyarev DP was in production from 1928. It was a generally tough gas-operated weapon that was perfectly suited to hard battlefield use, although its flat 42-round drum magazine was prone to damage. The DP fired the rimmed 7.62 x 54R (.03 x 2.1in) Soviet cartridge; its cyclical rate of fire was between 500 and 600rpm.

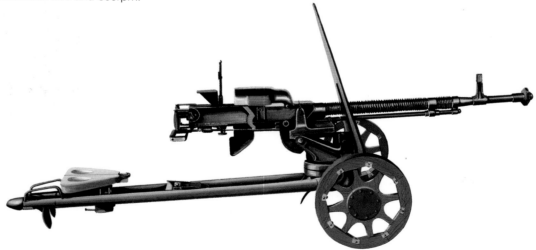

The DShK was the standard Soviet heavy machine gun of World War II, firing the hefty 12.7mm (0.5in) Soviet round to an effective range of 2000m (6600ft). Its main drawback was its weight, particularly when mounted on the infantry carriage seen here, but its long-range power was appreciated for area fire and anti-aircraft applications.

Private
Red Army

Armed with a Degtyarev DP machine gun, a Soviet machine-gunner mans a defensive position within the rubble of Stalingrad. The DP was a characteristically tough Russian weapon, one that would stay in production until the 1950s. The soldier is wearing standard Red Army khaki uniform for late 1942. Note that new dress regulations of 1943 were to change the entire visual structure of the Red Army. The traditional collar patches were abolished and all rank badges were transferred onto piped shoulder boards.

SPECIFICATIONS	
Country:	Soviet Union
Date:	1942
Unit:	Red Army
Rank:	Private
Theatre:	Eastern Front
Location:	Stalingrad

Soviet Mounted, Armoured and Mechanized Troops 1941–44

Soviet armoured forces grew dramatically in scale throughout World War II, although mechanization was always limited and most Red Army soldiers still had to rely on their feet and horses to deploy into battle.

◀ Trooper
Cavalry Regiment

Here we see a questionable form of river-crossing equipment. The outfit consisted of a large, inflatable rubber ring strapped around the waist, complete with harness straps and a set of integral waders. Once the soldier was floating, he would use the small oars to propel himself, while the long rod was used for depth readings.

SPECIFICATIONS	
Country:	Soviet Union
Date:	1941
Unit:	Cavalry Regiment
Rank:	Trooper
Theatre:	Eastern Front
Location:	Leningrad

Junior Sergeant ▶
Armoured
Regiment, Red Army

The tankman here is wearing the sun hat that was first introduced in March 1938 for military personnel serving in the Central Asian, North Caucasian and Trans-Caucasian commands, and in the Crimea. On his collar he wears patches indicating his arm-of-service, plus a tank badge.

SPECIFICATIONS	
Country:	Soviet Union
Date:	1941
Unit:	Armoured Regiment
Rank:	Junior Sergeant
Theatre:	Eastern Front
Location:	Crimea

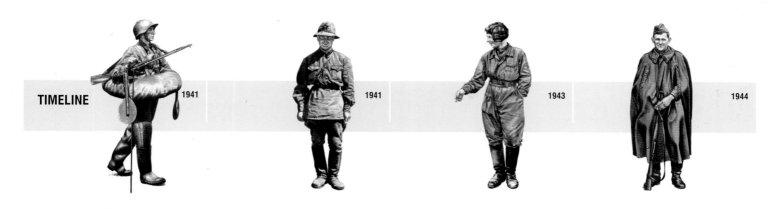

◀ Tankman
II Guards Tank Corps

The standard tankman uniform for operations was a one-piece overall worn over the standard tunic and trousers, this overall featuring a single, large chest pocket and one on the thigh, plus two slash pockets, one on each side.

SPECIFICATIONS	
Country:	Soviet Union
Date:	1943
Unit:	II Guards Tank Corps
Rank:	Tankman
Theatre:	Eastern Front
Location:	Kursk

Private ▶
Guards Motorized Division

This Red Army private is wearing a side cap (*pilotka*) and waterproof cape over the standard field uniform. The Russian ground sheet was designed so that it could be worn as a hooded cape, as illustrated here. The soldier is armed with the 7.62mm (0.3in) M44 Mosin-Nagant rifle.

SPECIFICATIONS	
Country:	Soviet Union
Date:	1944
Unit:	Guards Motorized Division
Rank:	Private
Theatre:	Eastern Front
Location:	Crimea

Soviet Officer in Stalingrad

At the beginning of World War II, the Soviet Union had the largest army in Europe, estimated at around 1.8 million men. Maintaining a continuous supply of uniforms and equipment for this manpower was a major undertaking, which meant that many Red Army soldiers wore uniforms designed at the beginning of the century. Others, such as the officer at Stalingrad here, were luckier.

The TT33 was a standard-issue Soviet handgun, alongside the Nagant M1895 revolver. It fired the 7.62 x 25mm Tokarev cartridge, eight of which could be held in the detachable box magazine. The TT-33 was a short-recoil weapon; it remains in use to this day in many conflict zones, such is its reliability and wide distribution.

The ZiS-5 was a prolific range of trucks produced in the Soviet Union between 1933 and the 1950s – in total, one million were manufactured. Weighing 3100kg (6800lb), it had a road speed of up to 65km/h (40mph) and served as the framework for variants ranging from artillery tractors to ambulances. The ZiS-5V was a simplified wartime version, and it is here fitted with a DShK machine gun for air defence.

Officer
Guards Motorized
Division

The Red Army officer pictured here took part in the Stalingrad battles. He wears the 1940-pattern *ushanka* fur cap and the sheepskin coat, the *polaschubuk*, with 1935-pattern leather equipment for officers. The sheepskin coat was normally issued to both mounted and armoured personnel. However, it is worth noting that the image of Soviet troops being fully equipped with warm winter clothing is wrong. Like the Germans, Soviet troops also suffered from exposure, not least because of problems with the logistical system.

SPECIFICATIONS	
Country:	Soviet Union
Date:	1942
Unit:	Guards Motorized Division
Rank:	Officer
Theatre:	Eastern Front
Location:	Stalingrad

Red Army Air Force 1940–44

The Red Air Force suffered from poor standards of tactics and training at the beginning of Operation *Barbarossa*. It lost up to 20,000 aircraft in 1941 alone, but Soviet industrial muscle and combat experience eventually turned it into an effective military force.

◀ **Major**
Red Army Air Force

As part of the Red Army, the Soviet Air Force during World War II was basically dressed as army personnel, though with some differences of colouration. The air force colour was blue, and this colour also featured on the cap band, the collar patches and the piping on the cuffs and trousers.

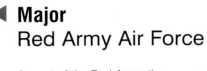

SPECIFICATIONS	
Country:	Soviet Union
Date:	1940
Unit:	Red Army Air Force
Rank:	Major
Theatre:	Eastern Front
Location:	Kiev

Lieutenant ▶
Red Army Air Force

This fighter pilot is wearing a pre-war leather flying coat with flying helmet. Note the rank badges displayed on the collar patches. Lieutenants were identified by square red enamel badges, in this case two, plus the winged propeller. Officers were also issued with double-breasted greatcoats.

SPECIFICATIONS	
Country:	Soviet Union
Date:	1941
Unit:	Red Army Air Force
Rank:	Lieutenant
Theatre:	Eastern Front
Location:	Murmansk

| TIMELINE | 1940 | 1941 | 1942 | 1944 |

◄ Senior Political Officer
Red Army Air Force

The senior political officer pictured here is wearing the 1935-pattern blue service dress of the Red Army Air Force, although the black piping on his collar patches identifies him as a commissar. Red Army regulations stated that commissars were required to wear a red cloth five-pointed star on both cuffs, although here they are removed.

SPECIFICATIONS	
Country:	Soviet Union
Date:	1942
Unit:	Red Army Air Force
Rank:	Senior Political Officer
Theatre:	Eastern Front
Location:	Leningrad

Lieutenant ►
Red Army Air Force

Regulations introduced on 15 January 1935 brought many changes to the uniforms of Red Army Air Force officers. New tunics were issued for the purpose of showing insignia, and all officers had shoulder boards of gold lace for parade and service uniform or plain cloth ones, as seen here, for field dress.

SPECIFICATIONS	
Country:	Soviet Union
Date:	1944
Unit:	Red Army Air Force
Rank:	Lieutenant
Theatre:	Eastern Front
Location:	Kiev

Luftwaffe, Eastern Front 1941–44

On the Eastern Front, the *Luftwaffe* was initially dominant, establishing air superiority over many areas of the battlefield. For the initial invasion of the Soviet Union, the Germans deployed nearly 4400 combat aircraft.

◄ Major
Jagdgeschwader 51

Here we see Major Werner Mölders, one of Germany's leading air aces. He wears a side cap displaying the *Luftwaffe* eagle and the national cockade, and a non-regulation black leather flying jacket, over which he has the self-inflating life-jacket issued to all pilots of single-engined aircraft.

SPECIFICATIONS	
Country:	Germany
Date:	1941
Unit:	*Jagdgeschwader* 51
Rank:	Major
Theatre:	Eastern Front
Location:	West of Moscow

Captain ▶
Luftwaffe, Army Group Centre

Captain Hans Phillipp, pictured here, was one of Germany's most highly decorated pilots on the Eastern Front. He was awarded the Swords to the Knight's Cross of the Iron Cross with Oak Leaves for downing 82 Allied aircraft, the decoration here hung around his neck.

SPECIFICATIONS	
Country:	Germany
Date:	1942
Unit:	*Luftwaffe*
Rank:	Captain
Theatre:	Eastern Front
Location:	Ukraine

TIMELINE 1941 1942 1944 1944

◄ **1st Lieutenant**
Jagdgeschwader 52,
Army Group Centre

This 1st lieutenant is wearing the peaked cap with *Jagdfliegerknicke* (literally, 'pilot's nick'), an effect achieved by removing the wire stiffener from the cap and squashing the cap flat. His other items are the *Luftwaffe* leather flying jacket, blue-grey trousers and *Luftwaffe* leather and suede flying boots.

SPECIFICATIONS	
Country:	Germany
Date:	1944
Unit:	*Jagdgeschwader* 52
Rank:	1st Lieutenant
Theatre:	Eastern Front
Location:	East Prussia

Major ▶
Stukageschwader 2

The major is wearing what was often termed the 'Invasion Suit', a one-piece flying overall in field-grey, with zip fastenings at the front and down the insides of the legs, the latter so that the outfit could be removed even while wearing boots or shoes. The large patch pockets served to store maps and navigational aids.

SPECIFICATIONS	
Country:	Germany
Date:	1944
Unit:	*Stukageschwader* 2
Rank:	Major
Theatre:	Eastern Front
Location:	Western USSR

Luftwaffe Field Divisions

In late 1942, the decision was taken to transfer surplus personnel from the air force into the army. Hermann Göring, however, insisted that these personnel be organized as *Luftwaffe* field divisions under air force control, a move that ensured they suffered on the battlefield, as the officers and other ranks had no experience of combat.

The Model 24 *Stielhandgranate* is one of the most recognizable weapons of the *Wehrmacht* during World War II, although its origins actually date back to 1915. The explosive charge was contained in the metal head, and a pull cord ran through the handle to a friction igniter at the base of the detonator – pulling the cord set off a fuse that burned for five seconds before detonating the main charge.

The Kar 98k was a shortened version of the Mauser Gewehr 98, which had been the standard German rifle of World War I. The newer rifle also fired the 7.92mm (.31in) Mauser M98 cartridge, and its Mauser action was known for its rugged reliability under any combat conditions. Some 11.5 million of the rifles were manufactured by war's end.

Private
Luftwaffe Field Division

The uniform worn by the field divisions was the same as in other *Luftwaffe* branches, although collar patches were often omitted from tunics and flying jackets. The most distinctive item of the uniform was the camouflage smock. The smock featured a camouflage pattern of angular segments or splinters in three colours; it was identical to that used by the army for camouflaged shelter quarters, helmet covers and smocks. The soldier here is armed with an MP40 submachine gun, and two Model 39 grenades sit alongside the map case at the front.

SPECIFICATIONS	
Country:	Germany
Date:	1944
Unit:	*Luftwaffe* Field Division
Rank:	Private
Theatre:	Eastern Front
Location:	Lvov

Other Axis Air Forces, Eastern Front

Non-German Axis air forces made a small but significant contribution to Hitler's air power on the Eastern Front. The Romanian Air Force, for example, had a force of 621 aircraft at the start of Operation *Barbarossa*.

◀ ## Officer
Romanian Air Force

Here we see an officer of the Romanian Air Force in 1942. He is wearing the standard two-piece uniform of the time, the tunic featuring two breast patch pockets and two large hip pockets. A white shirt and black tie are worn beneath. His silver aircrew wings are displayed on the left breast.

SPECIFICATIONS	
Country:	Romania
Date:	1942
Unit:	Romanian Air Force
Rank:	Officer
Theatre:	Eastern Front
Location:	Ukraine

Captain ▶
Croat Air Force

Officers of the Croat Air Force wore the grey-blue service dress of the former Yugoslav Air Force, but with new insignia. Croatian versions of *Luftwaffe* rank badges were worn on the collar patches and the shoulder straps, but on the latter the German star was replaced by a metal trefoil.

SPECIFICATIONS	
Country:	Croatia
Date:	1942
Unit:	Croat Air Force
Rank:	Captain
Theatre:	Eastern Front
Location:	Russia

TIMELINE 1942 1942 1943 1944

◀ Lieutenant
Hungarian Air Force

Beneath his German sheepskin flying jacket, this lieutenant of the Hungarian Air Force is wearing standard Hungarian Army khaki service dress, including a khaki field cap with brown leather peak. The army uniform was worn by all air and ground personnel.

SPECIFICATIONS	
Country:	Hungary
Date:	1943
Unit:	Hungarian Air Force
Rank:	Lieutenant
Theatre:	Eastern Front
Location:	Southern Russia

Corporal ▶
Romanian Air Force

This corporal of the Romanian Air Force is ground crew rather than flying crew, and he wears standard service dress for other ranks. His trousers tuck into leather buckled gaiters, and his rank is displayed simply on the shoulder straps.

SPECIFICATIONS	
Country:	Romania
Date:	1944
Unit:	Romanian Air Force
Rank:	Corporal
Theatre:	Eastern Front
Location:	Unknown

Soviet Navy 1942–44

At the beginning of the war against Nazi Germany, the Red Navy lacked anti-submarine warfare vessels, minesweepers and support craft. As a consequence, during the first six months of the war in the Baltic the Soviets lost 25 submarines for the loss of only three German cargo ships.

◄ Seaman
Baltic Fleet, Red Navy

The seaman illustrated here is wearing the 1940-pattern steel helmet and waterproof foul-weather coat. His earphone and speaker are part of the ship's gunnery control equipment. The rubber attachments on his greatcoat skirts were for hitching this equipment to his belt.

SPECIFICATIONS	
Country:	Soviet Union
Date:	1942
Unit:	Baltic Fleet, Red Navy
Rank:	Seaman
Theatre:	Eastern Front
Location:	Leningrad

Petty Officer 2nd Class ►
Caspian Flotilla, Red Navy

This petty officer of the Caspian Flotilla wears the black and blue square rig uniform of the Red Navy. It is typical navy clothing: a black jumper with white-striped blue jean collar (a *forminka*) over a blue and white T-shirt, black naval belt, bell-bottomed trousers and black shoes.

SPECIFICATIONS	
Country:	Soviet Union
Date:	1943
Unit:	Caspian Flotilla, Red Navy
Rank:	Petty Officer 2nd Class
Theatre:	Eastern Front
Location:	Caspian Sea

Petty Officer 2nd Class ▶
Black Sea Fleet, Red Navy

This petty officer, 2nd class, is one of thousands of Soviet seamen who ended up fighting on land. He wears the uniform of the Red Army, while proudly retaining the striped vest to denote his naval affiliations. On this quilted jacket he wears the Medal for the Defence of Sevastopol. The pouch holds a magazine for his PPSh-41.

SPECIFICATIONS	
Country:	Soviet Union
Date:	1944
Unit:	Black Sea Fleet, Red Navy
Rank:	Petty Officer 2nd Class
Theatre:	Eastern Front
Location:	Sevastopol

Rear Admiral ▶
Pacific Fleet, Red Navy

This senior officer of the submarine service is wearing the standard uniform of the Red Navy. Line officers wore gold insignia: cap badge, embroideries on the peaked cap's visor, cuff stripes, shoulder straps and buttons. The cap badge depicted a foul anchor on a cockade.

SPECIFICATIONS	
Country:	Soviet Union
Date:	1944
Unit:	Pacific Fleet, Red Navy
Rank:	Rear Admiral
Theatre:	East Asia
Location:	South China Sea

Allied Maritime Forces, Europe/Atlantic 1940–43

The Allied war in the Atlantic was one of the least glamorous theatres of the war. Yet it was the most important for the British, as it was vital that its maritime forces, merchant and naval, kept open the Atlantic supply lines.

◀ Lieutenant-Commander
Royal Navy

Lieutenant-Commander Kimmins is wearing the same uniform as was worn during a combined operation in Norway: a naval service dress under an army helmet and leather jerkin. His web equipment is the 1937 pattern, while the arrow on the top of the binoculars indicates that they are War Department property.

SPECIFICATIONS	
Country:	Britain
Date:	1941
Unit:	Royal Navy
Rank:	Lieutenant-Commander
Theatre:	Arctic
Location:	North Cape

Petty Officer ▶
Royal Navy

This petty officer serving aboard an escort vessel in the Atlantic Ocean is holding a shell for a 120mm (4.7in) gun. He wears a peaked cap that displays the special badge for petty officers. The rest of his uniform consists of a balaclava helmet, duffle coat and sea socks and boots.

SPECIFICATIONS	
Country:	Britain
Date:	1941
Unit:	Royal Navy
Rank:	Petty Officer
Theatre:	Atlantic
Location:	Atlantic Ocean

◀ Gunlayer 2nd Class
Royal Navy

This figure wears the typical action rig, which was worn by British naval gun crews during World War II. Over this he wears a one-piece blue overall with a canvas money belt. Under the steel helmet he has an anti-flash hood, while his hands are protected by special gauntlets.

SPECIFICATIONS	
Country:	Britain
Date:	1941
Unit:	Royal Navy
Rank:	Gunlayer 2nd Class
Theatre:	Atlantic
Location:	Atlantic Ocean

Petty Officer 1st Class ▶
Task Force 34

This Task Force 34 sailor is seen during the Allied landings in North Africa, which began on 8 November 1942. As a rating, he can be seen wearing the standard navy blue square rig uniform, which consisted of blue pullover with white-striped flap collar, black knotted scarf, matching blue trousers, black shoes and white cap.

SPECIFICATIONS	
Country:	United States
Date:	1942
Unit:	Task Force 34
Rank:	Petty Officer 1st Class
Theatre:	Mediterranean
Location:	Morocco

Allied Maritime Forces, Europe/Atlantic 1940–43

Despite the adoption of the convoy system, Allied losses at the hands of U-boats were massive. This was particularly the case in the period 1941–43, when U-boat packs roamed the ocean from their bases on the French Atlantic coast.

◄ Chief Petty Officer
Task Force 34

As a chief petty officer, this figure wears chevrons and a branch badge on the left sleeve. The rating badge consisted of an eagle, chevrons, arc and speciality badge. The eagle and branch badges were white. The sailor here has four stripes on his cuff, each one denoting four years' service.

SPECIFICATIONS	
Country:	United States
Date:	1942
Unit:	Task Force 34
Rank:	Chief Petty Officer
Theatre:	Mediterranean
Location:	North Africa

Lieutenant ►
Royal Canadian Women's Naval Service

This lieutenant's uniform matches that of British ranks except in the button details and hat ribbons, which illustrated the country of origin. She wears a standard lightweight uniform, but the three-cornered hat separates her as an officer from the round sailor's hat worn by NCOs and lower ranks.

SPECIFICATIONS	
Country:	Canada
Date:	1943
Unit:	Royal Canadian Women's Naval Service
Rank:	Lieutenant
Theatre:	Northwest Europe
Location:	London

TIMELINE   1942   1943   1943   1943

Sergeant ◀
No. 120 Squadron, Coastal Command

This airman is wearing the flying suit that was typical of those crews who flew with Coastal Command on long missions over the Atlantic and Arctic. His polo-neck sweater – called a Frock White sweater – and Irvin sheepskin jacket over a pre-war flying suit provided both comfort and practicality.

SPECIFICATIONS	
Country:	Britain
Date:	1943
Unit:	No. 120 Squadron, Coastal Command
Rank:	Sergeant
Theatre:	Atlantic
Location:	Bay of Biscay

Ensign ▶
US Atlantic Fleet

Here we see a US naval ensign (the lowest commissioned rank). The picture is dated by the length of the rank stripes on the cuff: before 1 January 1944, they looped around the entire cuff; after this they extended across only the outside half of the sleeve. The star displayed on the cuff indicates line-officer status.

SPECIFICATIONS	
Country:	United States
Date:	1943
Unit:	US Atlantic Fleet
Rank:	Ensign
Theatre:	Atlantic
Location:	Washington DC

The Women's Royal Naval Service

The Women's Royal Naval Service (WRNS) was formed in November 1917, its members becoming known as 'Wrens' on account of the service's initial letters. The service was disbanded after World War I, but reformed in 1939.

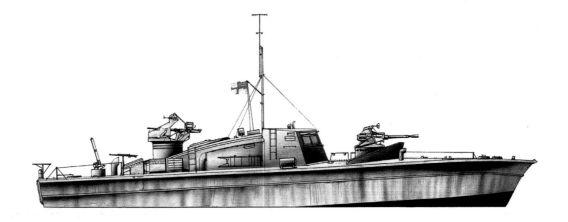

Although Wrens did not serve as naval combat crews, they did man various types of small power boats in coastal duties. Here is a British Power Boat 60ft Type craft, which had a length of 18.36m (60ft 3in) and a maximum speed of 33 knots. It was armed with eight machine guns and two 457mm (18in) torpedoes.

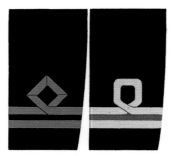

The two rank shoulder straps, both of the Women's Royal Naval Service, here belong to a 2nd officer (left) and a medical superintendent (right). In the Wrens there were five rating ranks, from Ordinary Wren to Chief Wren, and seven commissioned ranks, from 3rd Officer to Chief Commandant.

2nd Officer
Women's Royal Naval Service

The figure illustrated here holds the rank of 2nd officer, which was equivalent to the rank of lieutenant in the Royal Navy. All Wren officers wore special cap badges on their tricorne hats. These badges were smaller than those worn by their male colleagues and, in addition, the six-leaved wreath was embroidered in blue silk. Officers also wore special blue stripes on the cuff, as shown here, and shoulder straps with a diamond instead of a curl.

SPECIFICATIONS	
Country:	Britain
Date:	1942
Unit:	Women's Royal Naval Service
Rank:	2nd Officer
Theatre:	Northwest Europe
Location:	London

Kriegsmarine, Atlantic 1942–44

From 1942 the German *Kriegsmarine* underwent a significant strategic change. Its mighty surface warships – vessels such as the *Tirpitz* – were effectively kept out of harm's way for fear of their sinking, leaving the U-boats and small surface vessels to continue the war.

◄ Lieutenant
German Navy

The imposing figure here is that of a U-boat commander. Submarine service was hard on uniforms, hence this officer's uniform has a worn appearance. The Knight's Cross of the Iron Cross decoration hangs on a ribbon around his neck, while the Iron Cross 1st Class is displayed on his navy reefer jacket.

SPECIFICATIONS	
Country:	Germany
Date:	1942
Unit:	German Navy
Rank:	Lieutenant
Theatre:	Atlantic
Location:	France

Petty Officer ▶
German Navy

The black leather jacket and trousers worn here were actually work wear, donned typically by those working in engine rooms and around machines – the leather was a more stain-resistant fabric than cloth. Note that the jacket has little in the way of insignia, apart from on the shoulder straps.

SPECIFICATIONS	
Country:	Germany
Date:	1943
Unit:	German Navy
Rank:	Petty Officer
Theatre:	Atlantic
Location:	Unknown

TIMELINE	1942	1943	1943	1944

◀ Commander
German Navy

The German Navy commander here is wearing part of his poor-weather clothing system: a long double-breasted leather jacket, worn here without any form of rank insignia. The jacket could be worn with matching leather over-trousers; German Navy personnel tended to wear a wide variety of trousers when at sea.

SPECIFICATIONS	
Country:	Germany
Date:	1943
Unit:	German Navy
Rank:	Commander
Theatre:	Atlantic
Location:	France

Seaman ▶
German Naval Artillery

This soldier is a naval artilleryman, responsible for manning heavy coastal guns. The uniform is actually navy issue, despite its resemblance to the army uniform (the pocket configuration is different), but he is armed with the standard German Army rifle, the Mauser Kar 98k.

SPECIFICATIONS	
Country:	Germany
Date:	1944
Unit:	German Naval Artillery
Rank:	Seaman
Theatre:	Western Europe
Location:	France

Italian Navy 1941–43

At the outbreak of World War II, the Italian Navy fielded an impressive fleet of more than 300 combat vessels (including six battleships). Yet its contribution to Axis combat efforts was fairly minimal, and focused mainly on supply runs between Italy and North Africa.

◄ Seaman
Italian Navy

The seaman pictured here is wearing the Italian Navy square rig uniform, consisting of a navy blue jacket and trousers, the former with a blue denim collar. The naval cap bears the words 'Regia Marina' – translating as 'Royal Navy' – and the uniform is completed by a pair of black leather shoes.

SPECIFICATIONS	
Country:	Italy
Date:	1941
Unit:	Italian Navy
Rank:	Seaman
Theatre:	Mediterranean
Location:	Italy

Seaman ►
Italian Navy

At the beginning of the war, the Italian Navy had a total of 115 submarines in its arsenal. This seaman is a submarine crewman, as indicated by the dolphin emblem on his grey-green naval uniform. The black beret was also an item for submariners, although it was only worn aboard ship.

SPECIFICATIONS	
Country:	Italy
Date:	1942
Unit:	Italian Navy
Rank:	Seaman
Theatre:	Mediterranean
Location:	Unknown

TIMELINE

1941   1942   1942   1943

◀ **Ranking Lieutenant**
Taranto Command, Italian Navy

This officer of the Taranto Command wears
a blue reefer jacket and matching trousers,
and a peaked cap, the standard dress of
Italian Navy officers. The cap badge is
the Italian naval insignia: an oval shield
bracketed by laurel leaves and surmounted
by a crown, all in gold embroidery.

SPECIFICATIONS	
Country:	Italy
Date:	1942
Unit:	Taranto Command
Rank:	Ranking Lieutenant
Theatre:	Mediterranean
Location:	Taranto

Sub-Commander ▶
Italian Navy

The Italian Navy sub-commander seen here
is wearing an informal mix of uniform items,
adapted to the tropical climes of the
Mediterranean. A pair of possibly army
shorts are worn with a zipped jacket and
wellington boots; only the cap indicates
his naval and officer status.

SPECIFICATIONS	
Country:	Italy
Date:	1943
Unit:	Italian Navy
Rank:	Sub-Commander
Theatre:	Mediterranean
Location:	North Africa

Royal Navy, Mediterranean 1941–43

The Mediterranean Fleet was one of the Royal Navy's most prestigious commands. It was involved in several major actions, including the attack on the Italian fleet at Taranto in 1940 and the battle of Crete.

◄ Rating
HMS *Warspite*, Royal Navy

This gunner's uniform is designed to be hard-wearing. Over his naval dress he has a heavy toggle-fastened duffel coat and life-jacket. His trousers are bell-bottomed and tucked into rubber boots with heavy socks. Under his standard British steel helmet he also wears an asbestos anti-flash hood.

SPECIFICATIONS	
Country:	Britain
Date:	1941
Unit:	HMS *Warspite*
Rank:	Rating
Theatre:	Mediterranean
Location:	North Africa

Admiral ►
Mediterranean Fleet, Royal Navy

Here we see Admiral Sir John Cunningham, the Naval Commander-in-Chief Levant, wearing the regulation Royal Navy whites worn by officers on ceremonial or tropical duties. The cap could be made with a white top, but an option was to fit a white cover over the standard naval blue cap.

SPECIFICATIONS	
Country:	Britain
Date:	1943
Unit:	Mediterranean Fleet, Royal Navy
Rank:	Admiral
Theatre:	Mediterranean
Location:	Cairo

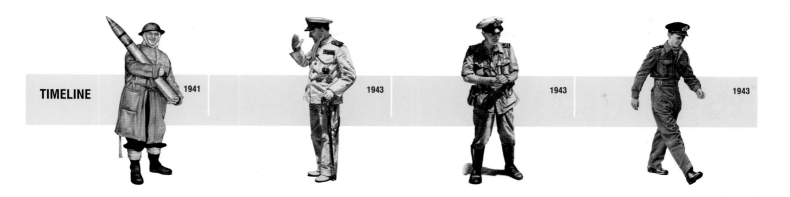

◀ Lieutenant
Royal Naval
Volunteer Reserve

This lieutenant is wearing the uniform issued for land operations in the tropics. During the war, the most popular uniform for wear in these conditions was the white-topped hat or khaki drill sun helmet, khaki drill shirt or Royal Marine-pattern tunic, and khaki drill long or short trousers.

SPECIFICATIONS	
Country:	Britain
Date:	1943
Unit:	RN Volunteer Reserve
Rank:	Lieutenant
Theatre:	Mediterranean
Location:	Sicily

Lieutenant ▶
Royal Navy

Here we see a British submarine commander, actually wearing British Army battledress modified with naval rank badges on the shoulder straps, plus the Royal Navy peaked cap. The roll-beck pullover beneath the tunic is also naval issue.

SPECIFICATIONS	
Country:	Britain
Date:	1943
Unit:	Royal Navy
Rank:	Lieutenant
Theatre:	Mediterranean
Location:	Unknown

French and US Navies, Mediterranean 1940–42

After the fall of France in the summer of 1940, the French Fleet was obliged to keep its ships under Axis control. The Royal Navy's attack on the French ports of Mers-el-Kébir and Dakar ensured that the Vichy Fleet remained hostile to the Allies.

◀ Lieutenant
Mediterranean Fleet, French Navy

The sailor here is a lieutenant of the Mediterranean Fleet, and he wears the blue service dress of the navy, although in tropical climates there was also a standard lightweight khaki uniform. His cap is blue with a black leather peak, and features a fouled anchor badge.

SPECIFICATIONS	
Country:	France
Date:	1940
Unit:	Mediterranean Fleet
Rank:	Lieutenant
Theatre:	Mediterranean
Location:	Toulon

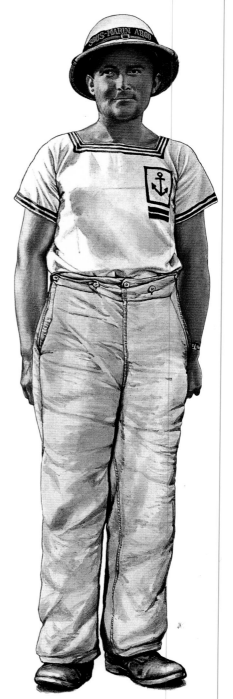

Leading Seaman ▶
Mediterranean Fleet, French Navy

In very hot weather, officers and ratings wore a white sun helmet as shown here. A metal version of the cap badge was worn by officers and petty officers, with a yellow metal anchor on the front for ratings, who also wore the cap ribbon illustrated.

SPECIFICATIONS	
Country:	France
Date:	1941
Unit:	Mediterranean Fleet
Rank:	Leading Seaman
Theatre:	Mediterranean
Location:	Marseille

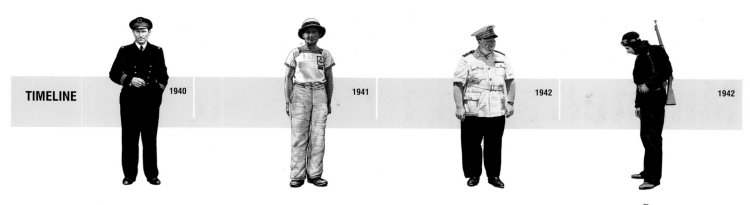

TIMELINE 1940 1941 1942 1942

◄ Rear Admiral
French Navy

Here we see a rear admiral of the French Navy in 1942 – his rank is indicated by the white metal stars in the centre of his highly embroidered cap band. With a pair of black trousers and shoes, he wears a naval short-sleeved white tropical jacket.

SPECIFICATIONS	
Country:	France
Date:	1942
Unit:	French Navy
Rank:	Rear Admiral
Theatre:	Mediterranean
Location:	Unknown

Seaman 2nd Class ►
US Navy

This US Navy seaman 2nd class is kitted out in winter working gear. The distinctive head cover provided warmth for the head and sides of the face, although he also has goggles for eye protection. An additional face mask could be fitted if the extreme weather conditions demanded.

SPECIFICATIONS	
Country:	United States
Date:	1942
Unit:	US Navy
Rank:	Seaman 2nd Class
Theatre:	Mediterranean
Location:	North Africa

Private, Italian Social Republic Marine, 1944

The Italian Social Republic was created in the north of Italy following Italy's capitulation to the Allies in 1943. It was essentially a Nazi puppet state – here is one of the few Italian Navy marines who decided to stick with the Axis regime.

The Beretta M1938 was a 9mm Parabellum weapon that gained a good reputation during World War II. It was produced in various models to suit wartime production needs, and it was fed from a 32-round box magazine, with a cyclical rate of fire of 600rpm.

The Modello 30 was one of a new breed of light machine guns design in Italy during the interwar years. Its feed mechanism consisted of a hinged integral box, which was opened, filled with 6.5 x 52mm M95 cartridges, and closed for firing. It was not a successful system.

Private
Italian Social
Republic Marine

Here we see a private of the Italian Social
Republic Marine in a distinctive grey-green
uniform, which was actually first introduced
for Italian Army parachute troops. Elements
that suggest the 'para' style include the
trousers fitted into the tops of the boots and
the close-fitting chest pouches, these
containing magazines for the soldier's
weapon, the Beretta M38 submachine gun.
The helmet is the standard Italian maritime
model. Insignia is limited to the collar, which
features the Lion of St Mark (previously worn
on the cuffs) and the *gladio* symbol.

SPECIFICATIONS	
Country:	Italy
Date:	1944
Unit:	Italian Social Republic Marine
Rank:	Private
Theatre:	Italy
Location:	North Italy

Balkan Armies 1940–45

In 1940, the Italian Army launched a disastrous campaign in the Balkans, invading Albania and Greece. Having met unexpectedly ferocious resistance, the Italians were eventually rescued in 1941 by German intervention.

◄ Private
Evzones, Greek Army

This soldier belongs to the *Evzones* infantry, an elite force within the Greek Army. This uniform shows elements of the *Evzones* traditional dress, including the shoes with woollen pompoms. The tight pantaloons and stockings are a military representation of civilian mountain dress. For warmth, the soldier has a goat-fleece cape.

SPECIFICATIONS	
Country:	Greece
Date:	1940
Unit:	*Evzones*, Greek Army
Rank:	Private
Theatre:	Balkans
Location:	Greece

Sergeant ►
Greek Army

Having a more conventional appearance than the infantryman above, this sergeant in the Greek Army wears a British Mk I steel helmet with a khaki uniform. Rank is given on the sleeve, while the collar displays arm-of-service tabs (infantry).

SPECIFICATIONS	
Country:	Greece
Date:	1940
Unit:	Greek Army
Rank:	Sergeant
Theatre:	Balkans
Location:	Greece

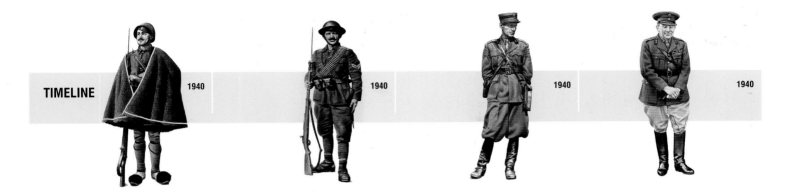

◄ Lieutenant
Artillery Regiment, Greek Army

As a mounted officer, this officer wears loose riding breeches and riding boots, these being worn with a three-quarter-length tunic fastened at the waist with a belt. The uniform is matched by a khaki kepi hat, this being adorned with a silver crown and also the blue and white Greek cockade.

SPECIFICATIONS	
Country:	Greece
Date:	1940
Unit:	Artillery Regiment
Rank:	Lieutenant
Theatre:	Balkans
Location:	Greece

Lieutenant-Colonel ►
II Corps, Greek Army

The Greek Army adopted a khaki uniform in 1912, and by the outbreak of World War II this incorporated many British features, especially the officers' uniform, as seen here. Indeed, the service dress worn here is almost identical to the British model.

SPECIFICATIONS	
Country:	Greece
Date:	1940
Unit:	II Corps, Greek Army
Rank:	Lieutenant-Colonel
Theatre:	Balkans
Location:	Greece

Balkan Armies 1940–45

Despite Mussolini's initial confidence in his Balkan invasion, Greek forces violently repelled the Italian onslaught through dextrous tactics, intimacy with the mountainous terrain and sheer aggression.

◀ Wing Commander
Fighter Squadron, Greek Air Force

The Greek Air Force uniform was designed around the British RAF model, and many Greek pilots underwent their primary combat training in the UK. A single-breasted jacket and matching trousers, both in blue-grey, was the standard uniform; it was worn with a white or grey shirt and black tie.

SPECIFICATIONS	
Country:	Greece
Date:	1941
Unit:	Fighter Squadron, Greek Air Force
Rank:	Wing Commander
Theatre:	Balkans
Location:	Greece

Able Seaman ▶
Greek Navy

Like the Greek Air Force to the Royal Air Force, the Greek Navy had a uniform similar to that of the Royal Navy. This able seaman wears the classic blue reefer jacket with matching trousers and Royal Navy-pattern anklets. As a rating, his rank is given on the sleeve in red.

SPECIFICATIONS	
Country:	Greece
Date:	1941
Unit:	Greek Navy
Rank:	Able Seaman
Theatre:	Balkans
Location:	Greece

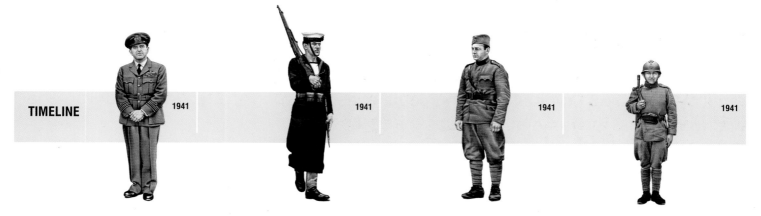

TIMELINE 1941   1941   1941   1941

◀ **Senior Sergeant**
Artillery Arm,
Yugoslav Army

This senior sergeant wears the standard uniform of the Yugoslav infantry. Yugoslavian military dress, however, had its origins in Serbian uniform, which in turn was indebted to Austro-Hungarian and Imperial Russian uniforms, so during the war variations were common, especially among officers.

SPECIFICATIONS	
Country:	Yugoslavia
Date:	1941
Unit:	Artillery Arm, Yugoslav Army
Rank:	Senior Sergeant
Theatre:	Balkans
Location:	Yugoslavia

Private ▶
Infantry Division,
Yugoslav Army

This particular soldier is dressed in the Serbian uniform of World War I. This was a double-breasted jacket with a stand collar – the colour of which indicated arm-of-service – baggy pantaloons tucked into knee-high puttees, black shoes and a French Adrian model helmet.

SPECIFICATIONS	
Country:	Yugoslavia
Date:	1941
Unit:	Infantry Division, Yugoslav Army
Rank:	Private
Theatre:	Balkans
Location:	Yugoslavia

Balkan Armies 1940–45

The Germans swiftly conquered the Balkans in 1941, but certain territories would not stay quiescent. Yugoslavia in particular was locked in a brutal guerrilla war, one that would cost over one million lives by 1945.

◀ Captain
Infantry Regiment, Yugoslav Army

Although this captain is wearing the more modern service tunic issued in the early 1940s, the ornamentation clearly casts a glance back to Imperial Russia. Chief among these features are the shoulder boards, while an aiguillette across the shoulder and chest add more ceremony.

SPECIFICATIONS	
Country:	Yugoslavia
Date:	1941
Unit:	Infantry Regiment, Yugoslav Army
Rank:	Captain
Theatre:	Balkans
Location:	Yugoslavia

Captain ▶
Fighter Flight, Yugoslav Air Force

This captain wears the Yugoslav grey-blue officers' service dress. This was a single-breasted tunic worn over a white shirt and black tie, with a matching pair of trousers and side cap. The rank of captain is shown on the shoulder boards.

SPECIFICATIONS	
Country:	Yugoslavia
Date:	1941
Unit:	Fighter Flight, Yugoslav Air Force
Rank:	Captain
Theatre:	Balkans
Location:	Yugoslavia

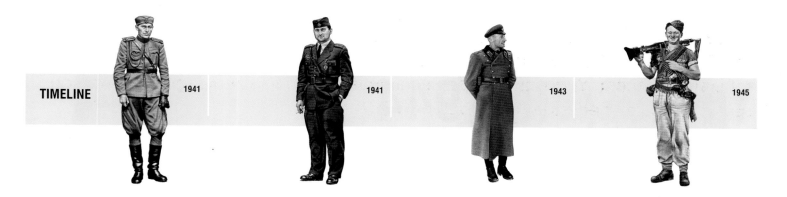

1941   1941   1943   1945

◀ Major
Cavalry Division, Bulgarian Army

This officer wears wartime Bulgarian service dress with a greatcoat, which for officers had scarlet lapels and scarlet piping around the collar, cuffs, down the front and on the half-belt, and featured pocket flaps at the back. The tunic had either a stand-and-fall or an open collar.

SPECIFICATIONS	
Country:	Bulgaria
Date:	1943
Unit:	Cavalry Division, Bulgarian Army
Rank:	Major
Theatre:	Balkans
Location:	Macedonia

Partisan ▶
Yugoslav People's Liberation Army

This Yugoslav partisan is wearing a mixture of clothing, including German shirt, Yugoslav Army cap, British khaki drill trousers and British anklets and ammunition boots. Note the five-pointed star on his cap, which was a standard communist designation.

SPECIFICATIONS	
Country:	Yugoslavia
Date:	1945
Unit:	Yugoslav People's Liberation Army
Rank:	Partisan
Theatre:	Balkans
Location:	Yugoslavia

Long-Range Desert Group, Yugoslavia 1944

The figure here is Lieutenant 'Tiny' Simpson, who was a member of the Long-Range Desert Group (LRDG). The LRDG was a British reconnaissance and intelligence-gathering unit raised in July 1940, and which served in North Africa, the Mediterranean and the Balkans.

The Besa machine gun was designed during the inter-war period purposely for mounting on vehicles. It was a gas-operated 7.92mm (0.31in) gun. The Mk 1 and Mk 2 variants had a rate selector to vary the rate of fire from 500 to 850rpm.

The Chevrolet WA, a Canadian 4 x 4 vehicle, found extensive use in the hands of the Long-Range Desert Group, modified for desert warfare and long-range patrols. The chassis was to form the basis of many light and medium trucks supplied to Allied forces, and the WA was adapted to specialist purposes ranging from ambulances to gun carriages.

Lieutenant
Long-Range Desert Group

Simpson wears the heavy knit 'commando' sweater favoured by many members of Britain's special forces during World War II. He wears it with battledress trousers and black ammunition boots. He also has a 1937-pattern web belt with pistol holder and ammunition pouch around his waist. On his head he has the black beret of the Royal Tank Regiment. Every LRDG man was issued with IS9 escape aids, a Bergen backpack, and the Thompson sleeping bag or the heavier Baxter, Woodhouse and Taylor version with waterproof cover.

SPECIFICATIONS	
Country:	Britain
Date:	1944
Unit:	Long-Range Desert Group
Rank:	Lieutenant
Theatre:	Balkans
Location:	Yugoslavia

German Forces, Balkans Theatre 1943–44

Although the Balkans were generally conquered with characteristic German efficiency in 1941, the campaigns did not all go to plan. The invasion of Crete in May, for example, cost the German paratroop arm 7000 casualties.

◀ **Private**
Infantry Regiment

This private in the German Army is wearing the typical uniform of troops serving on the so-called Adriatic Coast Line, an area that stretched from Trieste in Italy to the Greek islands in the Mediterranean. He is a machine gunner, armed with an MG42.

SPECIFICATIONS	
Country:	Germany
Date:	1943
Unit:	Infantry Regiment
Rank:	Private
Theatre:	Balkans
Location:	Adriatic coast

Lieutenant-Colonel ▶
Prinz Eugen Division

This *Waffen-SS* officer is kitted out with the standard mountain troop uniform, complete with ski cap, field blouse, mountain trousers, mountain boots and short elasticated puttees. The ski cap was soon replaced by the M1943 standard field cap.

SPECIFICATIONS	
Country:	Germany
Date:	1944
Unit:	*Prinz Eugen* Division
Rank:	Lieutenant-Colonel
Theatre:	Balkans
Location:	Yugoslavia

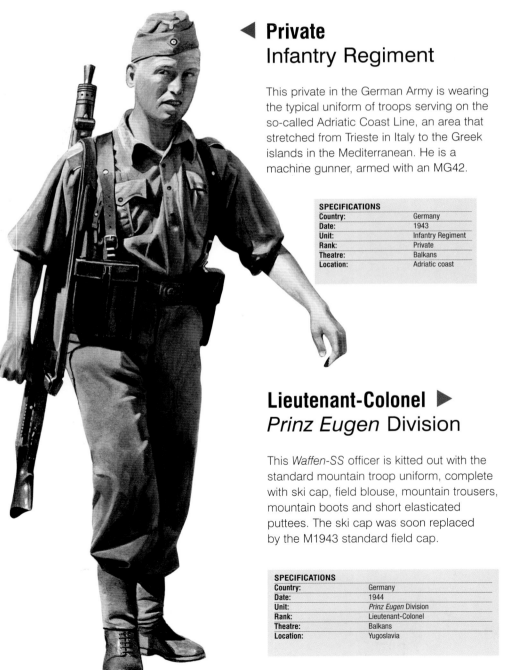

TIMELINE 1943   1944   1944   1944

◀ Senior Sergeant
Waffen-SS
Military Police

The 13th Waffen Mountain Division of the SS *Handschar* (1st Croatian) was a Yugoslavian volunteer formation, hence the regional style of headdress. National colours are also displayed on the tunic's left sleeve. Being a military policeman, this soldier also wears a duty metal gorget around his neck.

SPECIFICATIONS	
Country:	Yugoslavia
Date:	1944
Unit:	13th Waffen Mountain Division
Rank:	Senior Sergeant
Theatre:	Balkans
Location:	Bosnia

Artilleryman ▶
1st Cossack Cavalry
Division

Another foreign volunteer for German service, this soldier is serving in the 1st Cossack Cavalry Division in Yugoslavia. While most of the uniform has a German appearance, the traditional *papakha* Cossack fur cap is still worn.

SPECIFICATIONS	
Country:	Soviet Union
Date:	1944
Unit:	1st Cossack Cavalry Division
Rank:	Artilleryman
Theatre:	Balkans
Location:	Yugoslavia

Axis Forces, Balkans 1940–41

The Balkans were, and remain, an ethnically and politically complex region. The Germans could capitalize on age-old enmities to buy local allies, although there were plenty of enemies as well.

◀ Private
Army Group Albania

This Italian soldier is ill-equipped to fight the Balkan winter campaign of 1940/41. His greatcoat is made of a cheap, coarse cloth and is not even double-breasted. No special winter clothing was issued to Italians, apart from the mountain troops.

SPECIFICATIONS	
Country:	Italy
Date:	1940
Unit:	Army Group Albania
Rank:	Private
Theatre:	Balkans
Location:	Albania

Sergeant ▶
6th Regiment
Italian Army

A member of the elite *bersaglieri* riflemen, this sergeant presents arms with his 7.35mm (0.28in) M91 carbine, with its unusual folding bayonet extended. The black cockerel feathers were a traditional element of the *bersaglieri*, and were worn on various headdresses.

SPECIFICATIONS	
Country:	Italy
Date:	1941
Unit:	6th Regiment, Italian Army
Rank:	Sergeant
Theatre:	Balkans
Location:	Unknown

1940

1941

1941

1941

◀ Private
Bulgarian Army

A Russian style permeates this Bulgarian Army infantry uniform (the leather webbing is directly Russian), although German designs also began to have influence during the war, such as in the helmet shape. This soldier is armed with a copy of the 6.5mm (0.25in) Mannlicher Carcano 1891.

SPECIFICATIONS	
Country:	Bulgaria
Date:	1941
Unit:	Bulgarian Army
Rank:	Private
Theatre:	Balkans
Location:	Bulgaria

Rating ▶
Danube Flotilla,
Romanian Navy

This rating's uniform features a long, double-breasted greatcoat featuring two rows of gilt metal buttons, blue trousers and ankle boots, and a naval cap with the legend 'Marina Regala' on the band. This cap would have a ribbon hanging from the back. Ratings also wore a blue jumper with a blue jean collar.

SPECIFICATIONS	
Country:	Romania
Date:	1941
Unit:	Danube Flotilla, Romanian Navy
Rank:	Rating
Theatre:	Balkans
Location:	Black Sea

Fallschirmjäger, Crete 1941

The *Fallschirmjäger* were an elite force within Hitler's armies. They proved themselves during operations in Scandinavia and the Low Countries in 1940, but the sheer cost of the Crete invasion in May 1941 meant that thereafter the paras were used mainly as ground forces.

The 7.92mm (0.31in) *Fallschirmjägergewehr* 42 (FG 42) was developed specifically for German airborne forces, and was an innovative weapon on many levels. Its 'straight-in-line' design was excellent for handling recoil, and it could fire in both semi- and full-automatic modes, the latter at rates of up to 750rpm. It also came with an integral bipod, fitted near the muzzle.

The eagle surmounting a swastika was the famous motif of the German Air Force. Here we see two varieties of this emblem, in the form of patches displayed on the breast of the tunic. The uppermost one is that worn by an officer of general rank, while that below was worn by other ranks of officer.

Private
7th Air Division

This para wears the *Luftwaffe* parachute jump smock manufactured in pale green and grey cotton. The smock was of the step-in variety, which entailed the wearer stepping into the short legs of the garment, pulling the smock up over his body, pushing his arms into the sleeves and shrugging the jacket onto his shoulders. The smock was then buttoned up in the front from the crotch to the collar. Like the para helmet, the smock was designed to avoid all possibility of the wearer's kit or clothing becoming entangled in his parachute harness or being caught up on any projecting part of an aircraft's interior.

SPECIFICATIONS	
Country:	Germany
Date:	1941
Unit:	7th Air Division
Rank:	Private
Theatre:	Balkans
Location:	Crete

Italian Armed Forces 1940–44

Due to the defeats suffered by Italy in World War II, the average Italian serviceman has been viewed, unfairly, as a coward. Yet in reality Italy did not lack for courage, and more than 200,000 men were killed in the war.

◀ Corporal
Milizia Volontaria Per La Sicurezza

The *Milizia Volontaria Per La Sicurezza* was Mussolini's fascist militia organization. This soldier wears standard grey-green Italian Army uniform. His unit is distinguished by black additions to the uniform, including his black tie and shirt beneath the tunic.

SPECIFICATIONS	
Country:	Italy
Date:	1940
Unit:	Milizia Volontaria Per La Sicurezza
Rank:	Corporal
Theatre:	Mediterranean
Location:	Sicily

Private ▶
Italian Army

This Italian private is seen in the field service uniform typical of Italian infantry, including the distinctive breeches tucked into either woollen socks or (for motorized soldiers) leather leggings. He is armed with the M1891 Mannlicher-Carcano rifle.

SPECIFICATIONS	
Country:	Italy
Date:	1940
Unit:	Italian Army
Rank:	Private
Theatre:	Mediterranean
Location:	Italy

TIMELINE   1940   1940   1942   1943

◀ Sergeant-Major
Marine Infantry

Notwithstanding the blue and white navy collar, Italian Marine soldiers had little to distinguish them visually from the regular army, although the grey-green jumper (worn here with matching pantaloons and puttees) was usually blue in colour when issued to army troops.

SPECIFICATIONS	
Country:	Italy
Date:	1942
Unit:	Marine Infantry
Rank:	Sergeant-Major
Theatre:	Mediterranean
Location:	Sicily

Alpine 2nd Lieutenant ▶
Italian Army

Italy's Alpine troops were among its most respected forces, and their uniforms set them apart from the mass of infantry. This 2nd lieutenant has a felt Alpine cap featuring an eagle feather and a red woollen pompom. The cap badge is an eagle over crossed rifles and hunting horns.

SPECIFICATIONS	
Country:	Italy
Date:	1943
Unit:	Alpine Regiment, Italian Army
Rank:	2nd Lieutenant
Theatre:	Italy
Location:	Unknown

Italian Armed Forces 1940–44

Italy was one of the first countries to adopt a 'shirt and tie' uniform: a grey-green single-breasted tunic, which was designed to be worn open with a matching shirt and tie. In 1939, a new tunic with matching cloth belt was issued to other ranks in the infantry and dismounted arms.

◀ Major-General
Co-Belligerent Forces

Italy switched to the Allied side in 1943, and this senior officer of the Co-Belligerent Forces wears the Italian military uniform common in the later stages of the war – British battle dress with Italian insignia.

SPECIFICATIONS	
Country:	Italy
Date:	1944
Unit:	Co-Belligerent Forces
Rank:	Major-General
Theatre:	Italy
Location:	Southern Italy

Militiaman ▶
Legion Tagliamento

The paramilitary here is wearing the uniform that was typical of the fascist side in Italy at the end of the war. He is a legionary 'M' (for Mussolini) of the Republican National Guard (GNR). His black headdress is similar to that of the elite *bersaglieri* riflemen.

SPECIFICATIONS	
Country:	Italy
Date:	1944
Unit:	Legion Tagliamento
Rank:	Militiaman
Theatre:	Italy
Location:	Northern Italy

TIMELINE 1944 1944 1944 1944

◄ Seaman
Italian Social Republic Navy

The actual pattern of pre- and post-fascist Italian Navy uniform stayed roughly the same: a navy blue square rig uniform worn with either a sailor's cap, a steel helmet (as seen here), or a peaked cap for officer ranks. The real changes lay in the insignia.

SPECIFICATIONS	
Country:	Italy
Date:	1944
Unit:	Italian Social Republic Navy
Rank:	Seaman
Theatre:	Italy
Location:	Southern Italy

Major ►
Italian Social Republic Air Force

The uniform here is very like that worn by Italian forces in the North Africa campaign, including the *sahariana* jacket and loose-fitting trousers. The cap, however, is a late war variety, and this soldier's decorations include an Iron Cross 1st and 2nd class.

SPECIFICATIONS	
Country:	Italy
Date:	1944
Unit:	Italian Social Republic Air Force
Rank:	Major
Theatre:	Italy
Location:	Unknown

German Forces in Italy 1943–44

Although Winston Churchill famously called Italy the 'soft underbelly' of Europe, German forces in Italy inflicted terrible casualties upon a grindingly slow Allied advance, and proved their talents in defensive warfare.

Awarded (in its silver grade) from 1939, the Infantry Assault Badge was given to non-motorized infantry and mountain personnel who fought in combat. The bronze grade of medal, awarded to motorized troops, was instituted in 1940.

The 9mm (0.35in) Walther P38 was one of the finest handguns of the war, and it would serve well beyond the confines of World War II. It featured a safety indicator pin to show if there was a cartridge in the chamber, and it had a double-action lock.

2nd Lieutenant
German Army

This officer is wearing a mixture of uniform styles, bringing together elements of both tropical and temperate dress. Such was not uncommon during the Italian campaign, a theatre that brought a wide range of climatic conditions, particularly in the mountainous areas. His field cap and the right sleeve of the tunic, via the Edelweiss badge, reveal that he is a mountain soldier; he also has the Infantry Assault Badge and Wound Badge.

SPECIFICATIONS	
Country:	Germany
Date:	1944
Unit:	German Army
Rank:	2nd Lieutenant
Theatre:	Italy
Location:	Unknown

Allied Forces in Italy 1943–45

The average size of a British division in Italy was around 40,000 men. Attrition rates were high, however: between September 1943 and March 1944 the Eighth Army in Italy suffered 46,000 battle casualties.

◀ Lance-Corporal
Royal Military Police

This military policeman is serving with the 46th (North Midland and West Riding) Division in the Italian campaign. He wears a steel helmet with painted band and the letters 'MP' on it; on his right sleeve the blue armlet sports the same letters.

SPECIFICATIONS	
Country:	Britain
Date:	1943
Unit:	46th Division, Royal Military Police
Rank:	Lance-Corporal
Theatre:	Italy
Location:	Naples

Guardsman ▶
British Army

This guardsman is seen following the traumatic battle of Monte Cassino, hence his rough appearance. He wears the British Army double-breasted waistcoat, and carries extra ammunition in a bandolier for his Thompson M1928A1 submachine gun.

SPECIFICATIONS	
Country:	Britain
Date:	1943
Unit:	British Army
Rank:	Guardsman
Theatre:	Italy
Location:	Monte Cassino

TIMELINE	1943	1943	1943	1944

◀ ## Lieutenant
2nd Cameronians

What sets this lieutenant apart visually is his tam-o'-shanter hat displaying the regimental crest on a tartan background. Otherwise, he is wearing standard British Army officers' battle dress. The patch on the sleeve indicates the 5th Infantry Division, to which the 2nd Cameronians belonged.

SPECIFICATIONS	
Country:	Britain
Date:	1943
Unit:	2nd Cameronians
Rank:	Lieutenant
Theatre:	Italy
Location:	Central Italy

Lance-Corporal ▶
Royal Gurkha Rifles, Indian Army

This Gurkha lance-corporal is clothed in the British Army temperate-zone battledress. However, rank markings colouration is different – here rifle-green – and the sleeve also bears the formation sign of the Indian Army. He has 1938-pattern British webbing in khaki, worn in battle-order configuration.

SPECIFICATIONS	
Country:	Nepal/India
Date:	1944
Unit:	Royal Gurkha Rifles, Indian Army
Rank:	Lance-Corporal
Theatre:	Italy
Location:	Central Italy

Allied Forces in Italy 1943–45

The Italian campaign was just as hard for US forces as it was for the British. The US Fifth Army invaded mainland Italy at Salerno on 9 September 1943, but it took several bloody days to consolidate the initial beachhead.

◀ Private
II Polish Corps

This soldier is well-equipped in a mountain-warfare overall, a one-piece thickly padded and waterproof uniform, ideal for snowy, mountainous conditions. Instead of conventional webbing, he wears canvas chest packs with two No.36 hand-grenades.

SPECIFICATIONS	
Country:	Poland
Date:	1944
Unit:	II Polish Corps
Rank:	Private
Theatre:	Italy
Location:	Central Italy

Private ▶
4th Infantry Division, Eighth Army

The uniform of the typical 'Tommy' on the Italian campaign. On his back this private wears the 1937-pattern web equipment, under the top flap of which he has stowed his battledress. Standard equipment included a pick, which doubled as an entrenching tool.

SPECIFICATIONS	
Country:	Britain
Date:	1944
Unit:	4th Infantry Division, Eighth Army
Rank:	Private
Theatre:	Italy
Location:	Rome

| TIMELINE | 1944 | 1944 | 1944 | 1944 |

◀ **Corporal**
6th Rajputana Rifles, Eighth Army

The Indian headdress was normally the khaki puggaree, which varied in shape according to the religion and tribe of the wearer. Muslims wore the pointed kullah or skull cap inside the puggaree, while Sikhs wore the Sikh puggaree with their uncut hair in buns.

SPECIFICATIONS	
Country:	Indian
Date:	1944
Unit:	6th Rajputana Rifles, Eighth Army
Rank:	Corporal
Theatre:	Italy
Location:	Unknown

Private ▶
3rd Infantry Division

This US private here wears the standard M1 helmet, M1941 olive-drab field jacket, olive-drab trousers, canvas leggings and leather boots. His equipment consists of a haversack with entrenching tool, M1942 bayonet and a canteen suspended from the cartridge belt.

SPECIFICATIONS	
Country:	United States
Date:	1944
Unit:	3rd Infantry Division
Rank:	Private
Theatre:	Italy
Location:	Anzio

Allied Forces in Italy 1943–45

The Allied campaign in Italy was a truly multi-national affair. The US Fifth Army, for example, included British, French, Indian and Brazilian troops, although the majority of its divisions were American.

◀ Private
Royal Gurkha Rifles, Indian Army

The figure here is a private of the Royal Gurkha Rifles of the Indian Army. His uniform is typical of that worn during the Italian campaign; unlike in North Africa, in Italy the Indian Army troops were eventually issued with British uniforms in their entirety. This man is armed with a Thompson M1928.

SPECIFICATIONS	
Country:	Nepal/India
Date:	1944
Unit:	Royal Gurkha Rifles, Indian Army
Rank:	Private
Theatre:	Italy
Location:	Central Italy

Royal Marine ▶
No. 40 Commando, 2 Commando Brigade

The Royal Marines previously had worn army-pattern khaki service dress, but this was replaced at the beginning of the war with standard army khaki battledress, as seen here. This commando has 1937-pattern webbing and and anklets.

SPECIFICATIONS	
Country:	Britain
Date:	1945
Unit:	No. 40 Commando
Rank:	Royal Marine
Theatre:	Italy
Location:	Unknown

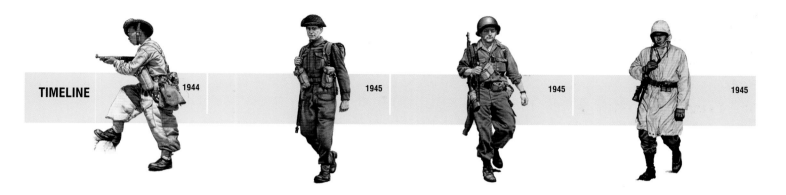

TIMELINE

1944

1945

1945

1945

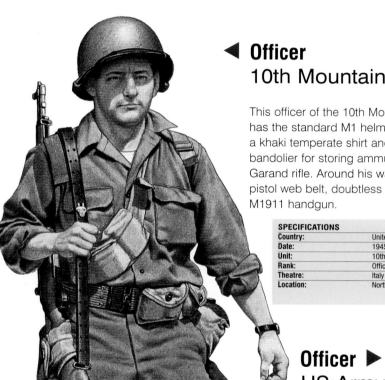

◀ **Officer**
10th Mountain Division

This officer of the 10th Mountain Division has the standard M1 helmet, wool trousers, a khaki temperate shirt and a cotton bandolier for storing ammunition for his M1 Garand rifle. Around his waist is an officer's pistol web belt, doubtless holding a Colt M1911 handgun.

SPECIFICATIONS	
Country:	United States
Date:	1945
Unit:	10th Mountain Division
Rank:	Officer
Theatre:	Italy
Location:	Northern Italy

Officer ▶
US Army

For all its sunny reputation, Italy produced a very hostile climate during the autumn and winter months. Here we see a late-war winter uniform issued to US troops, which included a snow smock and waterproof leggings tuck into M1943 combat boots.

SPECIFICATIONS	
Country:	United States
Date:	1945
Unit:	US Army
Rank:	Officer
Theatre:	Italy
Location:	Northern Italy

Pacific Land War 1941–42

The Pacific theatre presented a climate hostile to both men and uniforms. The combination of extreme heat and high humidity rotted fabrics and leathers, as well as rusting any metal items.

◀ Private
Imperial Japanese Army

This soldier is wearing the cotton khaki dress of a Japanese soldier in the tropical theatres of World War II. However, he is without the single-breasted khaki jacket with stand-and-fall collar, which was introduced in 1938 and that replaced an earlier jacket with a stiff collar.

SPECIFICATIONS
Country:	Japan
Date:	1941
Unit:	Imperial Japanese Army
Rank:	Private
Theatre:	Pacific
Location:	Luzon

Paratrooper ▶
Naval Parachute Troops

The soldier here is seen wearing the olive-drab jump overall issued to all naval paratroopers. It was worn over a matching shirt and pantaloons. The helmet is a Japanese Army para pattern in steel, but fitted with a canvas cover for camouflage.

SPECIFICATIONS
Country:	Japan
Date:	1941
Unit:	Naval Parachute Troops
Rank:	Paratrooper
Theatre:	Pacific
Location:	Southern Pacific

TIMELINE   1941   1941   1941   1942

◄ ## Private
Imperial Japanese Army

This Japanese Army tank crew member wears the standard cork helmet and goggles of armoured forces, plus a tankman's overall tucked into knee-high puttees. The only equipment here is a bayonet (left hip), haversack, water bottle and a gas mask.

SPECIFICATIONS	
Country:	Japan
Date:	1941
Unit:	Imperial Japanese Army
Rank:	Private
Theatre:	Pacific
Location:	Unknown

Private 1st Class ►
Imperial Japanese Army

Protection from heat and humidity were essential qualities of tropical uniforms. This Japanese soldier wears both his steel helmet and his field cap, the latter fitted with neckflaps. Note his shoes – canvas *tabi*, which were more suited to the jungle climate than leather boots.

SPECIFICATIONS	
Country:	Japan
Date:	1942
Unit:	Imperial Japanese Army
Rank:	Private 1st Class
Theatre:	Pacific
Location:	Pacific islands

Pacific Land War 1941–42

US industry had to gear itself up for war in short order. The US Marine Corps uniform in particular was conspicuously dated, although Marines often lagged behind the uniform issue of other arms-of-service anyway.

◀ Marine
1st Marine Defense Battalion

This Marine is wearing a World War I-pattern khaki shirt and trousers, with long, lace-up gaiters and a pair of brown leather shoes. His helmet is the M1917 helmet, modelled on that of the British Army. The large sack contains a gas mask.

SPECIFICATIONS	
Country:	United States
Date:	1941
Unit:	1st Marine Defense Battalion
Rank:	Marine
Theatre:	Pacific
Location:	Wake Island

Gunnery Sergeant ▶
US Marine Corps

The full dress uniform of the US Marines in World War II is shown on this gunnery sergeant during duties in Washington. He wears a 'Dress Blue' tunic with standing collar, lighter blue trousers with a red stripe running down the outside edge of each leg, and white and blue peaked dress cap bearing the USMC crest.

SPECIFICATIONS	
Country:	United States
Date:	1941
Unit:	US Marine Corps
Rank:	Gunnery Sergeant
Theatre:	USA
Location:	Washington DC

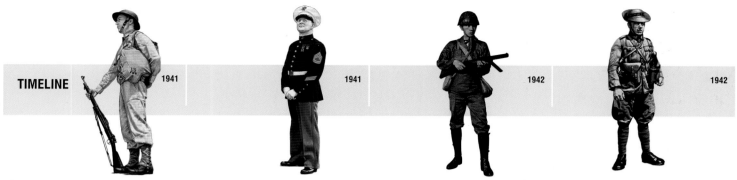

◄ Leading Seaman
Imperial Japanese Navy

Japanese marine troops wore high black leather boots and an olive-green uniform. This marine has fitted his steel helmet with a net cover for attaching camouflage.

A more notable piece of uniform is a crude bulletproof vest. He is armed with a Japanese version of the Swiss 7.62mm (0.3in) Bergmann 1920.

SPECIFICATIONS	
Country:	Japan
Date:	1942
Unit:	Imperial Japanese Navy
Rank:	Leading Seaman
Theatre:	Pacific
Location:	Dutch East Indies

Sergeant-Major ►
Royal Netherlands Marines

The most arresting part of this uniform is the distinctive straw hat, a part of Dutch ceremonial and non-combat dress replaced by a steel helmet during operations. Leather webbing, here holding a gas mask and pistol, is worn over grey-green uniform, and rank is displayed on the collar patches.

SPECIFICATIONS	
Country:	Netherlands
Date:	1942
Unit:	Royal Netherlands Marines
Rank:	Sergeant-Major
Theatre:	Pacific
Location:	Dutch East Indies

Japanese Private 1941

Japan mobilized 9.1 million men for its army, navy and air force, and its armed forces carried all before them in the Pacific and the Far East in 1941–42. Fanatical courage and resilience characterized Japan's fighting men.

The Type 100 was the only submachine gun Japan designed during World War II, with production beginning in 1942. It was a blowback weapon firing the 8mm (0.315in) Nambu cartridge, and was prone to jamming. Although a new model was brought out in 1944, the Japanese never produced enough of the Type 100 to match US infantry firepower.

The Arisaka 38th Year Rifle was the standard Japanese infantry rifle between 1907 and 1944. It fired a relatively low-powered 6.5mm (0.25in) cartridge, and its design was a mix of features from European Mannlicher and Mauser weapons. It gave generally good service in World War II, although material shortages resulted in many poor-quality guns in the last year of the war.

Private
Imperial Japanese Navy

This private is neatly attired in a new M98 uniform and webbing, the latter including two 30-round ammunition pouches at the front and a canvas gas mask case on the left hip. The pantaloons were usually bound to the knee with khaki tapes, these being a sensible measure when walking upon the insect-covered jungle floors of tropical Asia. As headgear, he wears the standard Japanese Army field cap, with a chin strap of brown leather and a removable neck sunguard. The cap could be worn beneath the Japanese steel helmet. Because of the temperatures in the Pacific theatre, it is uncommon to see the Japanese greatcoats.

SPECIFICATIONS	
Country:	Japan
Date:	1941
Unit:	Imperial Japanese Army
Rank:	Private
Theatre:	Pacific
Location:	Malaya

War in the Pacific 1943–45

The US Marine Corps numbered 20,000 men in 1939 and 65,881 by the time the United States entered the war in 1941. By the war's end, however, there were 450,000 marines – an army in itself.

◀ Marine
2nd Marine Division

This soldier is wearing the two-piece herringbone-twill uniform that became the dominant dress code of US Marines in the Pacific theatre, along with the coarser 'dungaree' uniform. Note the ammunition pouches worn around the waist.

SPECIFICATIONS	
Country:	United States
Date:	1943
Unit:	2nd Marine Division
Rank:	Marine
Theatre:	Pacific
Location:	Tarawa

Private ▶
US Marine Corps

This battle-weary marine in New Guinea wears the M1 helmet with webbing cover. The two-piece herringbone-twill fatigue suit shown here was introduced in 1942; the woven belt was usually only worn by officers, although this particular marine is wearing it with magazine and field dressing pouches attached.

SPECIFICATIONS	
Country:	United States
Date:	1943
Unit:	US Marine Corps
Rank:	Private
Theatre:	Pacific
Location:	New Guinea

1943   1943   1943   1943

◀ Marine
2nd Marine Division

This soldier belongs to the 2nd Marine Division, which first saw action in World War II when the 2nd Marines Regiment participated in the Guadalcanal operation. His M1 steel helmet features a 'beach' camouflage cover, indicative of the gradual introduction of camouflage into Marine combat uniform.

SPECIFICATIONS	
Country:	United States
Date:	1943
Unit:	2nd Marine Division
Rank:	Marine
Theatre:	Pacific
Location:	Tarawa

Marine ▶
US Marine Corps

A US Marine takes aim with his .45 ACP M3A1 'Grease Gun'. Like so many submachine guns of World War II, the M3 was designed specifically to meet the requirements of mass-production. This soldier wears a plain olive-green uniform with canvas leggings and leather shoes.

SPECIFICATIONS	
Country:	United States
Date:	1943
Unit:	US Marine Corps
Rank:	Marine
Theatre:	Pacific
Location:	Pacific islands

War in the Pacific 1943–45

The 'island-hopping' battles of 1943–45 were some of the bloodiest engagements in US history. The battle of Tarawa, for example, saw a total of nearly 1000 Marines killed on a central island less than 4km (2.5 miles) long.

◀ Private 1st Class
Imperial Japanese Army

The simplicity with which the Japanese soldier could operate was the envy of Allied logisticians. Here the soldier's equipment consists of nothing more than an ammunition pouch, water bottle and provisions sack. The submachine gun is the 8mm (0.315in) Type 100.

SPECIFICATIONS	
Country:	Japan
Date:	c. 1943
Unit:	Imperial Japanese Army
Rank:	Private 1st Class
Theatre:	Pacific
Location:	Unknown

Major-General ▶
US Sixth Army

The figure shown here is wearing a light khaki service uniform as worn by US officers in the Pacific theatre from 1943 onwards. All officers wore the 12.7mm (0.5in) olive-drab cuff bands, and those of general rank sported the letters 'US' in gold on the lapels of the tunic.

SPECIFICATIONS	
Country:	United States
Date:	1944
Unit:	US Sixth Army
Rank:	Major-General
Theatre:	Pacific
Location:	New Guinea

| TIMELINE | c. 1943 | 1944 | 1944 | 1945 |

◀ Major-General
1st Cavalry Division

Presenting a confident figure, Major-General Innis P. Swift of the 1st Cavalry Division is seen here in the Admiralty Islands in January 1944. He wears the light khaki trousers and shirt commonly worn by US Army personnel in the Pacific, and a map case and pistol hang over his right hip.

SPECIFICATIONS	
Country:	United States
Date:	1944
Unit:	1st Cavalry Division
Rank:	Major-General
Theatre:	Pacific
Location:	Los Negros, Admiralty Islands

Lieutenant ▶
US Marine Corps

The rank of this US Marine Corps lieutenant is defined by the silver bars on his tunic collar. His web belt supports a Colt M1911 pistol in a holster, an M4 knife bayonet, a field dressing pouch and a water bottle. He also has a camouflage poncho strapped to his pack.

SPECIFICATIONS	
Country:	United States
Date:	1945
Unit:	US Marine Corps
Rank:	Lieutenant
Theatre:	Pacific
Location:	Okinawa

War in the Pacific 1943–45

While the US armed forces slogged through the Pacific Ocean, British and Commonwealth troops fought equally harrowing campaigns in Southeast Asia, such as in the jungles of Burma and the Solomon Islands.

◀ Private
39th Australian Infantry

This soldier's bush hat bears the coloured flash of the 39th Australian Infantry Battalion. His equipment is of mixed US and British origin, including US herringbone-twill fatigue trousers, US gaiters and the British 1937-pattern web system. His firearm is the Australian 9mm (.35in) Owen.

SPECIFICATIONS	
Country:	Australia
Date:	1943
Unit:	39th Australian Infantry Battalion
Rank:	Private
Theatre:	Pacific
Location:	New Guinea

Lieutenant-General ▶
Imperial Japanese Army

This Japanese lieutenant-general presents a smart appearance, wearing his ceremonial sword from a fabric belt supported under the tunic. The sword could also be held in a scabbard attached to the traditional leather belt.

SPECIFICATIONS	
Country:	Japan
Date:	1944
Unit:	Imperial Japanese Army
Rank:	Lieutenant-General
Theatre:	Pacific
Location:	Unknown

TIMELINE

1943   1944   1944   1944

◀ **Colonel**
Imperial Japanese Army

The Japanese officer here has the classic white sunhat, although this also came in khaki colour, and his rank is presented on the tunic lapels. Another distinction of the officer class is the *tachi* sword, which was truly anachronistic in an age of modern firepower.

SPECIFICATIONS	
Country:	Japan
Date:	1944
Unit:	Imperial Japanese Army
Rank:	Colonel
Theatre:	Pacific
Location:	Burma

Lieutenant ▶
1st Battalion, Fiji Infantry

The New Zealand Army officer here looks from most perspectives like a British Army officer, the uniform, web anklets, ammunition boots and helmet being of British origin. His belt, however, is a US type, and on it he has a US .45-cal M1911 Colt pistol.

SPECIFICATIONS	
Country:	New Zealand
Date:	1944
Unit:	1st Battalion, Fiji Infantry
Rank:	Lieutenant
Theatre:	Pacific
Location:	Solomon Islands

US Marines, Pacific 1945

The key to the US victories in the Pacific theatre was American firepower. Even at a small-unit level, the US Army and Marine Corps troops generally outgunned their Japanese opponents.

The Portable Flamethrower M2-2 was first used in action by US forces on Guam in 1944. Worn on the back, it had a burn duration of up to nine seconds and could hurl a jet of flame up to 36m (118ft). The weapon was used mainly to burn out or suffocate Japanese soldiers in bunkers.

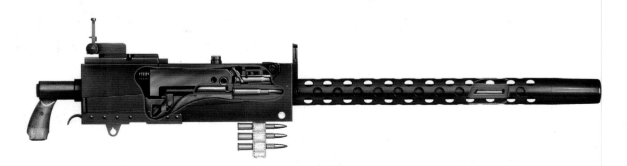

The Browning M1919 series of machine guns became the defining general-purpose machine guns of the US armed forces. Firing the 7.62mm (.3in) Browning round from 250-round fabric or metal-link belts, the M1919A4 was, like the other guns in the series, a short-recoil weapon, but one configured principally for infantry use. It could put down suppressive fire at a rate of 500rpm.

Marines
US Marine Corps

These members of a US Marine Corps squad show the increased emphasis on automatic firepower brought about by the Pacific fighting. Alongside riflemen armed with M1 Garand self-loading rifles, marines would carry 11.4mm (.45in) Thompson M1 submachine guns, which fired at up to 700rpm, and 7.62mm (.3in) M1 carbines. The central soldier, however, is armed with a man-portable flamethrower, useful for destroying Japanese bunkers and all those inside. Heavier firepower came from the Browning M1919 machine gun.

SPECIFICATIONS	
Country:	United States
Date:	1945
Unit:	US Marine Corps
Rank:	Marines
Theatre:	Pacific
Location:	Iwo Jima

Pacific Air War 1941–45

Air power was a critical decider of the outcome of the Pacific War. The Japanese opened the war with a carrier attack on Pearl Harbor in December 1941, but steadily lost air superiority over the following years.

◀ Lieutenant
US Navy,
USS *Enterprise*

Carrier pilots in the US Navy had a grey-green service dress consisting of tunic with four patch pockets, matching trousers and brown shoes. They also had a khaki drill shirt and black tie. His rank is displayed by the black lace stripes and stars on his tunic sleeve, and also on the shirt collar tips.

SPECIFICATIONS

Country:	United States
Date:	1941
Unit:	US Navy
Rank:	Lieutenant
Theatre:	Pacific
Location:	Central Pacific

Aircrewman ▶
Royal Netherlands
Indian Army Air Service

This aircrewman is armed with a Dutch 6.5mm (0.25in) M95 rifle, which would have provided little protection against the Japanese onslaught against his base in Singapore. His cap bears the national Dutch cockade, and the wings on his jacket indicate a bomber unit.

SPECIFICATIONS

Country:	Netherlands
Date:	1942
Unit:	Royal Netherlands Indian Army Air Service
Rank:	Aircrewman
Theatre:	Pacific
Location:	Singapore

◀ Pilot
US Marine Corps

The scorching and humid Pacific climate is reflected in this pilot's dress. He wears a one-piece tropical flight overall made in a light khaki cotton with a zip fastener. As a Marine Corps pilot he wears a matching infantry M1943 web belt. Survival clothing is in the shape of a yellow inflatable life-jacket.

SPECIFICATIONS	
Country:	United States
Date:	1943
Unit:	US Marine Corps
Rank:	Pilot
Theatre:	Pacific
Location:	Bougainville

Lieutenant-Colonel ▶
US Marine Corps

The fighter pilot shown here is Lieutenant-Colonel Harold W. Bauer. Before he was killed in November 1942, he shot down 11 Japanese aircraft, making him one of the first US Marine Corps aces. He is wearing a herringbone-twill utility overall instead of a flying suit.

SPECIFICATIONS	
Country:	United States
Date:	1942
Unit:	US Marine Corps
Rank:	Lieutenant-Colonel
Theatre:	Pacific
Location:	Guadalcanal

Pacific Air War 1941–45

The Pacific theatre presented harsh climatic challenges for air crews, from tropical temperatures at ground level to freezing conditions at high altitudes. This situation was amplified once Pacific islands close to Japan were captured and long-range, high-altitude US area bombing of the Japanese mainland began.

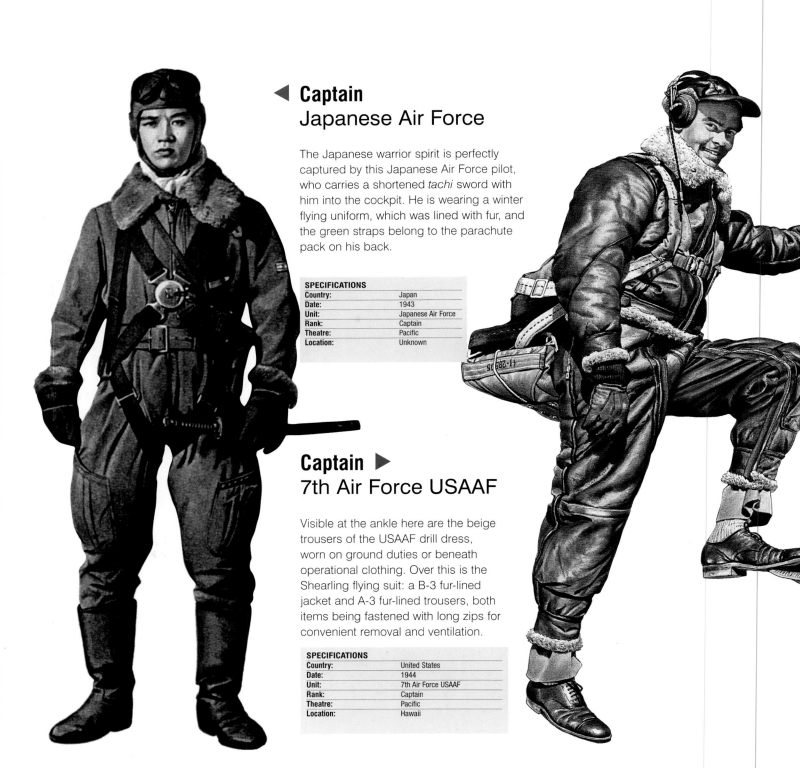

◀ **Captain**
Japanese Air Force

The Japanese warrior spirit is perfectly captured by this Japanese Air Force pilot, who carries a shortened *tachi* sword with him into the cockpit. He is wearing a winter flying uniform, which was lined with fur, and the green straps belong to the parachute pack on his back.

SPECIFICATIONS	
Country:	Japan
Date:	1943
Unit:	Japanese Air Force
Rank:	Captain
Theatre:	Pacific
Location:	Unknown

Captain ▶
7th Air Force USAAF

Visible at the ankle here are the beige trousers of the USAAF drill dress, worn on ground duties or beneath operational clothing. Over this is the Shearling flying suit: a B-3 fur-lined jacket and A-3 fur-lined trousers, both items being fastened with long zips for convenient removal and ventilation.

SPECIFICATIONS	
Country:	United States
Date:	1944
Unit:	7th Air Force USAAF
Rank:	Captain
Theatre:	Pacific
Location:	Hawaii

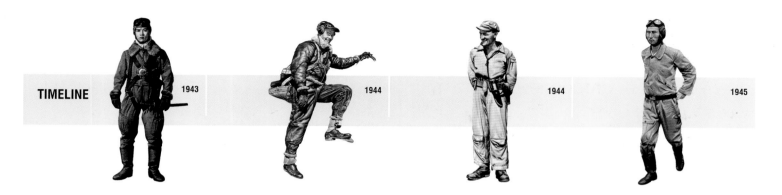

TIMELINE   1943   1944   1944   1945

◀ **Officer**
New Zealand Air Force

This officer in the New Zealand Air Force is mostly kitted out in American items of uniform, with the exception of the ankle boots, which are British. His pistol is also American, being a Colt M1911. The shoulder insignia, however, bear the words 'New Zealand'.

SPECIFICATIONS	
Country:	New Zealand
Date:	1944
Unit:	New Zealand Air Force
Rank:	Officer
Theatre:	Pacific
Location:	Unknown

Sub-Lieutenant ▶
Japanese Navy Air Service

While the Japanese figure on the opposite page wears the winter flying uniform, this airman is dressed in the summer equivalent, a two-piece outfit. The rank is displayed on the left sleeve. The Japanese Navy Air Service suffered appalling losses in the last two years of the war.

SPECIFICATIONS	
Country:	Japan
Date:	1945
Unit:	Japanese Navy Air Service
Rank:	Sub-Lieutenant
Theatre:	Pacific
Location:	Japan

Japanese Navy 1939–43

The Japanese Navy was the world's third largest navy during the interwar years, but was largely destroyed during World War II, losing most of its warships to US Navy carrier aircraft and submarines.

Seaman 1st Class
Imperial Japanese Navy

Here a Japanese sailor is seen equipped for a shore operation, mixing traditional naval dress with elements of infantry kit. A canvas provisions bag and a water bottle are hung from shoulder straps, while the belt supports two ammunition pouches for his 7.7mm (.303in) M38 rifle.

SPECIFICATIONS	
Country:	Japan
Date:	1939
Unit:	Imperial Japanese Navy
Rank:	Seaman 1st Class
Theatre:	East Asia
Location:	China

Commander ▶
Imperial Japanese Navy

This Japanese commander is well dressed for cold-weather conditions. He wears a double-breasted fur-lined watchcoat, on which he has rank markings on his shoulder straps. In the Japanese Navy, the colour of the binoculars strap also indicated rank.

SPECIFICATIONS	
Country:	Japan
Date:	1941
Unit:	Imperial Japanese Navy
Rank:	Commander
Theatre:	Pacific
Location:	Pacific

1939   1941   1942   1943

◄ **Rating**
Combined Fleet, Japanese Navy

This style of white rig uniform was worn by sailors who were undertaking administrative or service roles aboard a ship or at shore installations. It consists of a simple white tunic and trousers, all loose-fitting, worn with a pair of black leather shoes. Markings and insignia are minimal.

SPECIFICATIONS	
Country:	Japan
Date:	1942
Unit:	Combined Fleet, Japanese Navy
Rank:	Rating
Theatre:	Pacific
Location:	Philippine Sea

Lieutenant ►
5th Fleet, Japanese Navy

Japanese Navy uniforms were typically understated, as is the case here with this lieutenant of the 5th Fleet. He is seen in his regulation whites, composed of a single-breasted stand-collar tunic with five gold buttons and side-slash pockets, matching trousers and white leather shoes.

SPECIFICATIONS	
Country:	Japan
Date:	1943
Unit:	5th Fleet, Japanese Navy
Rank:	Lieutenant
Theatre:	Pacific
Location:	Tokyo

Pacific Naval War 1942–43

The US Navy became the indisputable naval power of the Pacific theatre from 1943. The British Royal Navy also played its part, but was much weaker in the Pacific when compared to the American presence.

◄ Lieutenant
Women's Auxiliary Volunteer Service

Many thousands of women served in the US Navy in support roles ranging from clerical duties through to communications and intelligence operatives. This lieutenant's rank is displayed via her blue sleeve stripes, plus the officers' cap badge. The collar tabs depict an anchor-and-propeller motif.

SPECIFICATIONS	
Country:	United States
Date:	1942
Unit:	Women's Auxiliary Volunteer Service
Rank:	Lieutenant
Theatre:	Pacific
Location:	USA

Petty Officer 3rd Class ►
USS *Saratoga*

The sailor shown here, Samoan by origin, is employed on the USS *Saratoga* as a cook, this job being identified by the US eagle badge with a 'C' underneath on his *lava-lava* (the wrapped skirt around his waist). Apart from this, he bears little resemblance to US ship personnel.

SPECIFICATIONS	
Country:	Samoa/United States
Date:	1943
Unit:	USS *Saratoga*
Rank:	Petty Officer 3rd Class
Theatre:	Pacific
Location:	Gilbert Islands

TIMELINE | 1942 | 1943 | 1943 | 1943

◄ Warrant Officer
Pacific Fleet

This British naval engineer stationed in the Pacific theatre is wearing working garb. His Royal Navy officers' peaked cap has a white cover that matches the colour of his overall. He has strong gloves on his hands and his laceless shoes can be kicked off quickly in an emergency.

SPECIFICATIONS	
Country:	Britain
Date:	1943
Unit:	Pacific Fleet
Rank:	Warrant Officer
Theatre:	Pacific
Location:	Indian Ocean

Marine ►
Royal Marines

This Royal Marine is wearing the older 1908-pattern webbing over his tropical uniform, featuring the multiple ammunition pouches for the his 7.7mm (.303in) SMLE rifle. The khaki puttees were useful for jungle operations, as they protected the lower legs against branches, sharp leaves, thorns and biting insects.

SPECIFICATIONS	
Country:	Britain
Date:	1943
Unit:	Royal Marines
Rank:	Marine
Theatre:	Pacific
Location:	Singapore

Landing Signals Officer

The landing signals officer shown here is signalling to the pilot of an aircraft coming in to land on the deck of the USS *Princeton* during the battle of Leyte Gulf. Though the *Princeton* was sunk during the battle, it played its part in crippling Japan's naval fleet and air force.

The Hellcat, along with the Corsair, formed the core of US carrier fighter strength during World War II. The F6F-5 version had an improved fighter-bomber capability, being armed with a combination of machine guns, cannon and underwing bombs or rockets.

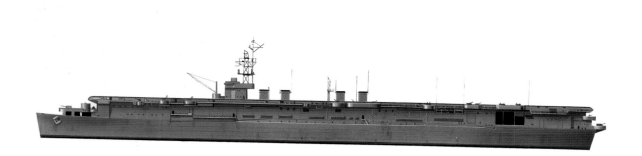

The USS *Princeton* was commissioned on 25 February 1943. It had a crew of more than 1500 men, and a complement of 18 combat aircraft. The carrier was sunk on 24 October 1944 after a single Japanese bomb penetrated her hold, causing a catastrophic fire.

Landing Signals Officer
USS *Princeton*

In the US Navy, flight deck personnel on aircraft carriers adopted coloured helmets, baseball caps, T-shirts and jackets with their name, rank and role often painted in black on the front and back. For example, aircraft captains wore red; aircraft handlers, grey; fire details and firemen, red; arresting gear details, green; hangermen, yellow; and ordnance men, pink. This LSO is wearing the light khaki cotton or poplin officers' service dress shirt with yellow slipover.

SPECIFICATIONS	
Country:	United States
Date:	1944
Unit:	USS *Princeton*
Rank:	Landing Signals Officer
Theatre:	Pacific
Location:	Leyte Gulf

Burma Theatre 1942–45

Both British and American forces deployed to the Burma theatre found that their uniforms often left a lot to be desired in the jungle conditions. Complaints led to improved patterns of tropical combat dress.

◄ Subedar-Major
20th Burma Rifles, Indian Army

Here we see a Viceroy Commission Officer of the Indian Army. The uniform is the British light khaki service dress, smartly presented with an infantry officer's sword by his side, which featured a steel hilt and black leather scabbard.

SPECIFICATIONS	
Country:	India
Date:	1942
Unit:	20th Burma Rifles
Rank:	Subedar-Major
Theatre:	Southeast Asia
Location:	Burma

Warrant Officer ►
77th Indian Brigade

At the beginning of the war in the Pacific, British Army troops wore the same khaki drill uniform as their comrades in the Middle East. This uniform was found to be unsuitable for jungle operations, as it was the wrong colour and was uncomfortable.

SPECIFICATIONS	
Country:	Britain
Date:	1943
Unit:	77th Indian Brigade
Rank:	Warrant Officer
Theatre:	Southeast Asia
Location:	Burma

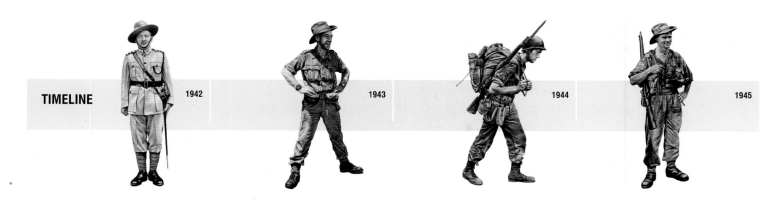

| TIMELINE | 1942 | 1943 | 1944 | 1945 |

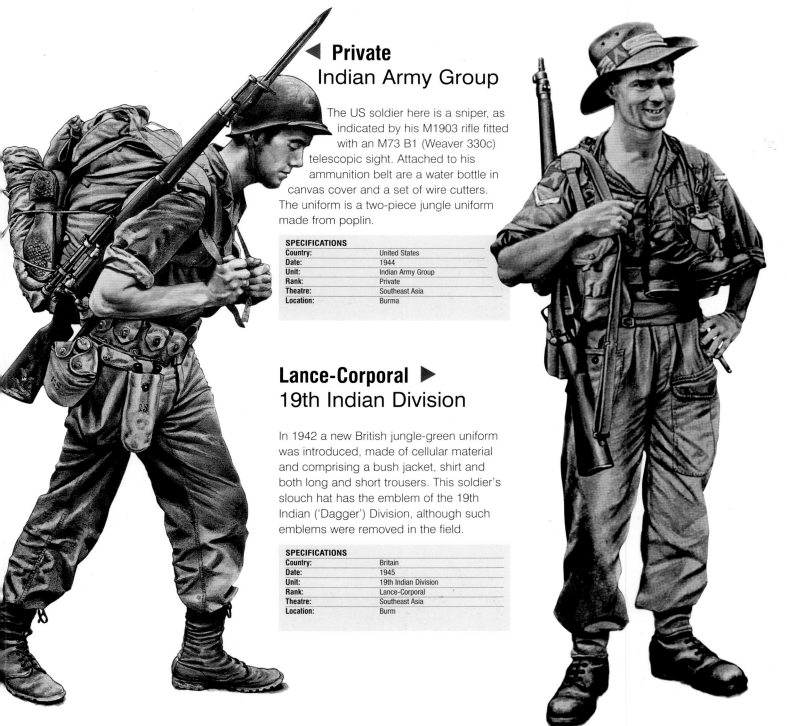

◀ Private
Indian Army Group

The US soldier here is a sniper, as indicated by his M1903 rifle fitted with an M73 B1 (Weaver 330c) telescopic sight. Attached to his ammunition belt are a water bottle in canvas cover and a set of wire cutters. The uniform is a two-piece jungle uniform made from poplin.

SPECIFICATIONS	
Country:	United States
Date:	1944
Unit:	Indian Army Group
Rank:	Private
Theatre:	Southeast Asia
Location:	Burma

Lance-Corporal ▶
19th Indian Division

In 1942 a new British jungle-green uniform was introduced, made of cellular material and comprising a bush jacket, shirt and both long and short trousers. This soldier's slouch hat has the emblem of the 19th Indian ('Dagger') Division, although such emblems were removed in the field.

SPECIFICATIONS	
Country:	Britain
Date:	1945
Unit:	19th Indian Division
Rank:	Lance-Corporal
Theatre:	Southeast Asia
Location:	Burm

Southeast Asia 1941–45

After the initial Japanese campaigns of conquest in 1941 and 1942, the war in Southeast Asia settled into a grinding, arduous war of attrition. British, Commonwealth, American and Chinese troops conducted a three-year campaign in Burma, in which disease was as big a danger as the fighting.

◀ Corporal
9th Gurkha Rifles, Indian Army

This Gurkha uniform resembles British Army tropical dress though with some variations, such as the wide-brimmed slouch hat, also known as a *saffa*. By his side, the soldier carries the fearsome *kukri* knife, a practical combat weapon in trained hands.

SPECIFICATIONS	
Country:	Britain
Date:	1941
Unit:	9th Gurkha Rifles, Indian Army
Rank:	Corporal
Theatre:	Southeast Asia
Location:	Burma

Senior NCO ▶
Indian National Army

Although this soldier is an Indian national, he falls under the auspices of the Japanese Army as a member of the anti-British Indian National Army (INA). A senior NCO, he retains the khaki field-drill uniform of the Indian Army, though Japanese uniforms were sometimes worn.

SPECIFICATIONS	
Country:	India
Date:	1942
Unit:	Indian National Army
Rank:	Senior NCO
Theatre:	Southeast Asia
Location:	Malaysia

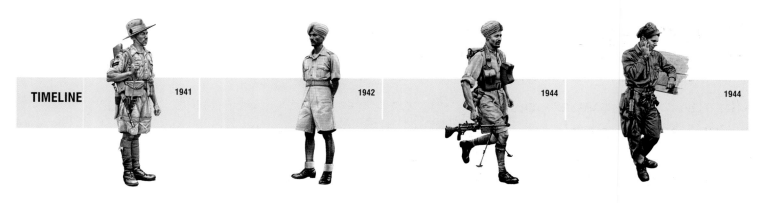

TIMELINE 1941 1942 1944 1944

◀ **Sepoy**
Indian Army

Apart from his turban, this Indian Army soldier largely wears the tropical uniform and kit of the British Army. However, he carries a Vickers-Berthier Indian Mk III machine gun, which the Indian Army used as an alternative to the Bren gun. Ammunition for the weapon is carried in the two large leather chest pouches.

SPECIFICATIONS	
Country:	Britain
Date:	1944
Unit:	Indian Army
Rank:	Sepoy
Theatre:	Southeast Asia
Location:	India

Pilot ▶
1st US Air Commando Force

US airpower had critical logistical functions in Burma, with air drops often being the only viable means of provisioning units in the jungle. Here we see a pilot from the 1st US Air Commando Force wearing an air force tunic with airborne soldier's trousers.

SPECIFICATIONS	
Country:	United States
Date:	1944
Unit:	1st US Air Commando Force
Rank:	Pilot
Theatre:	Southeast Asia
Location:	Burma

Southeast Asia 1941–45

With the end of the war in Europe in May 1945, the Far East became the remaining major combat deployment of British forces. The RAF alone had 207,632 men deployed there in July 1945.

◄ Groundcrew
Fire-Fighting Unit, Royal Air Force

This groundcrew wears the full protective fire suit, made from asbestos and with full-body coverage and the minimum of joints that might be wrenched open by blast. The asbestos jacket is double-breasted and secured with a metal clasp and a chain.

SPECIFICATIONS	
Country:	Britain
Date:	1945
Unit:	Fire-Fighting Unit, Royal Air Force
Rank:	Groundcrew
Theatre:	Southeast Asia
Location:	Malaysia

Squadron Leader ►
Royal Air Force Volunteer Reserve

This officer from the RAFVR is wearing the RAF's tropical dress, but has kept the cap from the blue-grey service uniform. His rank insignia is worn on the shoulder straps, and his reserve status is indicated by the letter's 'VR' on the collar.

SPECIFICATIONS	
Country:	Britain
Date:	1945
Unit:	Royal Air Force Volunteer Reserve
Rank:	Squadron Leader
Theatre:	Southeast Asia
Location:	India

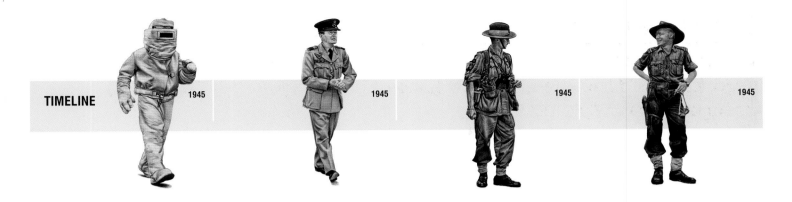

TIMELINE   1945   1945   1945   1945

◄ Brigadier
Indian Army

The man portrayed here is Brigadier Denham-Young, commander of the 5th Indian Division (the divisional sign is on his sleeve). The uniform he wears is rendered in tropical green, ideal for jungle combat. Note also the officer's non-standard leather pistol ammunition bandolier.

SPECIFICATIONS	
Country:	Britain
Date:	1945
Unit:	Indian Army
Rank:	Brigadier
Theatre:	Southeast Asia
Location:	British India

Pilot Officer ►
Royal Air Force

This Royal Air Force pilot officer displays a medley of uniform items. They include a wide-brimmed slouch hat, a tropical shirt, canvas anklets and fatigue trousers. His pistol holster has a thigh strap to keep the holster flat when the pistol was drawn.

SPECIFICATIONS	
Country:	Britain
Date:	1945
Unit:	Royal Air Force
Rank:	Pilot Officer
Theatre:	Southeast Asia
Location:	India

German Forces, Northwest Europe 1943–45

With the opening of the Allied Second Front in June 1944, German forces faced an impossible demand fighting on numerous fronts. On the Western Front, they were steadily pushed back to and across the borders of the Reich.

◀ **2nd Lieutenant**
Security Police

All Germany's police forces ultimately fell under SS authority; this German *Sipo* (Security Police) officer has a *Waffen-SS* uniform, with rank displayed on the shoulder straps and on the left collar tab only. In this case, the sleeve chevron indicates Nazi Party service, not rank.

SPECIFICATIONS	
Country:	Germany
Date:	1943
Unit:	Security Police
Rank:	2nd Lieutenant
Theatre:	Northwest Europe
Location:	France

Private ▶
Panzergrenadier, German Army

The Panzergrenadier here wears a reversible army camouflage smock, over which he has his leather webbing, which includes ammunition pouches for his Mauser 98k rifle. He has also stuck a *Stielgranate* (Stick Grenade) Model 24 in his belt.

SPECIFICATIONS	
Country:	Germany
Date:	1944
Unit:	Panzergrenadier, German Army
Rank:	Private
Theatre:	Northwest Europe
Location:	Normandy

1943

1944

1944

1944

◄ **Corporal**
German Army

This late-war variety of German Army uniform features a tunic with two large patch pockets, breeches tucked into riding boots (indicating a mounted soldier) and light grey insignia. The ribbon on the tunic indicates that he survived a winter on the Eastern Front.

SPECIFICATIONS

Country:	Germany
Date:	1944
Unit:	German Army
Rank:	Corporal
Theatre:	Northwest Europe
Location:	France

Senior Sergeant ▶
916th Infantry Regiment

This German *Feldwebel* (sergeant) shows the equipment carried by German infantry soldiers in 1944. The most recognizable item is the cylindrical gas-mask case. Beneath this to the right is the tent quarter/poncho, a canvas bread bag and a water bottle in leather cover.

SPECIFICATIONS

Country:	Germany
Date:	1944
Unit:	916th Infantry Regiment
Rank:	Senior Sergeant
Theatre:	Northwest Europe
Location:	Normandy

Hitlerjugend Soldier 1944

By 1944, camouflage was making widespread appearance in many German units, though mainly those units with elite status. While much of this camouflage was confined to the Eastern Front initially, the threat of a second front in France forced Hitler to relocate some SS units there.

The MG42 was arguably the best general-purpose machine gun in history. It had a blisteringly fast rate of fire – up to 1200rpm – and was consequently named 'Hitler's buzzsaw' by the Allies. A barrel change could be performed in a matter of seconds. On tripod or vehicular mounts the MG42 could operate in sustained-fire or anti-aircraft roles.

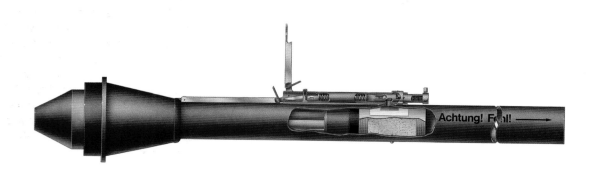

The Panzerfaust (lit. 'armour fist') was a single-shot, hand-held anti-tank weapon in service with Axis forces between 1943 and 1945. Its shaped-charge warhead, in the most powerful variants, could punch through 220mm (8.7in) of armour. The Allies lost hundreds of tanks to the weapon, particularly in urban combat environments.

Private
Hitlerjugend Division

This *Hitlerjugend* trooper is wearing an Italian-pattern camouflage smock and trousers, the helmet also being covered in a matching cloth. The period 1944–45 saw many German units adopting surplus Italian military clothing, as Germany's own supplies ran short and industry could not produce enough to meet demand. This accounts for an increasing lack of consistent appearance among German troops on all fronts. The *Hitlerjugend* division was largely formed from former members of the Hitler Youth. This trooper is armed with the MG42 machine gun.

SPECIFICATIONS	
Country:	Germany
Date:	1944
Unit:	*Hitlerjugend* Division
Rank:	Private
Theatre:	Northwest Europe
Location:	Normandy

US Airborne/Ranger Forces, Northwest Europe 1944

Although the US Army was traditionally averse to the idea of elite units, during the Normandy campaign the fighting was spearheaded in many locales by specialist Ranger and airborne forces.

◄ Sergeant Grade 4
101st Airborne Division

This soldier is dressed in the specially designed para uniform introduced into airborne forces in the early 1940s. The standard jump-uniform was a two-piece olive-green tunic and trousers, the latter featuring reinforced sections on the knees. Instead of a para helmet, he wears the standard M1.

SPECIFICATIONS	
Country:	United States
Date:	1944
Unit:	101st Airborne Division
Rank:	Sergeant Grade 4
Theatre:	Northwest Europe
Location:	Normandy

Major-General ►
82nd Airborne Division

The major-general seen here is wearing the M1944 field jacket, popularly known as the 'Ike' jacket, after General Eisenhower. His membership of the 82nd Airborne is denoted by several elements of insignia on this jacket, most distinctly the army paratrooper badge on the left breast.

SPECIFICATIONS	
Country:	United States
Date:	1944
Unit:	82nd Airborne Division
Rank:	Major-General
Theatre:	Northwest Europe
Location:	Britain

TIMELINE 1944   1944   1944   1944

◀ Private
1st Ranger Battalion

The 1st Rangers wore a one-piece herringbone-twill work suit during training and on operations, as seen here. This Ranger is wearing the M1 helmet, which replaced the M1917A1 helmet in autumn 1942. He also carries the M1928 haversack on his back, and a water bottle is fitted to his belt.

SPECIFICATIONS	
Country:	United States
Date:	1944
Unit:	1st Ranger Battalion
Rank:	Private
Theatre:	Northwest Europe
Location:	North Carolina

Officer ▶
82nd Airborne Division

This officer of the 82nd Airborne Division shows the convoluted levels of kit needed to make a combat parachute jump. Any loose equipment was bound in with webbing tape prior to the operation.

SPECIFICATIONS	
Country:	United States
Date:	1944
Unit:	82nd Airborne Division
Rank:	Officer
Theatre:	Northwest Europe
Location:	Britain

US 101st Airborne Soldier, Ardennes 1944

US soldiers facing the winter in northern Europe in 1944/5 were lucky that the issue of M1943 combat uniforms had begun. As the temperatures plunged below zero, US troops in the Ardennes also had to face Hitler's last-ditch offensive in the West.

Here is the US 101st Airborne Division's Combat Service Identification badge, worn on the uniform sleeve by those soldiers who had seen active service. The eagle motif used by the 101st Airborne led to their popular title, the 'Screaming Eagles'.

The C-47 Skytrain (known as the DC-3 Dakota in RAF service) was the primary aircraft for deploying US paratroopers during World War II. It had accommodation inside for 28 troops, and also served as a glider tower and transport aircraft. Whatever the use, the aircraft was revered for its reliability.

Private
101st Airborne Division

The M1943 uniform utilized an advanced (for the time) layering principle, whereby the soldier could combine a waterproof and windproof jacket and overtrousers with additional layers of warm clothing. However, by November 1944 the issue of this uniform was not complete, as is evident for this soldier with the M1943 jacket (distinguished from the older M1941 jacket by chest patch pockets) but also older khaki woollen service trousers. He has rubber waterproof covers for his leather combat boots, these having snap fastenings. He carries a variety of equipment and acquisitions, including an M1 Garand rifle, a cooking pot hung from his belt and an entrenching tool around the left hip.

SPECIFICATIONS	
Country:	United States
Date:	1944
Unit:	101st Airborne Division
Rank:	Private
Theatre:	Northwest Europe
Location:	Ardennes

US/Canadian Infantry, Northwest Europe 1944

Some 175,000 Allied troops would participate in the D-Day landings of 6 June 1944, including the men of the US First Army and several Canadian units. The US infantry at 'Omaha Beach' suffered the highest losses of the day – some 3000 casualties.

◀ Private
Le Regiment de Levis, Canadian Army

This soldier's general uniform would have been a close match for that of a British soldier, but the 'Canada' badge on his upper sleeve leaves no doubt as to his provenance. There are further distinctions; the cap is Canadian-pattern, and has the regimental badge on the front.

SPECIFICATIONS	
Country:	Canada
Date:	1944
Unit:	Le Regiment de Levis, Canadian Army
Rank:	Private
Theatre:	Northwest Europe
Location:	England

Lieutenant ▶
US Army

Over his M1941 combat jacket and olive fatigues, this soldier wears a mass of equipment for the amphibious landings. The half-inflated pouch centred over his chest is a flotation bag, intended to provide some protection from drowning during the landings. A map case hangs at the front.

SPECIFICATIONS	
Country:	United States
Date:	1944
Unit:	US Army
Rank:	Lieutenant
Theatre:	Northwest Europe
Location:	Southern England

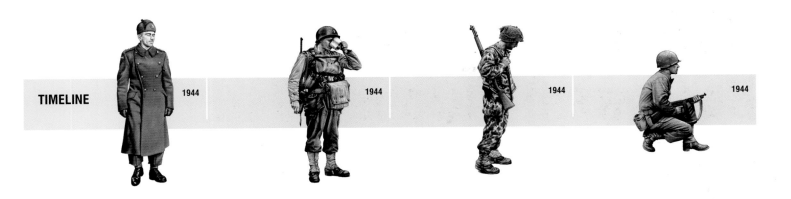

TIMELINE   1944   1944   1944   1944

◄ **Private**
Infantry Division, 1st Army

For the campaign in Normandy in June 1944, the US Army issued this two-piece camouflage suit to some units, not realizing that the *Waffen-SS* sported similar camouflage uniforms. As well as his M1 Garand rifle, this soldier has a captured Walther automatic pistol in a holster.

SPECIFICATIONS	
Country:	United States
Date:	1944
Unit:	Infantry Division, 1st Army
Rank:	Private
Theatre:	Northwest Europe
Location:	Normandy

Private ▶
US Army

By the time of the Normandy landings, the US Army had produced a practical and hard-wearing uniform for its frontline divisions: M1 steel helmet, M1941 field jacket, olive-drab trousers, canvas gaiters and russet leather ankle boots, as seen on this private.

SPECIFICATIONS	
Country:	United States
Date:	1944
Unit:	US Army
Rank:	Private
Theatre:	Northwest Europe
Location:	Normandy

British Army, Northwest Europe 1944

By June 1944, the British Army had already been fighting for nearly five years. Although financial pressures were being felt in many aspects of kit and equipment, the British still provided the second-largest Allied force in Northwest Europe.

◀ **Private**
British Commandos

Here we see a British commando ready for participation in the assault landings on the Normandy coast. His commando status is declared by the defining green beret and a name badge at the top of the sleeve, under which is a Combined Operations badge. His rifle is the SMLE No.4.

SPECIFICATIONS	
Country:	Britain
Date:	1944
Unit:	British Commandos
Rank:	Private
Theatre:	Northwest Europe
Location:	Normandy

Lieutenant ▶
1st Glider Pilot Regiment

The treacherous nature of glider landings is suggested by the fibre crash-helmet this pilot wears over the Type C flying helmet. Furthermore, a Type F oxygen mask speaks of the lack of pressurization in the basic Horsa gliders.

SPECIFICATIONS	
Country:	Britain
Date:	1944
Unit:	1st Glider Pilot Regiment
Rank:	Lieutenant
Theatre:	Northwest Europe
Location:	Normandy

TIMELINE 1944
1944
1944
1944

◄ Corporal
Royal Corps of Signals

This soldier is a despatch rider, hence the motorcycle helmet and the biker's boots. He also wears a leather jerkin, which would help to keep the rest of his uniform clean. The armlet indicates his membership of the Royal Corps of Signals.

SPECIFICATIONS	
Country:	Britain
Date:	1944
Unit:	Royal Corps of Signals
Rank:	Corporal
Theatre:	Northwest Europe
Location:	Normandy

Trooper ►
Royal Tank Regiment

Here we have a trooper of the Royal Tank Regiment, the black beret being standard regimental dress. His clothing consists of a one-piece canvas overall, made from water-repellent material and fitted with numerous pouches and pockets.

SPECIFICATIONS	
Country:	Britain
Date:	1944
Unit:	Royal Tank Regiment
Rank:	Trooper
Theatre:	Northwest Europe
Location:	Normandy

Royal Air Force, Europe 1942–44

From 1942, the Royal Air Force had two major combat roles: delivering its part in the strategic bombing campaign against Germany, and providing tactical air support to Allied ground forces.

◄ Squadron Leader
Royal Air Force

This RAF officer – actually deployed to Russia as an instructor – wears the bulky M1940 flying suit, its fur-lined collar clearly visible, plus a 1932-pattern life-jacket. Other items of dress include the 1937-pattern web belt and the standard RAF officers' blue peaked cap.

SPECIFICATIONS	
Country:	Britain
Date:	1942
Unit:	Royal Air Force
Rank:	Squadron Leader
Theatre:	Eastern Front
Location:	Northern Russia

Head Officer ►
Royal Observer Corps

Although in military dress, this officer is actually part of the civilian Observer Corps. In 1941, the Corps finally moved from civilian to military clothing. This new uniform was the RAF grey-serge battledress. The tunic featured the badge of the ROC surmounted by a crown, this badge being repeated on the cap.

SPECIFICATIONS	
Country:	Britain
Date:	1944
Unit:	Royal Observer Corps
Rank:	Head Officer
Theatre:	Western Europe
Location:	Britain

TIMELINE   1942   1944   1944   1944

◀ Flying Officer
Royal Air Force

The most distinctive part of this officer's dress is the outer US 'flak suit', so called because it provided protection from anti-aircraft shell splinters. Further protection comes from the Type C flying helmet, reinforced with strips of steel. Beneath the flak jacket he wears the RAF battledress.

SPECIFICATIONS	
Country:	Britain
Date:	1944
Unit:	Royal Air Force
Rank:	Flying Officer
Theatre:	Western Europe
Location:	Britain

Flying Officer ▶
No. 617 Squadron,
Royal Air Force

This Lancaster pilot wears the standard RAF battledress, over which he has an inflatable life vest. On his upper left arm can be seen a nationality badge, indicating his Australian origins – large numbers of foreign nationals served in the RAF.

SPECIFICATIONS	
Country:	Australia/Britain
Date:	1944
Unit:	No. 617 Squadron, Royal Air Force
Rank:	Flying Officer
Theatre:	Western Europe
Location:	Britain

Wing Commander, 617 Squadron 1944

Pictured here is the legendary Wing Commander Guy Gibson, leader of the 'Dambuster' No. 617 squadron. His uncompromising and skilled leadership led to the smashing of the Ruhr dams and his award of the Victoria Cross.

The crest of 617 Squadron remembers the squadron's most famous wartime raid – the attack on the Möhne, Eder and Sorpe dams in the Ruhr in May 1943. It shows lightning striking a dam structure, shattering it open and releasing a rush of water. The French motto beneath, *Après moi le déluge*, translates as 'After me, the flood'.

The insignia here, worn on the cuff by the highest ranks of RAF officer, are (from left to right): Marshal of the RAF; Air Chief Marshal; Air Marshal; Air Vice-Marshal and Air Commodore. The next three descending ranks are Group Captain, Wing Commander and Squadron Leader.

Wing Commander
No. 617 Squadron

Gibson's uniform is the standard blue-grey battledress issued to RAF personnel, with additions for operational status. Over the uniform he wears the yellow Type LS inflatable life-jacket, while clutched in his right hand is the Type C leather flying helmet. His headgear in this case is his officer's service cap, with a black band and the RAF eagle and badge. Rank is displayed on the shoulder straps. One item of interest is his fleece-lined flying boots, which provided good heat retention for the pilot, even at high altitudes. However, if he was shot down, he could cut away the top of the boots and leave a functional pair of ground boots.

SPECIFICATIONS	
Country:	Britain
Date:	1944
Unit:	No. 617 Squadron
Rank:	Wing Commander
Theatre:	Western Europe
Location:	Britain

US Army Air Force in Europe 1944–45

The USAAF brought huge destructive capability to the European theatre. At the peak of its strength, the 8th Air Force alone numbered just over 40 heavy bombardment, 15 fighter and two reconnaissance groups.

◀ Captain
8th Army Air Force

The captain here is the pilot of a P-51B Mustang, seen at the fighter base back in East Anglia. He is wearing typically informal USAAF fighter-pilot uniform. Standard drill uniform was olive-drab trousers with light khaki tunic and matching shirt and tie.

SPECIFICATIONS	
Country:	United States
Date:	1944
Unit:	8th Army Air Force
Rank:	Captain
Theatre:	Western Europe
Location:	East Anglia

Aircrewman ▶
8th Army Air Force

This aircrewman is fitting himself with the flak suit designed by Brigadier-General Grow and manufactured by the Wilkinson Sword company. The flak suit was introduced from 1943 in an attempt to deal with the shrapnel injuries to bomber crews from exploding anti-aircraft shells.

SPECIFICATIONS	
Country:	United States
Date:	1944
Unit:	8th Army Air Force
Rank:	Aircrewman
Theatre:	Western Europe
Location:	East Anglia

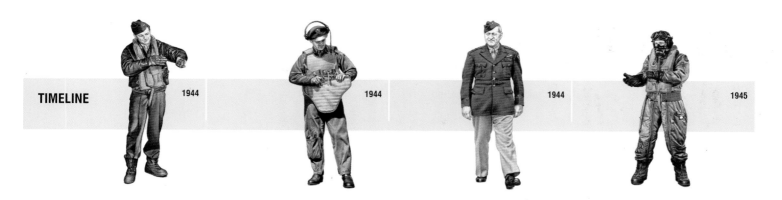

TIMELINE | 1944 | 1944 | 1944 | 1945

◀ **Major-General**
9th Army Air Force

This senior officer is wearing the typical service dress for members of the USAAF in the European Theatre of Operations (ETO). Rank insignia is worn on the shoulder straps and on the left side of the overseas cap (two stars for a major-general).

SPECIFICATIONS

Country:	United States
Date:	1944
Unit:	9th Army Air Force
Rank:	Major-General
Theatre:	Western Europe
Location:	East Anglia

Bomber Crewman ▶
8th Army Air Force

This aviator is a crewman aboard a B-17 Flying Fortress. He is wearing a one-piece flying suit lined with wool and alpaca, over this donning an olive-drab flying jacket with a formation badge on the sleeve. Extra warmth is provided by fleece-lined gloves and zip-on overboots.

SPECIFICATIONS

Country:	United States
Date:	1945
Unit:	8th Army Air Force
Rank:	Aircrewman
Theatre:	Western Europe
Location:	East Anglia

US Airman, 322nd Bombardment Group 1944

This figure is 1st Lieutenant Benjamin McCartney, who is wearing the light uniform of the USAAF. The 322nd Bombardment Group was attached to the 3rd Bomb Wing, and on 16 October 1944 the group was assigned to the Ninth Air Force.

The Boeing B-17G was the most powerful bomber in the USAAF strategic air campaign against Germany. Its defensive armament consisted of 13 12.7mm (0.5in) machine guns, and it could carry a maximum bomb load of 6983kg (17,600lb) over a range of 2897km (1800 miles).

Here we see the USAAF 'wings', granted to a qualified pilot. Wings were not only worn by USAAF pilots, but also by those of the US Navy, US Marine Corps and various civilian/military auxiliary and training units.

Bombardier
322nd Bombardment Group

Under McCartney's life-jacket is a light khaki shirt, the rest of his clothing being khaki dress trousers, russet shoes and the standard officers' peaked cap. On his shirt collar is a single silver bar to denote his rank. Aviation personnel used the rank insignia of their parent service. Thus the USAAF had those of the US Army. McCartney's unit, the 322nd Bombardment Group, was activated in Florida on 19 June 1942 and comprised the 449th, 450th, 451st and 452nd Squadrons.

SPECIFICATIONS	
Country:	United States
Date:	1944
Unit:	322nd Bombardment Group
Rank:	Bombardier
Theatre:	Western Europe
Location:	England

Italian and German Air Forces 1942–44

The pressures on the Axis air forces became insurmountable between 1942 and 1945, when the United States added its industrial muscle to the air war. Much of Germany's air power became devoted to protecting the Reich itself.

◀ Major
Southern Zone, Italian Air Force

The pilot here is wearing a leather flying jacket over his service dress, and a leather flying helmet. On his cuffs are his rank badges: officers' ranks stripes were made of gold lace. On his left breast he wears a torpedo-bomber qualification badge.

SPECIFICATIONS	
Country:	Italy
Date:	1942
Unit:	Southern Zone, Italian Air Force
Rank:	Major
Theatre:	Mediterranean
Location:	Italy

Officer ▶
Luftwaffe

This *Luftwaffe* officer is wearing the leather greatcoat issued to all officers of the German Air Force. A double-breasted, ankle-length item, it was a fine piece of dress, and here the officer complements it with a Sam Browne belt, despite its being discontinued in the *Luftwaffe* in 1939.

SPECIFICATIONS	
Country:	Germany
Date:	1942
Unit:	*Luftwaffe*
Rank:	Officer
Theatre:	Europe
Location:	Unknown

TIMELINE   1942   1942   1944   1944

◀ ## Major-General
Italian Social Republic Air Force

By the late stage of the war, here October 1944, many fascist Italian airmen were serving alongside *Luftwaffe* personnel, or had been trained by the German Air Force. As a result, they wore German Air Force uniforms with German or Italian rank badges.

SPECIFICATIONS	
Country:	Italy
Date:	1944
Unit:	Italian Social Republic Air Force
Rank:	Major
Theatre:	Italy
Location:	Northern Italy

Captain ▶
Luftwaffe

The trousers of this late-war German Air Force uniform are very distinctive. Known as *Kanalhosen* ('Channel trousers'), they had large pockets at the front for storing survival kit. The rest of the uniform consists of a 1943-model flying cap and zippered jacket.

SPECIFICATIONS	
Country:	Germany
Date:	1944
Unit:	*Luftwaffe*
Rank:	Captain
Theatre:	Europe
Location:	Unknown

Last Battles for the Reich 1944–45

The final battles for Germany in 1944 and 1945 saw the Third Reich scrape the bottom of the barrel with its military personnel, as young and old were drawn into the fight.

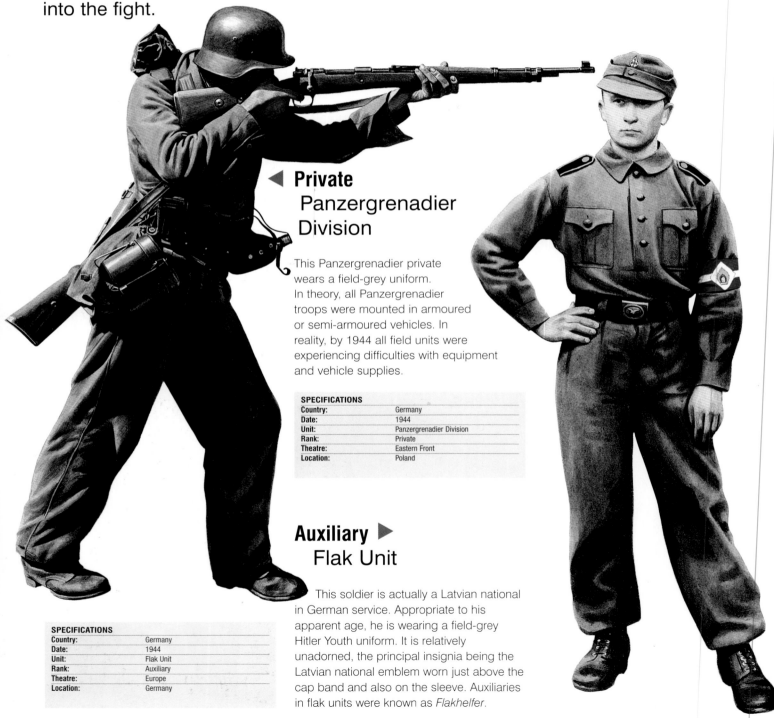

◀ Private
Panzergrenadier Division

This Panzergrenadier private wears a field-grey uniform. In theory, all Panzergrenadier troops were mounted in armoured or semi-armoured vehicles. In reality, by 1944 all field units were experiencing difficulties with equipment and vehicle supplies.

SPECIFICATIONS	
Country:	Germany
Date:	1944
Unit:	Panzergrenadier Division
Rank:	Private
Theatre:	Eastern Front
Location:	Poland

Auxiliary ▶
Flak Unit

This soldier is actually a Latvian national in German service. Appropriate to his apparent age, he is wearing a field-grey Hitler Youth uniform. It is relatively unadorned, the principal insignia being the Latvian national emblem worn just above the cap band and also on the sleeve. Auxiliaries in flak units were known as *Flakhelfer*.

SPECIFICATIONS	
Country:	Germany
Date:	1944
Unit:	Flak Unit
Rank:	Auxiliary
Theatre:	Europe
Location:	Germany

TIMELINE	1944		1944		1945		1945

◀ Private
Infantry Division, Romanian Army

This soldier's uniform is the standard Romanian khaki combat dress, though here the trousers are worn with knee-high puttees. Instead of the M1928 steel helmet, he wears an unadorned khaki field cap.

SPECIFICATIONS	
Country:	Romania
Date:	1945
Unit:	Infantry Division, Romanian Army
Rank:	Private
Theatre:	Eastern Front
Location:	Austria

Paratrooper ▶
82nd Airborne Division

This soldier wears the standard American paratrooper uniform, which was similar to the M1943 combat dress but had different pocket arrangements. Note the water bottles attached to his woven waistbelt. His weapon is the .45-calibre M1 Thompson.

SPECIFICATIONS	
Country:	United States
Date:	1945
Unit:	82nd Airborne Division
Rank:	Paratrooper
Theatre:	Europe
Location:	Germany

Last Battles for the Reich 1944–45

While US and British forces pushed over the German borders from the West, it was left to the Soviet Union to take Berlin and finally bring Adolf Hitler's regime crashing down.

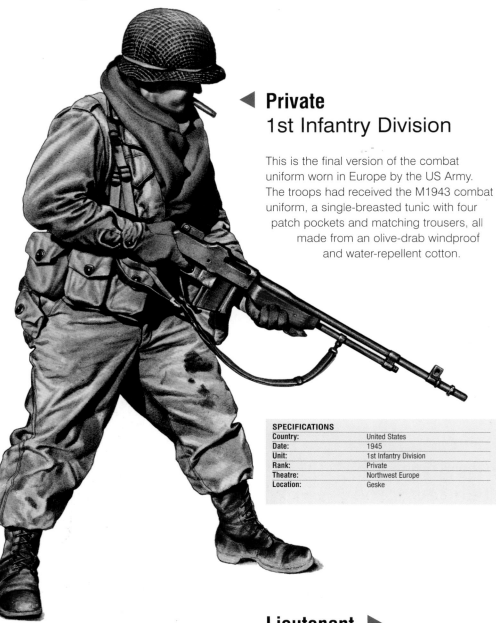

◄ Private
1st Infantry Division

This is the final version of the combat uniform worn in Europe by the US Army. The troops had received the M1943 combat uniform, a single-breasted tunic with four patch pockets and matching trousers, all made from an olive-drab windproof and water-repellent cotton.

SPECIFICATIONS	
Country:	United States
Date:	1945
Unit:	1st Infantry Division
Rank:	Private
Theatre:	Northwest Europe
Location:	Geske

Lieutenant ►
Red Army Rifles

This officer is an infantryman, as indicated by the red piping and band on the peaked cap and the red piping on the shoulder straps. He is wearing the 1943-pattern shirt with belt and pistol holder. In 1943, junior ranks and soldiers in the Red Army were issued with a brown leather belt.

SPECIFICATIONS	
Country:	Soviet Union
Date:	1945
Unit:	Red Army Rifles
Rank:	Lieutenant
Theatre:	Eastern Front
Location:	Berlin

◄ Junior Lieutenant
Belorussian Front, Red Army

The new dress regulations of 1943 were to change the entire structure of the Red Army. The traditional collar patches were abolished and all rank badges were transferred to piped shoulder boards. The tunic had no pocket at the front.

SPECIFICATIONS	
Country:	Soviet Union
Date:	1945
Unit:	Belorussian Front
Rank:	Junior Lieutenant
Theatre:	Eastern Front
Location:	Berlin

Private ►
2nd Moroccan Division

This figure here represents the final uniform worn by the Free French troops in World War II. The uniform was overwhelmingly American in style, with American khaki wool trousers, and the American winter combat jacket with slit pockets.

SPECIFICATIONS	
Country:	Morocco
Date:	1945
Unit:	2nd Moroccan Division
Rank:	Private
Theatre:	Europe
Location:	Germany

Reichsmarschall Hermann Göring

Here we see one of the most recognizable faces of World War II, the portly figure of Reichsmarschall Herman Göring. Although he was commander of the *Luftwaffe*, he was also intricately involved in some of the Third Reich's crimes against humanity.

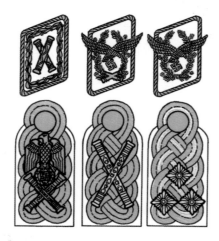

The shoulder straps (lower level) and collar tabs here show the very highest ranks of the *Luftwaffe*. Göring's rank of *Reichsmarschall* is seen on the far left, while next to it is the rank of field marshal then colonel-general.

The Focke-Wulf Fw 190 was one of the best all-round fighters of World War II. It could develop top speeds of more than 600km/h (373mph) and was armed with four 20mm (0.79in) cannon in the wings and two 7.92mm (0.31in) machine guns in the nose.

German High Command
Reichsmarschall

Göring was known for being a highly vain character, and his uniform displays this fact. This uniform was actually unique, its elements designed largely by Göring himself. Here he has a long leather coat, on which his rank is displayed on the shoulder straps and collar patches. Around his neck he wears the Grand Cross of the Iron Cross, while in his right hand he carries an everyday version of the field marshal's baton.

SPECIFICATIONS	
Country:	Germany
Date:	Unknown
Unit:	German High Command
Rank:	*Reichsmarschall*
Theatre:	Europe
Location:	Berlin

MODERN WARFARE 1945– PRESENT

The technological changes in land, naval and air warfare in the second half of the 20th century utterly transformed the way in which conflicts were fought.

Although some armies remained rudimentary, those in the developed world quickly achieved extraordinary sophistication, partly through advances in science and computerization, and partly through the arms race within the Cold War. Soldiers became capable of entirely new levels of destruction and firepower.

Left: Modern US troops in action, wearing advanced uniform and kit. The soldier on the right has a hydration tube attached to a water bladder on his back, and they all have mounting brackets on their helmets for night-vision systems.

Chinese Communist and Nationalist Forces 1945

The Chinese Civil War between 1945 and 1949 laid the theoretical groundwork for revolutionary warfare in the 20th century. Despite the greater material strength of the Nationalists, the Communists won through their better motivation and tactics and their superior levels of organization.

The Taisho 11 was a Japanese light machine gun introduced in 1922, and stocks of this weapon found their way into Chinese hands during the civil war. Its most unusual element was its feed mechanism: chargers for the 6.5mm (0.25in) 38th Year Rifle were fed into a hopper on the left side of the gun, and the hopper stripped out the rounds and fed them into the gun.

This high-quality US submachine gun went into production in 1942, and which served mainly in East Asia. It was a 9mm (0.35in) Parabellum weapon, although versions were also produced in .45 ACP in an attempt to draw buyers away from the Thompson submachine gun.

▼ Private
Chinese Nationalist Army

The United States supplied Nationalist forces with copious amounts of weaponry and equipment, as is clear from this private's .45-calibre Thompson M1A1 submachine gun. In terms of uniform, the soldier's dress is of World War II type: a light khaki tunic and trousers, with knee-high woollen puttees, black shoes and a peaked forage cap. Insignia is minimal; the only apparent badge is the 'white sun blue sky' badge on the cap.

SPECIFICATIONS (right)	
Country:	China
Date:	1945
Unit:	Chinese Nationalist Army
Rank:	Private
Theatre:	China
Location:	Southern China

◄ Private
Chinese Communist Army

The soldier on the left is an example of the better-equipped end of the spectrum of Chinese Communist troops in the mid-1940s. His uniform is Chinese Army issue, including the distinctive knee-high woollen puttees and the stand-and-fall collar shirt. His submachine gun is an interesting feature. The US 9mm (0.35in) United Defense Model 42 was a high-quality gun that was fairly rare in terms of distribution. This weapon was probably acquired via US Officer of Strategic Services (OSS) units in the Dutch East Indies.

SPECIFICATIONS (left)	
Country:	China
Date:	1945
Unit:	Chinese Communist Army
Rank:	Private
Theatre:	China
Location:	Northern China

Indochina 1945–54

The French war in Indochina between 1945 and 1954 in many ways mirrored the experience the United States would later have fighting in Vietnam. Communist forces weakened the French with an insurgency, but built up to the epic set-piece battle, and final French defeat, at Dien Bien Phu.

◀ Captain
Foreign Legion
Parachute Brigade

SPECIFICATIONS	
Country:	France
Date:	1952
Unit:	Foreign Legion Parachute Brigade
Rank:	Captain
Theatre:	Indochina
Location:	Unknown

This para captain wears a camouflage US jungle-warfare jacket matched with the trousers of British airborne forces. The M1 helmet is American, as are the M1910 canteen cover and enamel water bottle, the ammunition pouch for pistol magazines and the folding-stock M1A1 carbine.

Legionnaire ▶
French Foreign Legion

This soldier's combat trousers and camouflaged jacket are of US pattern; the former is from standard US fatigues, while the latter is a French adaptation of the US jacket issued to infantry combatants for the D-Day landings.

SPECIFICATIONS	
Country:	France
Date:	1952
Unit:	French Foreign Legion
Rank:	Legionnaire
Theatre:	Indochina
Location:	Central Indochina

◀ Guerrilla Fighter
Viet Minh

This Viet Minh guerrilla wears the black 'pyjama' uniform, which was simply a shirt and trousers dyed black, usually worn with a Vietnamese cork helmet, but here with a French slouch hat. Weaponry was from many sources – here a French MAT 49.

SPECIFICATIONS	
Country:	Vietnam
Date:	1954
Unit:	Viet Minh
Rank:	Guerrilla Fighter
Theatre:	Indochina
Location:	Dien Bien Phu

Private ▶
Vietnamese Army

This olive-drab uniform is probably of local origin, the ankles of the trousers featuring buttons to keep out the insect life of the jungle floor. The private holds aloft a hat made from woven reeds covered with cloth – little physical protection in itself, but cooling in the Vietnamese climate.

SPECIFICATIONS	
Country:	Vietnam
Date:	1954
Unit:	Vietnamese Army
Rank:	Private
Theatre:	Indochina
Location:	Hanoi

SAS Soldier, Borneo 1965–66

In both Borneo and Malaya, the SAS proved their capability for fighting in jungle environments. They also showed that they could fight with their heads as well as their hearts, building good relations with local people to increase British popularity and maintain local support.

The SAS badge is one of the most famous military insignia in history. It shows a flaming sword and displays the motto 'Who Dares Wins'. The badge is typically worn on a sand-coloured beret.

Prior to the introduction of assault rifles, such as the one seen opposite, the British Army was equipped with the Lee-Enfield No. 4 rifle. It offered all the qualities of reliability and power of previous generations of Lee-Enfields, but was essentially obsolete by the late 1940s.

SPECIFICATIONS

SPECIFICATIONS	
Country:	Britain
Date:	1965–66
Unit:	22 SAS Regiment
Rank:	Corporal
Theatre:	Southeast Asia
Location:	Indonesia

Corporal
22 SAS Regiment

The usual SAS lack of orthodoxy prevails in the uniform of this 22 SAS Regiment corporal, although he is perfectly clothed and equipped for jungle warfare. His tattered forage cap is worn over a sweat rag, providing combined protection against sun and perspiration. The olive-green trousers and shirt are generic military issue of unidentified origin. These are worn with lightweight jungle boots and short puttees, the latter being an excellent preventative measure against exposing ankles to insects and stinging plants on the jungle floor. His operational priorities are illustrated by the pouches on his standard 1958-pattern web belt: two ammunition pouches; a 1944-pattern compass holder (seen just off-centre to his left); and a 1944-pattern water-bottle carrier (to his far left).

South and Southeast Asia 1945–60s

In the aftermath of World War II, many East Asian countries that had been liberated from the Japanese were reluctant to return to their former colonial arrangements. The result was a flowering of independence insurgencies throughout the region.

◀ Private
Dutch Army

The Dutch forces that went into action immediately to fight the independence movement in the Dutch East Indies were clothed and equipped mainly in war surplus. This camouflage jungle overall is actually of US derivation, and was the type used by US soldiers during the Pacific campaign.

SPECIFICATIONS	
Country:	Netherlands
Date:	1946
Unit:	Dutch Army
Rank:	Private
Theatre:	Indonesia
Location:	Surabaya

Trooper ▶
18th Independent Infantry Brigade

Wearing a lightweight British Army tropical uniform, this soldier is armed with a non-standard combat weapon – a Browning Auto-5 (Remington Model 11) semi-auto 12-gauge shotgun. Firing 00 shot, this weapon had devastating short-range firepower.

SPECIFICATIONS	
Country:	Britain
Date:	1950s
Unit:	18th Independent Infantry Brigade
Rank:	Trooper
Theatre:	Southeast Asia
Location:	Malaya

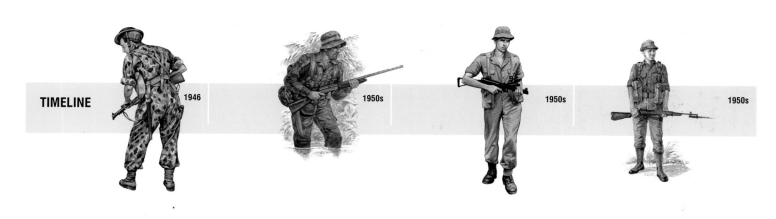

◀ Trooper
British Army

The British soldier here is armed with the 9mm L2A3 Sterling submachine gun. The folding stock and lightweight reliability made the Sterling a popular choice with troops such as drivers and artillerymen, who may have had to store their weapon inside the confines of a vehicle.

SPECIFICATIONS	
Country:	Britain
Date:	1950s
Unit:	British Army
Rank:	Trooper
Theatre:	Southeast Asia
Location:	Malaya

Corporal ▶
British Army

Another British infantryman in Malaya, this one wearing distinctive suede and canvas tropical boots (the fabric sections were more resistant to rotting than leather); these were similar in pattern to the desert boots worn by the Afrika Korps in World War II.

SPECIFICATIONS	
Country:	Britain
Date:	1950s
Unit:	British Army
Rank:	Corporal
Theatre:	Southeast Asia
Location:	Malaya

South and Southeast Asia 1945–60s

The British Army in Malaya most commonly conducted its operations in small units; they combined aggressive patrol and ambush initiatives with an effective programme of intelligence-gathering.

◄ Marine
Royal Marines

This Marine wears a combination of items ideally suited for manoeuvres in the hot and humid Southeast Asian jungles. An olive-drab fatigue shirt is worn with Marine-issue trousers. Equipment is held in 1944-pattern webbing, and the weapon is the exceptionally durable Australian 9mm (0.35in) Owen submachine gun.

SPECIFICATIONS	
Country:	Britain
Date:	1952
Unit:	Royal Marines
Rank:	Marine
Theatre:	Southeast Asia
Location:	Malaya

Guerrilla ►
Malayan Races
Liberation Army

This soldier of the MRLA in many respects resembles a Japanese infantryman of World War II. This is partly due to massive stocks of war-surplus Japanese clothing and equipment left over in Southeast Asia after Japanese occupation.

SPECIFICATIONS	
Country:	Malaya
Date:	1953
Unit:	Malayan Races Liberation Army
Rank:	Guerrilla
Theatre:	Southeast Asia
Location:	Malaya

TIMELINE 1952 1953 1962 1966

◀ Marine
42 Commando

This Marine wears standard tropical cotton dress and his boots are fitted with a short pair of woollen puttees. Also standard for the time is the 1958-pattern web equipment; visible here are the soldier's two ammunition pouches and the bayonet for his 7.62mm (0.3in) L1A1 rifle.

SPECIFICATIONS	
Country:	Britain
Date:	1962
Unit:	42 Commando
Rank:	Marine
Theatre:	Southeast Asia
Location:	Brunei

Rifleman ▶
7th Gurkha Rifles

This Gurkha soldier is carrying the US M16A1 rifle on this jungle patrol in 1966, instead of the standard British Army rifle, the L1A1 SLR. The Gurkhas chose the lighter and shorter M16 because their smaller frames could better handle it; it also had considerably less recoil than the SLR.

SPECIFICATIONS	
Country:	Britain
Date:	1966
Unit:	7th Gurkha Rifles
Rank:	Rifleman
Theatre:	Southeast Asia
Location:	Borneo

Greek Civil War 1947

During the post-war conflict between the nationalist government of Greece and communist revolutionaries, Britain and the United States sponsored government resistance with both men and materiel. The British were initially involved as a combat force, but economic austerity at home forced their withdrawal.

British military equipment was much in evidence during the Greek Civil War, such as this 7.7mm (0.303in) Bren light machine gun. Unusually for such weapons, the Bren was fed from a top-mounted 30-round magazine, the operator aiming via an offset sight. The gun was, however, very accurate and reliable.

The Enfield .38 revolver went into production for British armed forces during the 1920s. It was a double-action revolver, and in most senses it was a copy of the Webley Mk VI, with modifications to the trigger and safety mechanisms.

Private
Greek National Army

Guerrila
Greek Democratic Army

SPECIFICATIONS (right)

Country:	Greece
Date:	1947
Unit:	Greek Democratic Army
Rank:	Guerrilla
Theatre:	Balkans
Location:	Greece

The two figures here show opposing sides of the Greek Civil War. The main on the left belongs to the Greek National Army. His shirt, pullover, beret, anklets and trousers are standard British Army uniform (the trousers are 'denims', a working version of combat uniform). By contrast, the submachine gun is the US .45in Thompson M1A1. The female warrior is from the insurgent Greek Democratic Army. She wears a civilian blouse and waistcoat, but with trousers from British Army combat dress, here dyed black. The web anklets are also British Army stock. The weapon, however, is the German 9mm (0.35in) MP40 submachine gun.

SPECIFICATIONS (left)

Country:	Greece
Date:	1947
Unit:	Greek National Army
Rank:	Private
Theatre:	Balkans
Location:	Greece

Soviet Forces 1945–89

Despite World War II being over, the wartime-era style of uniform dominated Soviet infantry dress until well into the 1960s. A replacement uniform filtered through only in about 1970, when the Red Army began modernizing.

◀ Junior Sergeant
Soviet Armoured Regiment

This tankman wears a hat that predates 1939 – a sun hat issued to troops in 1938 in the commands of Central Asia, North Caucasia and Trans Caucasia. The rest of his uniform follows a standard Soviet pattern that lasted well into the 1970s.

SPECIFICATIONS	
Country:	Soviet Union
Date:	1945
Unit:	Soviet Armoured Regiment
Rank:	Junior Sergeant
Theatre:	Europe
Location:	East Germany

Private ▶
Soviet Infantry

Here we see a khaki tunic with an uncomfortable-looking stand collar and shoulder straps for the rank insignia. Two pouches are carried: the bag suspended around his neck carries a gas mask, while the pouch on his left hip holds ammunition.

SPECIFICATIONS	
Country:	Soviet Union
Date:	1956
Unit:	Soviet Infantry
Rank:	Private
Theatre:	Europe
Location:	Hungary

1945

1956

1968

1970s

◀ Tank Driver
Armoured Forces

By the late 1960s, Soviet tank crews were wearing a two-piece black uniform as their operational clothing (here worn over the standard Soviet Army infantry tunic and trousers); this later became a one-piece overall.

SPECIFICATIONS	
Country:	Soviet Union
Date:	1968
Unit:	Armoured Forces
Rank:	Tank Driver
Theatre:	Europe
Location:	Czechoslovakia

Captain 2nd Rank ▶
Soviet Naval Infantry

The two stars on the collar of this soldier's field service dress indicate that he is a captain, 2nd rank (there were three ranks of captain), in the Soviet Navy. His special forces status is alluded to by the striped T-shirt beneath his tunic, and he is armed with a 5.45mm (0.21in) PSM handgun.

SPECIFICATIONS	
Country:	Soviet Union
Date:	1970s
Unit:	Soviet Naval Infantry
Rank:	Captain 2nd Rank
Theatre:	Europe
Location:	Unknown

Soviet Forces 1945–89

During the 1970s and 1980s, camouflage uniforms started to be introduced in greater quantities into the Soviet Army, particularly for special forces and operational units in war zones such as Afghanistan.

▼ Captain
Armoured Regiment

Head protection for this tankman comes from the padded leather helmet, this featuring built-in communications. The socket for a RT/IC radio-to-vehicle transmitter is hanging down his left shoulder, while around his neck is a throat microphone.

SPECIFICATIONS	
Country:	Soviet Union
Date:	1970s
Unit:	Armoured Regiment
Rank:	Captain
Theatre:	Europe
Location:	Russia

Starshina ▲
Technical Troops

A *Starshina* was a senior rank of NCO in the Soviet Army; the shoulder boards indicate both the rank and membership of a technical troops unit. The uniform is a 'rain' pattern common in Warsaw Pact armies.

SPECIFICATIONS	
Country:	Soviet Union
Date:	1970s
Unit:	Technical Troops
Rank:	*Starshina*
Theatre:	Europe
Location:	Unknown

TIMELINE 1970s 1970s c. 1975 1988

Infantryman ▲
East German Army

This East German infantryman is wearing the M-56 pattern of steel helmet, here fitted with netting to attach camouflage. The weapon is the legendary AK-47, the solid-stock version. The AK-47 was the standard Soviet infantry rifle issue from 1948, and was known for its absolute reliability.

SPECIFICATIONS	
Country:	East Germany
Date:	c. 1975
Unit:	East German Army
Rank:	Infantryman
Theatre:	Europe
Location:	East Germany

Sergeant ▶
Ministry of State Security (MVD)

When not wearing the *ushanka* fur cap (seen here), Soviet troops in the late 1980s would generally wear either the SSh-40 or newer SSh-60 helmet, or a simple forage cap that replaced the *pilotka* sidecap in 1984. However, MVD troops could also be seen in broad-brimmed, officer-style caps.

SPECIFICATIONS	
Country:	Soviet Union
Date:	1988
Unit:	Ministry of State Security (MVD)
Rank:	Sergeant
Theatre:	Europe
Location:	Moscow

Soviet Naval Infantry 1980s

This soldier's physical control and aggression indicate the elite capabilities of the Naval Infantry, the oldest of the former Soviet Union's special forces. The defining emblem of the Naval Infantry is the fouled anchor cap badge worn by all ranks on the traditional black beret.

The fouled anchor symbol on the Cadet's parade uniform (left) is a traditional symbol of the Soviet/Russian naval infantry. The other ranks shown are Cadet with two years' experience (centre) and Cadet with three years' experience (right).

The AKSU-74 is essentially a shortened version of the AK-74, firing the same 5.45mm (0.21in) Soviet round. With its stock folded it measures just 527mm (20.7in), the compact dimensions appreciated by special forces soldiers. Note the flared flash hider at the muzzle – shortened weapons often produce excessive muzzle blast.

Corporal
Naval Infantry

Within the Naval Infantry of the 1980s, a red
triangular flash bearing another anchor motif
was often worn on the beret. In combat, a
black steel helmet was worn with a red star
in the centre and an anchor stencilled on
the left. A trademark piece of clothing for the
Naval Infantry was, and remains, a blue and
white striped T-shirt worn by most Soviet
Special Forces, although here this is
covered by a one-piece lightweight
camouflage combat uniform. Naval Infantry
units with Guard status also wear a Guards
badge over their right uniform pocket and all
usually have a gold anchor insignia on the
sleeve. Markings on the broad steel belt
buckle indicate to which of four naval fleets
the soldier belongs (Northern, Baltic, Black
Sea and Pacific). Clutched in his hands are
bayonets for the AK series of firearms; these
can also act as wire-cutters.

SPECIFICATIONS	
Country:	Soviet Union
Date:	1980s
Unit:	Naval Infantry
Rank:	Corporal
Theatre:	Europe
Location:	None

Chinese and Korean Forces, Korean War 1950–53

The communist forces of North Korea and China did not have the sophisticated levels of equipment possessed by United Nations (particularly US) forces, but they did have copious manpower and decent small arms.

◀ Private
Korean People's Army

This soldier is extremely well dressed for the severe Korean winter climate. His jacket and trousers are made from thickly quilted material, the jacket featuring a double-breasted design with zipper fastening to reduce penetration by wind chill.

SPECIFICATIONS	
Country:	North Korea
Date:	1950
Unit:	Korean People's Army
Rank:	Private
Theatre:	Korea
Location:	Near Pyongyang

Private ▶
Chinese People's Liberation Army

This soldier wears a fully quilted jacket and trousers, with archaic puttees. The cap is fur-lined, with extensive earflaps to prevent frostbite. Ammunition for his Type 88 Hanyang rifle is held in cotton bandoliers across the chest.

SPECIFICATIONS	
Country:	China
Date:	1951
Unit:	Chinese People's Liberation Army
Rank:	Private
Theatre:	Korea
Location:	South Korea

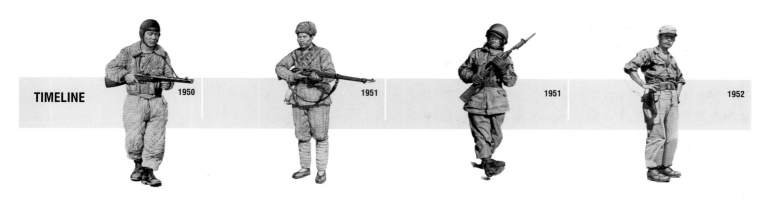

◄ Private
Army of the Republic of South Korea

This soldier shows his indebtedness to US supplies. His clothing is the US M1943 battledress, a uniform that worked on a layering system. The outer layers had good properties of wind- and rain-resistance, while inner layers provided warmth. The US M1 helmet is worn on top of a woollen cap.

SPECIFICATIONS	
Country:	South Korea
Date:	1951
Unit:	Army of the Republic of South Korea
Rank:	Private
Theatre:	Korea
Location:	South Korea

Trooper ►
UN Partisan Infantry

The UN Partisan Infantry was around 22,000 strong and fought a vigorous and effective guerrilla war against the North Korean regime from within North Korea itself. The uniform is US World War II surplus; the shirt is from the herringbone-twill jungle dress issued to US troops in the Pacific theatre.

SPECIFICATIONS	
Country:	North Korea
Date:	1952
Unit:	UN Partisan Infantry
Rank:	Trooper
Theatre:	Korea
Location:	North Korea

Royal Australian Regiment, Korea 1951

During the Korean War, Australia contributed two infantry battalions, one fighter squadron and selected naval forces to the UN resistance against North Korea. In April 1951, Australian soldiers fought part of a massive counter-attack by communist forces near Kapyong, for which the 3rd Battalion won a US Presidential citation.

Despite its rather ungainly appearance, courtesy of its top-mounted magazine, the Owen was actually an excellent submachine gun, proving to be extremely durable and reliable. It had a cyclical rate of fire of 700rpm, feeding from a 33-round magazine, and it served into the 1960s.

Another submachine gun of Commonwealth forces, the Sten Mk V was introduced into British service in 1944. Its improvements over previous versions of the Sten were mainly cosmetic, and the weapon's unreliable feed mechanism was preserved.

Private
3rd Bn, Royal Australian Regiment

This soldier is a member of the 3rd Battalion, Royal Australian Regiment. He wears the wide-brimmed slouch hat characteristic of Australian ground troops. British and US influences run through the rest of his outfit and equipment. The jacket and trousers are from the US M1943 combat dress; they are made of a light windproof and rain-resistant material, with warmth coming from the standard Australian fatigues worn underneath, the leather gloves and the thick wool scarf. The brown leather boots are worn with a pair of US-style gaiters secured by two buckle straps on each gaiter. British Commonwealth associations come through in the webbing (British 1937-pattern) and the weapons.

SPECIFICATIONS	
Country:	Australia
Date:	1951
Unit:	3rd Bn, Royal Australian Regiment
Rank:	Private
Theatre:	Korea
Location:	Near Kapyong, South Korea

British and US Forces, Korean War 1950–53

The United Nations force deployed to Korea in the early 1950s was truly multi-national, with more than 20 nations contributing. The United States and the British provided the largest foreign contingents.

◀ Marine
Royal Marines

Although this soldier is a Royal Marine Commando, his uniform and kit are US-supplied, issued to the Marines in Japan prior to their deployment to the Korean conflict. The M1943 combat dress was a seminal advance in post-war uniform design, working on a layered principle.

SPECIFICATIONS	
Country:	Britain
Date:	1950
Unit:	Royal Marines
Rank:	Marine
Theatre:	Korea
Location:	Chosin

Marine ▶
US Marine Corps

This US Marine is carrying ammunition for his M1 .30-calibre rifle in his M1923 cartridge belt and also in the cotton bandoliers across his chest, around 200 rounds in total. His main uniform item is a set of olive-drab M1944 fatigues.

SPECIFICATIONS	
Country:	United States
Date:	1950
Unit:	US Marine Corps
Rank:	Marine
Theatre:	Korea
Location:	Inchon

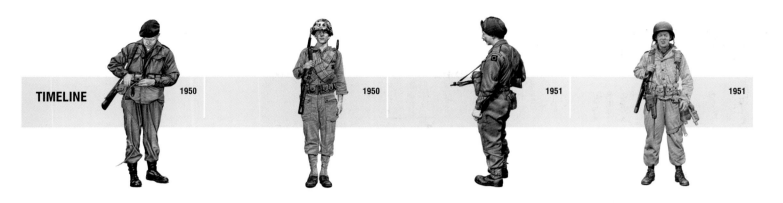

◀ Corporal
Gloucestershire Regiment

This soldier is kitted out in the British 1950-pattern battledress, based on the US M1943 layered uniform system. Here the soldier is wearing the basic serge shirt and trousers, although there was also a weather-proof smock for further protection.

SPECIFICATIONS	
Country:	Britain
Date:	1951
Unit:	Gloucestershire Regiment
Rank:	Corporal
Theatre:	Korea
Location:	Imjin River

Private ▶
US Airborne Forces

Although this soldier wears the M1943 trousers, he has yet to be issued with the jacket and instead has the older-pattern M1941 jacket. His webbing and kit is arranged very much in battle order. He carries ammunition for his M1 Garand rifle in a six-pouch rifleman's belt.

SPECIFICATIONS	
Country:	United States
Date:	1951
Unit:	US Airborne Forces
Rank:	Private
Theatre:	Korea
Location:	Around the 38th Parallel

327

Private, Gloucestershire Regiment 1951

In the Korean War, British soldiers' uniforms had to be adapted for conditions in the field. This Gloucestershire Regiment soldier shows a warranted attention to protection against cold and wind, most visible in his large white winter mittens, which were designed to be worn over the standard-issue woollen gloves.

The Bedford MWD was designed prior to World War II, but it served the British Army as a light utility vehicle until the late 1950s. Originally, the vehicle was fitted with a canvas hood and collapsible windscreen, but these were replaced in 1943 by a solid cab.

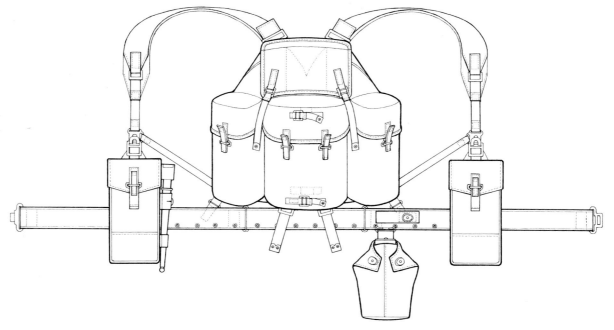

The 1944-pattern webbing system was the standard load-carrying equipment for many British and Commonwealth soldiers during the Korean War. Here, a central three-section rucksack is flanked by two ammunition pouches for the SMLE No. 4 rifle; a water bottle hangs beneath the belt.

Corporal
Gloucestershire
Regiment

Common to British soldiers in the Korean War was the 1950-pattern combat dress, with extra protective elements that formed the 'cold/wet weather' uniform. This soldier wears the additional camouflaged clothing issued to the 29th Brigade, which included the Gloucestershire Regiment, and must have provided a good degree of heat retention when combined with the sheepskin-like texture of the combat smock and trousers. The woollen cap was also a standard feature of many soldiers' uniforms. Worn over the uniform is 1944-pattern webbing, a practical system that carried a rucksack, ammunition pouches, a bayonet and a water bottle. In this case, ammunition is for the .303 Lee Enfield No. 4 rifle.

SPECIFICATIONS	
Country:	Britain
Date:	1951
Unit:	Gloucestershire Regiment
Rank:	Corporal
Theatre:	Korea
Location:	Imjin River

African Guerrilla Forces 1950s–80s

As with East Asia, Africa was rocked by independence and revolutionary wars in the aftermath of World War II. Many of these conflicts attracted foreign fighters, serving as either ideological warriors or simply as mercenaries.

◀ Guerrilla
National Liberation Front

This Algerian guerrilla serving in the National Liberation Front (FLN) is armed, like many insurgent armies, with a weapon captured from his enemy – a French MAS 49/56 semi-auto rifle. His clothing is entirely civilian.

SPECIFICATIONS	
Country:	Algeria
Date:	1950s
Unit:	National Liberation Front
Rank:	Guerrilla
Theatre:	North Africa
Location:	Algeria

Guerrilla ▶
Algerian National Liberation Army

This revolutionary soldier has several items of US source. His jacket is from the US M1943 uniform; his rifle is the US M2 carbine, a .30-calibre weapon with a short range but a full-automatic capability.

SPECIFICATIONS	
Country:	Algeria
Date:	1960
Unit:	Algerian National Liberation Army
Rank:	Guerrilla
Theatre:	North Africa
Location:	Tunisian/Algerian border

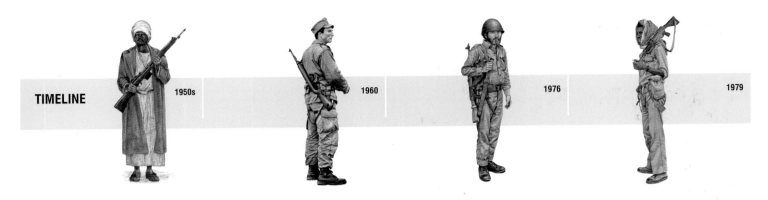

TIMELINE

1950s   1960   1976   1979

◀ Private
Cuban Army

Cuban forces were involved in substantial numbers in Angolan affairs from the mid-1970s. Cuban kit is mainly of Russian manufacture. The Soviet AKM assault rifle is seen here, with its innovative bayonet and scabbard: the two components lock together to form a wire-cutter.

SPECIFICATIONS	
Country:	Cuba
Date:	1976
Unit:	Cuban Army
Rank:	Private
Theatre:	Africa
Location:	Angola

Guerrilla ▶
Eritrean Liberation Front

This soldier is mostly wearing civilian clothing. However, he has managed to acquire a British 1937-pattern web belt and ammunition pouch; the pouch is used to store magazines for his Czech Cz58 assault rifle, which fired M1943 rounds.

SPECIFICATIONS	
Country:	Eritrea
Date:	1979
Unit:	Eritrean Liberation Front
Rank:	Guerrilla
Theatre:	Africa
Location:	Eritrea

African Mercenaries 1960s–80s

The numerous conflicts in Africa provided fertile recruiting grounds for foreign mercenaries. They came to Africa looking for money and adventure, although many lost their lives in the process.

◄ Mercenary
5 Commando

This mercenary is clearly identified on his sleeve as a member of 5 Commando, one of the more unified and focused mercenary groups operating in the Congo. His green beret is the distinguishing mark of a commando, while the beret badge is of a Belgian armoured battalion.

SPECIFICATIONS	
Country:	Unknown
Date:	1964
Unit:	5 Commando
Rank:	Mercenary
Theatre:	Africa
Location:	Congo

Major ►
5 Commando

Typical for mercenaries in the Congo at this time, the rank insignia here generally follows the form of the Belgian Army, the insignia of major being a single yellow bar and star: the dagger motif is a commando addition. The web belt is a British 1944-pattern.

SPECIFICATIONS	
Country:	Unknown
Date:	1964
Unit:	5 Commando
Rank:	Major
Theatre:	Africa
Location:	Congo

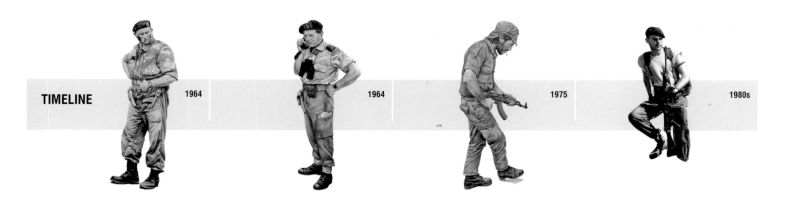

| TIMELINE | 1964 | 1964 | 1975 | 1980s |

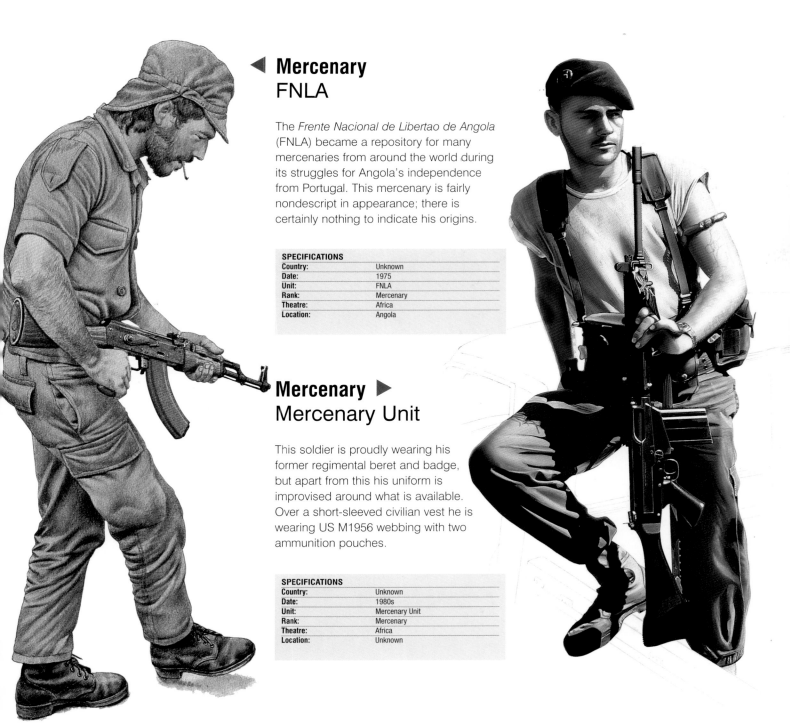

◀ Mercenary
FNLA

The *Frente Nacional de Libertao de Angola* (FNLA) became a repository for many mercenaries from around the world during its struggles for Angola's independence from Portugal. This mercenary is fairly nondescript in appearance; there is certainly nothing to indicate his origins.

SPECIFICATIONS	
Country:	Unknown
Date:	1975
Unit:	FNLA
Rank:	Mercenary
Theatre:	Africa
Location:	Angola

Mercenary ▶
Mercenary Unit

This soldier is proudly wearing his former regimental beret and badge, but apart from this his uniform is improvised around what is available. Over a short-sleeved civilian vest he is wearing US M1956 webbing with two ammunition pouches.

SPECIFICATIONS	
Country:	Unknown
Date:	1980s
Unit:	Mercenary Unit
Rank:	Mercenary
Theatre:	Africa
Location:	Unknown

African/Colonial Armies 1950s–70s

Amid numerous independence, civil and revolutionary wars throughout Cold War Africa, many African armies continued to uphold traditions of professionalism. Others, however, were little more than armed rabbles.

◄ Private
British Army

The uniform of this soldier, who is fighting in Kenya's insurgency war of the 1950s, consists of khaki drill trousers and a khaki shirt, over which he wears a pullover. The hat, ideal for guarding against the equatorial sun, is a simple, wide-brimmed slouch hat. The trousers are closed at the bottom using grey anklets.

SPECIFICATIONS	
Country:	Britain
Date:	1953
Unit:	British Army
Rank:	Private
Theatre:	Africa
Location:	Kenya

Private ►
French 10th Parachute Division

This private is carrying a 7.5mm (0.29in) M1952 (AAT Mle 52) machine gun, and he is wearing the standard M51 tropical parachute uniform. By this time, all French troops were wearing camouflage, a change that occurred in 1960.

SPECIFICATIONS	
Country:	France
Date:	1961
Unit:	10th Parachute Division
Rank:	Private
Theatre:	Africa
Location:	Algeria

◀ Warrant Officer
Belgian Paracommando Regiment

The paracommando here wears the paras' maroon beret, the SAS badge on which refers to the first Belgian para company, which conducted operations with the SAS in World War II. His jacket is a Belgian version of the British paras' Denison smock.

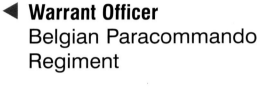

SPECIFICATIONS	
Country:	Belgium
Date:	1964
Unit:	Belgian Paracommando Regiment
Rank:	Warrant Officer
Theatre:	Africa
Location:	Congo

Private ▶
Biafran Army

This soldier's shirt and jacket are of unknown origin, although probably taken from the Soviet-supplied kit that flooded many countries of Africa during the Cold War period. For armament, he carries a 7.62mm (0.3in) Vz58 assault rifle – a Czech copy of the Kalashnikov AK-47.

SPECIFICATIONS	
Country:	Biafra
Date:	1968
Unit:	Biafran Army
Rank:	Private
Theatre:	Africa
Location:	East Nigeria

African/Colonial Armies 1950s–70s

The wars in Africa were frequently proxy conflicts for the superpowers. For this reason, Europe, the United States and the Soviet Union all pumped arms, equipment and uniforms into the continent.

◀ Private
Nigerian Federal Army

This soldier is seen wearing green fatigues, which, alongside a khaki version, formed the standard uniform of the NFA. His fairly anonymous shirt and trousers are worn with British 1958-pattern webbing with two large ammunition/utility pouches and a water bottle with a 1944-pattern cover.

SPECIFICATIONS	
Country:	Nigeria
Date:	1968
Unit:	Nigerian Federal Army
Rank:	Private
Theatre:	Africa
Location:	Nigeria

Crewman ▶
Chadian National Army

This soldier is most likely the crewman of a French Panhard AML-60 or ALM-90 armoured car, the armoured mainstay of the post-independence Chadian Army. He wears French AFV communication headphones, and his paratrooper's shirt and suede boots are also of French origin.

SPECIFICATIONS	
Country:	Chad
Date:	1970
Unit:	Chadian National Army
Rank:	Crewman
Theatre:	Africa
Location:	Chad

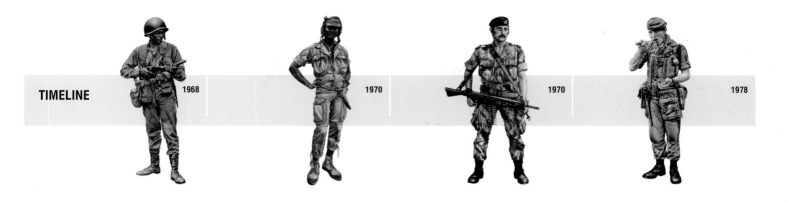

1968   1970   1970   1978

◀ Corporal
Portuguese Parachute Regiment

This is a corporal of the Portuguese Parachute Regiment, a unit typical of the elite forces used in Portugal's colonial conflicts. He wears a 1950 French pattern of camouflage in a distinctive green, brown and olive-green colour scheme.

SPECIFICATIONS	
Country:	Portugal
Date:	1970
Unit:	Portuguese Parachute Regiment
Rank:	Corporal
Theatre:	Africa
Location:	Mozambique

Corporal ▶
French Foreign Legion

This para corporal, his rank indicated by the green chevrons attached to his chest, wears a 'Satin 300' uniform, an outfit designed specifically for the use of the Legion and characterized by a short, wide-collared jacket with double-zip compartments.

SPECIFICATIONS	
Country:	France
Date:	1978
Unit:	French Foreign Legion
Rank:	Corporal
Theatre:	Africa
Location:	Zaire

Rhodesia/South Africa 1970s–80s

In 1965, Rhodesia declared itself independent from the United Kingdom, and during the 1970s fought a bitter bush war against revolutionary insurgents. South Africa, meanwhile, fought its own insurgency in Namibia and Angola.

◀ **Private**
Rhodesian African Rifles

The Rhodesian African Rifles proved itself one of the best counter-insurgency forces in post-war African history. This soldier is wearing a foliage pattern of camouflage on his shirt and trousers. He also wears a matching peaked field cap featuring the RAR badge.

SPECIFICATIONS	
Country:	Rhodesia
Date:	1976
Unit:	Rhodesian African Rifles
Rank:	Private
Theatre:	Africa
Location:	Rhodesia

Private ▶
Selous Scouts

A staggering 68 per cent of nationalist guerrilla fatalities can be laid at the door of the Selous Scouts. On operations, the Scouts travelled extraordinarily light and informally. This soldier is dressed in a camouflage shirt, woollen hat, British 1958-pattern webbing and hockey boots, also known as 'tackies'.

SPECIFICATIONS	
Country:	Rhodesia
Date:	1977
Unit:	Selous Scouts
Rank:	Private
Theatre:	Africa
Location:	Rhodesia

TIMELINE
1976
1977
1979
1980

◀ Guerrilla Fighter
Rhodesian Patriotic Front

This guerrilla's green beret and T-shirt are civilian, but the trousers are the camouflage combat trousers of the Rhodesian Army. His rifle is the excellent 7.62mm (0.3in) Heckler & Koch G3; he carries the magazines for this in the series of chest pouches.

SPECIFICATIONS	
Country:	Rhodesia
Date:	1979
Unit:	Rhodesian Patriotic Front
Rank:	Guerrilla
Theatre:	Africa
Location:	Rhodesia

Private ▶
South African Army

This soldier wears a cotton two-piece khaki uniform, the shirt and trousers having covered pocket buttons to stop them snagging on foliage when on patrol. His webbing system features two large ammunition pouches, each holding two magazines for his FN FAL rifle

SPECIFICATIONS	
Country:	South Africa
Date:	1980
Unit:	South African Army
Rank:	Private
Theatre:	Africa
Location:	Namibia

Sergeant, SA Recon Commando 1990s

The South African Recon Commandos are South Africa's counter-insurgency elite, specializing in deep penetration into the African bush as well as urban combat and specialist parachute techniques. Only about 8 per cent of people who begin Recon training pass the course.

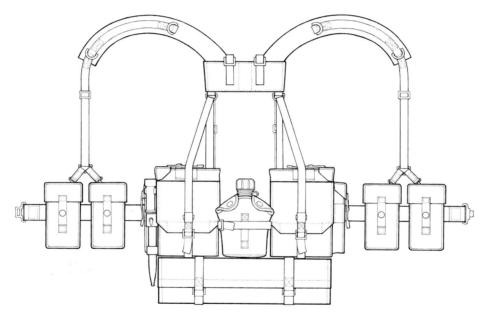

This South African Army webbing consists, in the centre, of two kidney pouches (the left-hand pouch has an FN FAL bayonet attached) framing a water bottle, with a poncho roll underneath. The rest of the belt is occupied by four FN FAL ammunition pouches.

Before it adopted the Vektor R4 rifle seen in the figure artwork, the South African Army used the dependable Belgian FN FAL rifle. Here we see the FN FAL (HB) (Heavy Barrel), which featured a more substantial barrel and a bipod to giving it a light support capacity.

Private
South African Army

Here a heavily armed 'Recce' is on patrol, his uniform the standard khaki shirt, trousers and slouch hat worn by all South African soldiers. However, Recces are also seen in several foliage-pattern camouflages, including varieties that mix vivid blues and mustards. His load-carrying equipment is South African; the Recces had a double-sided rucksack made for them that sat a parachute in the middle, so that packs could be standardized across airborne and ground operations. His rifle, the South African 5.56mm (0.22in) R4, is supplemented by two IMI rifle-grenades.

SPECIFICATIONS	
Country:	South Africa
Date:	1980
Unit:	South African Army
Rank:	Private
Theatre:	Africa
Location:	Namibia

Middle Eastern Insurgencies 1950s–70s

The British Army maintained its military presence in the Middle East for much of the Cold War period. As well as conducting peacekeeping and order operations, it also prosecuted several major counter-insurgency campaigns.

◀ **Trooper**
22 SAS Regiment

This SAS soldier's jacket is the British paratrooper's Denison smock, zipper-fastened at the collar and camouflaged in natural foliage shades. He also wears standard British Army battledress trousers and gaiters.

SPECIFICATIONS	
Country:	Britain
Date:	1959
Unit:	22 SAS Regiment
Rank:	Trooper
Theatre:	Middle East
Location:	Oman

Corporal ▶
Argyll and Sutherland Highlanders

Here operating in patrol and search roles, this corporal shows his regimental pride through the visually strong blue glengarry cap with badge, red and white band and small red pompom. The rest of his uniform is composed of standard British Army items.

SPECIFICATIONS	
Country:	Britain
Date:	1967
Unit:	Argyll and Sutherland Highlanders
Rank:	Corporal
Theatre:	Middle East
Location:	Aden

TIMELINE   1959   1967   1973   1973

◀ **Guerrilla**
Dhofari Guerrilla Forces

This fighter is dressed in traditional civilian skirt and headdress, supplemented by supplies from the Soviet Union and Eastern Bloc. His weapon is the AKM, the modernized version of Kalashnikov's AK-47. His East German jacket is rendered in a leaf-pattern camouflage.

SPECIFICATIONS	
Country:	Oman
Date:	1973
Unit:	Dhofari Guerrilla Forces
Rank:	Guerrilla
Theatre:	Middle East
Location:	Oman

Trooper ▶
22 SAS Regiment

The trooper here is armed with the powerful 7.62mm (0.3in) General Purpose Machine Gun made by FN Herstal. His webbing is the SAS-designed Lightweight Combat Pack, made from three packs hung by nylon mesh 'breathable' shoulder pieces.

SPECIFICATIONS	
Country:	Britain
Date:	1973
Unit:	22 SAS Regiment
Rank:	Trooper
Theatre:	Middle East
Location:	Oman

Arab–Israeli Wars 1940s–50s

The Middle East had a long history of ethnic, territorial and political strife even before Israel achieved independence in 1948. This event, however, and other upheavals, meant that the Middle East remained familiar with conflict.

◀ Irregular
Palmach Infantry

In 1948, the Palmach, an elite irregular Israeli unit, had to equip themselves with whatever war surplus was to hand. This soldier has a US drill shirt matched with British drill trousers; the webbing is a US Army cartridge belt and the water canteen has an M1910 cover. Armament in this case is the Czech 7.92mm (0.31in) Model 24.

SPECIFICATIONS	
Country:	Israel
Date:	1948
Unit:	Palmach Infantry
Rank:	Irregular
Theatre:	Middle East
Location:	Israel

Private ▶
Egyptian Army

This soldier's webbing, boots and weaponry allude clearly to Egypt's close links with the United Kingdom at this time. The uniform itself is of Egyptian manufacture – a simple khaki denim one-piece overall, fly-fronted, and with a standing collar.

SPECIFICATIONS	
Country:	Egypt
Date:	1948
Unit:	Egyptian Army
Rank:	Private
Theatre:	Middle East
Location:	Southern Israel

1948   1948   1948   1956

◀ Sergeant
Arab Legion

The sergeant here is preparing to fire a British 9mm Sten Mk V submachine gun, a model distinguished from earlier Stens by a pistol grip and a muzzle like the No.4 service rifle. The rest of his uniform is almost entirely of British manufacture.

SPECIFICATIONS	
Country:	Jordan
Date:	1948
Unit:	Arab Legion
Rank:	Sergeant
Theatre:	Middle East
Location:	West Bank

Corporal ▶
French Colonial
Parachute Regiment

The soldier here shows the typical French para uniform of the mid-1950s. The camouflage shirt and trousers are from the M51 parachute uniform; he also wears French webbing holding six rifle grenades for his MAS 1936 rifle.

SPECIFICATIONS	
Country:	France
Date:	1956
Unit:	French Colonial Parachute Regiment
Rank:	Corporal
Theatre:	Middle East
Location:	Suez

British Paratrooper, Suez 1956

The Suez invasion of 1956, spurred by Gamal Nasser's nationalization of the Suez Canal, was a political disaster for the British and the French. The week-long military operation (29 October–6 November 1956) also cost British forces a total of 16 killed and 96 wounded.

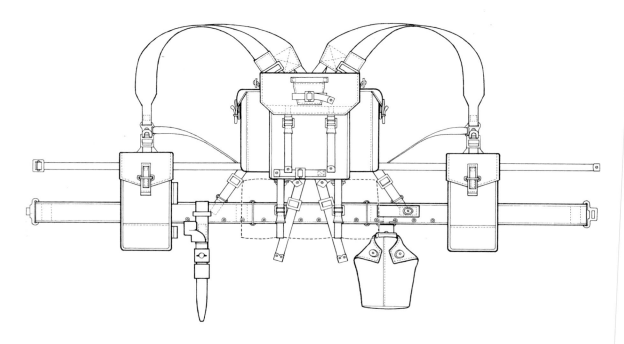

The webbing system shown here is the 1944-pattern. A double-belt system supports a backpack (with waterproof central container) and a bedding roll (in outline), plus two ammunition pouches, a No. 9 bayonet and a water bottle.

The cap badge of the Parachute Regiment, adopted in 1943, features a parachute flanked by wings and surmounted by a crown and lion. The motto of the regiment is *Utrinque Paratus* (Ready for Anything).

Private
3rd Battalion, The
Parachute Regiment

When in operational clothing, from 1941
British paras often wore the Denison smock,
consisting of a thigh-length waterproof and
windproof jacket. It came in a camouflage
mix of olive-green, ochre and yellows. On
the sleeve of his smock this para wears the
regiment's wings in white on a khaki field.
Beneath that insignia is a green flash, which
signifies his drop zone and membership of
3 Para. He wears 1950-pattern khaki
battledress and a sand-coloured helmet,
with commando-type boots with thick,
heavily treaded rubber soles. Like most
paras on operations, he carries large
amounts of kit in the 1944-pattern webbing
system: a backpack and bedding roll, an
oilskin for wrapping weapons in, a water
bottle, a first-aid pack, and ammunition
pouches at the front.

SPECIFICATIONS	
Country:	Britain
Date:	1956
Unit:	3rd Battalion, The Parachute Regiment
Rank:	Private
Theatre:	Middle East
Location:	Suez

Israel Defence Forces, Six-Day War 1967

The Six-Day War of 1967 was Israel's brilliantly executed pre-emptive strike against the surrounding Arab nations. In less than a week of fighting, Israel took control of the Gaza Strip, Sinai Peninsula, West Bank, East Jerusalem and the Golan Heights.

◄ Private
Sayeret Golani

The Sayeret Golani are an elite reconnaissance and combat unit within the regular Golani Brigade of the Israeli Army. This soldier wears an olive-green Israeli battledress zippered jacket, with 'lizard' pattern camouflage trousers commonly seen on specialist Israeli troops.

SPECIFICATIONS	
Country:	Israel
Date:	1967
Unit:	Sayeret Golani
Rank:	Private
Theatre:	Middle East
Location:	Mount Hermon

1st Lieutenant ►
Israeli Armoured Corps

This Israeli tank commander is shown in full communications gear. His vented and padded helmet is of US World War II type, made of fibre and leather. Into the helmet are built receivers and a boom-arm microphone; the junction box for the communications system can be seen on his chest.

SPECIFICATIONS	
Country:	Israel
Date:	1967
Unit:	Israeli Armoured Corps
Rank:	1st Lieutenant
Theatre:	Middle East
Location:	Sinai

◄ Private
Golani Brigade

The rippled battledress here is of French origin, and is worn over a thin open-neck jumper. The soldier's head is protected by the US M1 helmet with a camouflaged netting cover; the helmet was a precursor to the lighter ballistic nylon headgear worn by Israeli forces today.

SPECIFICATIONS	
Country:	Israel
Date:	1967
Unit:	Golani Brigade
Rank:	Private
Theatre:	Middle East
Location:	Golan Heights

Private ►
Israeli Army

This Israeli soldier, dressed in simple olive-green fatigues, is carrying the 9mm Uzi submachine gun. The advantages of the Uzi for this soldier are its compact dimensions, its light weight and its high rate of fire (600 rounds per minute).

SPECIFICATIONS	
Country:	Israel
Date:	1967
Unit:	Israeli Army
Rank:	Private
Theatre:	Middle East
Location:	Jerusalem

Israel Defence Forces, Infantryman 1967

Although it was to be Israel's use of air and armour forces that would provide the defining victories of the Six-Day War, there was much hard fighting on the ground between Israeli infantry and their Arab opponents.

The 9mm Uzi submachine gun was a standard Israeli weapon from 1950 until the late 1960s. It used a telescoping bolt design to reduce the overall dimensions, and the magazine inserted directly into the pistol grip, giving the weapon a balanced centre of gravity.

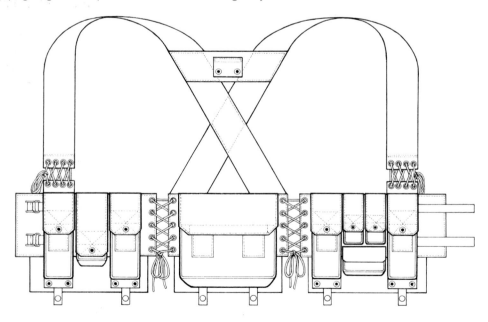

In its first decades, the IDF often had to rely on a mixture of foreign items to make up its equipment. This webbing is a case in point – the two ammunition pouches on the belt are British, while the water bottle and first-aid pouch between them are American, as is the entrenching tool on the pack in the centre.

Private
Israeli Army

The uniform and equipment of the infantryman pictured here is thoroughly eclectic, coming from French, US and Belgian influences, as well as from Israel. The clothing is a mix of French paratroop trousers rendered in jungle camouflage and a woollen shirt, probably made locally. Headgear is the US M1 steel helmet covered with a camouflage net and secured by a large rubber band. In terms of equipment carried, the Israeli-produced webbing belt and straps appear to be based on the British 1944-pattern system, while the ammunition pouches are of the British 1958-pattern.

SPECIFICATIONS	
Country:	Israel
Date:	1967
Unit:	Israeli Army
Rank:	Private
Theatre:	Middle East
Location:	Jerusalem

Arab Forces, Six-Day War 1967

The Six-Day War was a catastrophic defeat for the combined Arab forces. The conflict not only revealed the strengths of the Israel Defence Forces, but it also exposed serious problems of command and control in Arab units.

◀ Private
Egyptian Army Commandos

Although this soldier is wearing mostly local uniform and equipment, the Soviet influence is seen in the Russian infantryman's helmet and also the gas-mask pack, which can just be seen on the left hip. The water bottle is American issue, however.

SPECIFICATIONS	
Country:	Egypt
Date:	1967
Unit:	Egyptian Army Commandos
Rank:	Private
Theatre:	Middle East
Location:	Sinai

Private ▶
Egyptian Army

This soldier carries a blanket around his shoulders for the desert nights, when the temperatures can drop precipitously. Soviet kit is again in evidence. He has no webbing system, just a civilian leather belt fitted with a water bottle and a Soviet-issue haversack.

SPECIFICATIONS	
Country:	Egypt
Date:	1967
Unit:	Egyptian Army
Rank:	Private
Theatre:	Middle East
Location:	Sinai

◀ **Private**
Jordanian Army

The British influence in Jordanian history is apparent here in the British Army Mk 1 steel helmet with camouflage cover, while the 1937-pattern webbing is also of British manufacture. The weapon is US – the M1 Garand. Ammunition for this is carried in British battle-order pouches on the belt.

SPECIFICATIONS	
Country:	Jordan
Date:	1967
Unit:	Jordanian Army
Rank:	Private
Theatre:	Middle East
Location:	West Jordan

Crewman ▶
Egyptian Army

This Egyptian crewman wears a simple cotton khaki overall of Egyptian 1955-issue pattern. His headgear, of Soviet origin, features an internal headset for receiving radio communications; over his left shoulder hangs the throat microphone. The other lead is for the RT/IC internal communications radio.

SPECIFICATIONS	
Country:	Egypt
Date:	1967
Unit:	Egyptian Army
Rank:	Crewman
Theatre:	Middle East
Location:	Sinai

Israeli Elite Units 1970s–90s

Compared to some Western armies, the Israeli forces could appear highly informal. Yet their discipline and training were unquestionable, and they have fielded some of the world's best special forces units.

Crewman ▶
Aeromedical Evacuation Unit

The uniform of Israeli aeromedical units in the 1970s was a copy of the US K2B flight suit. This was a one-piece overall with large, zippered pockets and elasticated ankles. It was held at the waist with a simple web belt. Pistols and water bottles were usually the only types of equipment carried on the body.

SPECIFICATIONS	
Country:	Israel
Date:	1973
Unit:	Aeromedical Evacuation Unit
Rank:	Crewman
Theatre:	Middle East
Location:	Sinai

Corporal ▶
202nd Parachute Brigade

This Israeli soldier patrolling in the Lebanon is wearing the standard olive-green field uniform of the IDF, capped by a ballistic-nylon helmet that acted as the replacement for the old steel variety. The webbing is also Israeli issue, and can be distinguished from foreign supply by the 'boot-lace' fittings connecting the straps to the belt. The rifle is the Israeli Galil.

SPECIFICATIONS	
Country:	Israel
Date:	1982
Unit:	202nd Parachute Brigade
Rank:	Corporal
Theatre:	Middle East
Location:	South Lebanon

TIMELINE 1973 1982 1985 1990s

◀ **1st Lieutenant**
Sayeret Tzanhanim

The Sayeret Tzanhanim is the elite
reconnaissance arm of the Israeli parachute
brigade. This soldier evidently belongs to
an armoured deployment, as indicated by
the Type 602 crewman's helmet, a copy
of US designs, containing full
communications headset.

SPECIFICATIONS	
Country:	Israel
Date:	1985
Unit:	Sayeret Tzanhanim
Rank:	1st Lieutenant
Theatre:	Middle East
Location:	Lebanon

Private ▶
202nd Parachute Brigade

This soldier wears a modern olive-drab
uniform, with kevlar body armour to protect
against small-arm rounds and shell
splinters. He also carries the US M16A2
with the M203 40mm (15.7in) grenade-
launcher attachment.

SPECIFICATIONS	
Country:	Israel
Date:	1990s
Unit:	202nd Parachute Brigade
Rank:	Private
Theatre:	Middle East
Location:	Gaza Strip

Arab and Israeli Forces 1970s–90s

Following the Six-Day War in 1967, the Arab–Israeli conflict rumbled on in the War of Attrition (1967–70), then exploded again with the Yom Kippur War of 1973, which once again led to a major Arab defeat.

◀ Private
Syrian Army

This private on the Golan Heights is dressed in uniform and equipment that is almost entirely of Soviet- or communist-Europe issue. He holds an AK-47 assault rifle, which had such an impact during the Yom Kippur War that it forced the Israelis to redevelop and improve their own small arms.

SPECIFICATIONS	
Country:	Syria
Date:	1973
Unit:	Syrian Army
Rank:	Private
Theatre:	Middle East
Location:	Golan Heights

Gunman ▶
Phalange Militia

This Phalange Party militiaman has patched together a uniform of sorts, mixing a civilian jacket and balaclava helmet with camouflage trousers and combat books. The AK-47 became an insurgent's favourite weapon.

SPECIFICATIONS	
Country:	Lebanon
Date:	1970s
Unit:	Phalange Militia
Rank:	Gunman
Theatre:	Middle East
Location:	Lebanon

1973

1970s

1982

1985

Insurgent ▶
Palestine Liberation Organization

This insurgent of the Palestine Liberation Organization (PLO) is, like many guerrilla fighters, dressed in local civilian clothing. His weapon is the Belgian Samopal 62 'Skorpion', a diminutive 7.65mm (0.32in) submachine gun designed for armoured vehicle crews.

SPECIFICATIONS	
Country:	Palestine/Israel
Date:	1985
Unit:	Palestine Liberation Organization
Rank:	Insurgent
Theatre:	Middle East
Location:	Unknown

◀ Corporal
Syrian Army

This soldier's green beret indicates that he is probably a special forces soldier, although uniforms became somewhat unorthodox during the conflict in Beirut. His uniform is a plain olive-drab trousers and shirt in a Soviet pattern. Syrian commandos could also be seen in a lizard-pattern camouflage.

SPECIFICATIONS	
Country:	Syria
Date:	1982
Unit:	Syrian Army
Rank:	Corporal
Theatre:	Middle East
Location:	Lebanon

Arab and Israeli Forces 1970s–90s

Israel is essentially a militarized nation, with much of the population acting as a ready reserve for times of emergency. It was this capability that made the IDF so respected, although in return it struggled to cope with the growing Arab insurgency during the 1970s and 1980s.

▼ Sniper
Israeli Army

The Israeli soldier here is a sniper, and he is looking through the sight of his 7.62mm (0.3in) M21 Sniper Weapon System rifle. The M21 is a US rifle, and is an accurized development of the M14 rifle. Unlike many sniper weapons, it is gas-operated rather than bolt-action.

SPECIFICATIONS	
Country:	Israel
Date:	1980s
Unit:	Israeli Army
Rank:	Sniper
Theatre:	Middle East
Location:	Unknown

Private ▶
Lebanese Army

This soldier, caught up in the street fighting in Beirut that ravaged the city in the 1980s, is carrying a US M16A1 rifle with plentiful ammunition in Lebanese Army web pouches on the belt. The sling on the M16 is a custom attachment.

SPECIFICATIONS	
Country:	Lebanon
Date:	1982
Unit:	Lebanese Army
Rank:	Private
Theatre:	Middle East
Location:	Lebanon

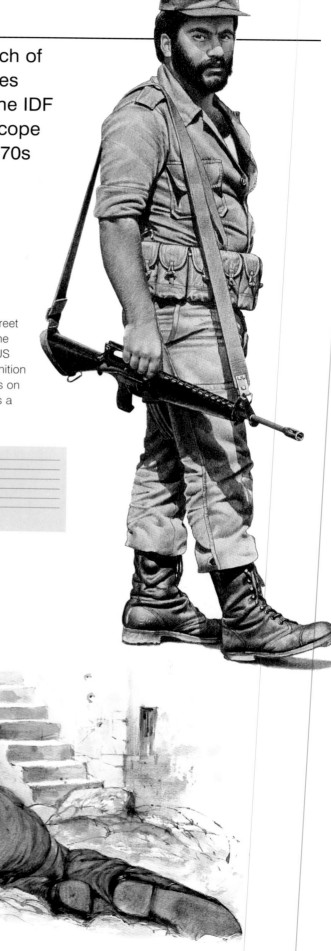

1980s

1982

1990s

1990s

Private ▲
Israeli Army

This soldier is protecting a patrol using the firepower of a 5.56mm (0.22in) Galil rifle fitted with a grenade-firing attachment. The IMI bullet-trap rifle grenades here used could be fired with any type of 5.56mm ammunition and fitted directly onto the muzzle of the Galil.

SPECIFICATIONS	
Country:	Israel
Date:	1990s
Unit:	Israeli Army
Rank:	Private
Theatre:	Middle East
Location:	Gaza Strip

◄ Private
Golani Infantry Brigade

The absence of headgear on this particular Golani infantryman is not unusual, as the IDF often exhibits an informality of dress in operational circumstances (less so in recent times). A brown beret is sometimes worn by those soldiers who have successfully completed their training.

SPECIFICATIONS	
Country:	Israel
Date:	1990s
Unit:	Golani Infantry Brigade
Rank:	Private
Theatre:	Middle East
Location:	Lebanese border

Latin American Insurgencies 1950s–80s

South and Central America became hotbeds of revolutionary fervour from the 1950s, giving rise to brutal civil and insurgency conflicts. Naturally, US arms and equipment were much in evidence in the fighting.

◀ **Guerrilla**
Cuban Revolutionary Forces

Underneath his civilian jacket – emblazoned with a revolutionary Cuban patch – this Cuban fighter wears a standard US herringbone-twill combat uniform. The webbing is US-type, and the rifle is the venerable Springfield M1903.

SPECIFICATIONS	
Country:	Cuba
Date:	1959
Unit:	Cuban Revolutionary Forces
Rank:	Guerrilla
Theatre:	Latin America
Location:	Cuba

Gunner ▶
Royal Artillery

This Royal Artillery soldier in British Guiana is wearing khaki drill trousers, short puttees and a temperate uniform shirt with its sleeves rolled up. The only regimental piece of kit is the dark blue beret of the RA. He is armed with a Sterling SMG.

SPECIFICATIONS	
Country:	Britain
Date:	1964
Unit:	Royal Artillery
Rank:	Gunner
Theatre:	Latin America
Location:	British Guiana

TIMELINE   1959   1964   1980   1980s

◀ **Private**
Salvadorian Army

The entire uniform is US-produced, the shirt
and trousers being simple olive-drab
fatigues, while the helmet is the vintage
M1 steel helmet. Webbing is the US M1943
pattern with an M1956 belt, but the rifle is
German in origin – a 7.62mm (0.3in) Heckler
& Koch G3A3.

SPECIFICATIONS	
Country:	El Salvador
Date:	1980
Unit:	Salvadorian Army
Rank:	Private
Theatre:	Latin America
Location:	El Salvador

Guerrilla ▼
Contras

The Contras were a US-backed insurgent
movement in Nicaragua, active between the
late 1970s and the 1990s. This guerrilla has
put a US camouflage jacket and webbing
over civilian clothes, topped with an olive-
green field cap. He is armed with a heavy-
calibre revolver.

SPECIFICATIONS	
Country:	Nicaragua
Date:	1980s
Unit:	Contras
Rank:	Guerrilla
Theatre:	Latin America
Location:	Nicaragua

North/South Vietnamese Forces, Vietnam War 1963–75

Although the South Vietnamese forces had the full industrial and military support of the United States, the North Vietnamese Army (NVA) and the Viet Cong (VC) demonstrated greater strategic focus and personal motivation.

◀ Guerrilla
Viet Cong

This soldier is wearing the classic black 'pyjamas' we now associate with the VC, although civilian clothing of many different types was equally, if not more, prevalent. He wears a palm-leaf peasant hat, while his footwear consists of rubber sandals of the sort that were often cut from car tyres.

SPECIFICATIONS	
Country:	South Vietnam
Date:	1966
Unit:	Viet Cong
Rank:	Guerrilla
Theatre:	Vietnam
Location:	South Vietnam

Guerrilla ▶
Viet Cong

This guerrilla holds an AK-47 and carries ammunition for it in the 'ChiCom' chest pouches (for 'Chinese Communist', after the nation that pioneered the style) used by many Viet Cong. It was ideal for jungle warfare, as it was comfortable. Each pouch held two AK magazines.

SPECIFICATIONS	
Country:	South Vietnam
Date:	1967
Unit:	Viet Cong
Rank:	Guerrilla
Theatre:	Vietnam
Location:	South Vietnam

TIMELINE   1966   1967   1967   1969

◄ Guerrilla
Viet Cong

This Viet Cong fighter is dressed with ultimate simplicity, his provisions carried in nothing more than a simple cloth roll. His firearm is distinctive – it is the Danish Madsen M50 submachine gun, a 9mm Parabellum weapon.

SPECIFICATIONS	
Country:	South Vietnam
Date:	1967
Unit:	Viet Cong
Rank:	Guerrilla
Theatre:	Vietnam
Location:	South Vietnam

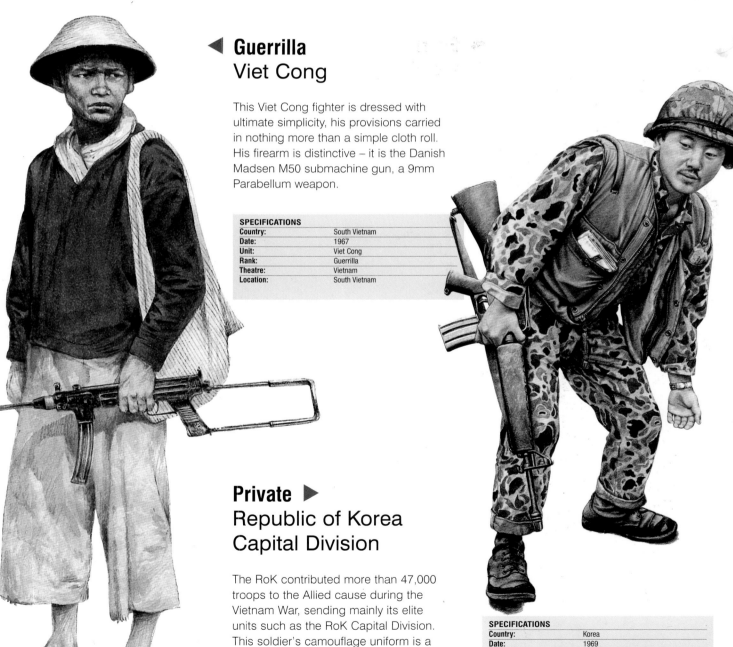

Private ►
Republic of Korea
Capital Division

The RoK contributed more than 47,000 troops to the Allied cause during the Vietnam War, sending mainly its elite units such as the RoK Capital Division. This soldier's camouflage uniform is a Korean version of the foliage patterns used by certain US units in the Pacific in World War II.

SPECIFICATIONS	
Country:	Korea
Date:	1969
Unit:	Republic of Korea Capital Division
Rank:	Private
Theatre:	Vietnam
Location:	South Vietnam

Army of the Republic of Vietnam, Soldier 1970

Despite huge investment by the US in the materiel and training of the Army of the Republic of Vietnam (ARVN), and despite having some truly elite units, the ARVN never fulfilled its potential as a military force and was constantly weakened by factionalism and poor morale.

The Browning Automatic Rifle (BAR) was developed during World War I, but it served in some ARVN units until the late 1960s. It was a gas-operated gun that fired up to 550rpm, despite the fact that it only had a 20-round magazine.

The M16A1 rifle was distributed to the ARVN in huge numbers by the United States. It was a 5.56mm (0.22in) weapon that fired its bullets at extremely high velocities – 1000mps (3280ft/sec). It had an effective range of about 500m (1640ft).

SPECIFICATIONS

SPECIFICATIONS	
Country:	South Vietnam
Date:	1970
Unit:	ARVN
Rank:	1st Lieutenant
Theatre:	Vietnam
Location:	South Vietnam

1st Lieutenant
ARVN

This soldier is pictured in 1970, a time when the US was withdrawing from the Vietnam War and leaving South Vietnam to a fated future. His camouflage uniform is in the 'tiger-stripe' pattern, designed by the Vietnamese Marine Corps in 1959 and worn by many US Special Forces soldiers. It features a shirt and trousers, with a matching slouch hat displaying two gold blossoms, the rank marking of a 1st lieutenant. His webbing is Vietnamese-made and has nylon mesh panels instead of straps for coolness. His M16 ammunition is contained in the chest pouches, while on his US M1967 belt are two M26A2 fragmentation-grenades.

US and Allied Forces, Vietnam War 1963–73

Customization was a major feature of many US soldiers' equipment and uniform throughout the Vietnam War, with many troops making adaptations using local sources, and adding their own artwork and slogans.

◄ Captain
5th Special Forces Group

This Special Forces captain is wearing the olive-green fatigues worn by most US soldiers in the early part of the Vietnam War. This initial pattern had slanting patch pockets on the shirt and exposed buttons. The webbing is the M1956 load-carrying equipment.

SPECIFICATIONS	
Country:	United States
Date:	1965
Unit:	5th Special Forces Group
Rank:	Captain
Theatre:	Vietnam
Location:	South Vietnam

Trooper ►
US 1st Air Cavalry Division

As was usual for US personnel in Vietnam at this time, this soldier is wearing the standard green fatigues. He is very heavily armed; the three bags suspended from his left shoulder each carries a Claymore anti-personnel mine.

SPECIFICATIONS	
Country:	United States
Date:	1966
Unit:	US 1st Air Cavalry Division
Rank:	Trooper
Theatre:	Vietnam
Location:	South Vietnam

TIMELINE   1965   1966   1967   1968

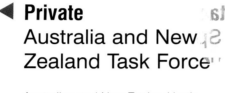

◀ Private
Australia and New Zealand Task Force

Australian and New Zealand both contributed combat troops to the Vietnam conflict. This New Zealander private has covered his webbing straps in waterproof plastic; the Vietnamese jungle climate could quickly eat through exposed cloth straps.

SPECIFICATIONS	
Country:	New Zealand
Date:	1967
Unit:	Australian and New Zealand Task Force
Rank:	Private
Theatre:	Vietnam
Location:	South Vietnam

Private 1st Class ▶
US Marine Corps

Although Marines tended towards older kit issues, this soldier has modern equipment in his M1956 webbing. His plastic water bottles are the latest pattern (previously the water bottles were black enamel). As a seasonal touch, he carries a miniature Christmas tree.

SPECIFICATIONS	
Country:	United States
Date:	1968
Unit:	US Marine Corps
Rank:	Private 1st Class
Theatre:	Vietnam
Location:	Hue

US and Allied Forces, Vietnam War 1963–73

The Vietnam War saw the development and heavy use of US Special Forces units, in missions that took them across the borders of South Vietnam into neighbouring Laos and Cambodia.

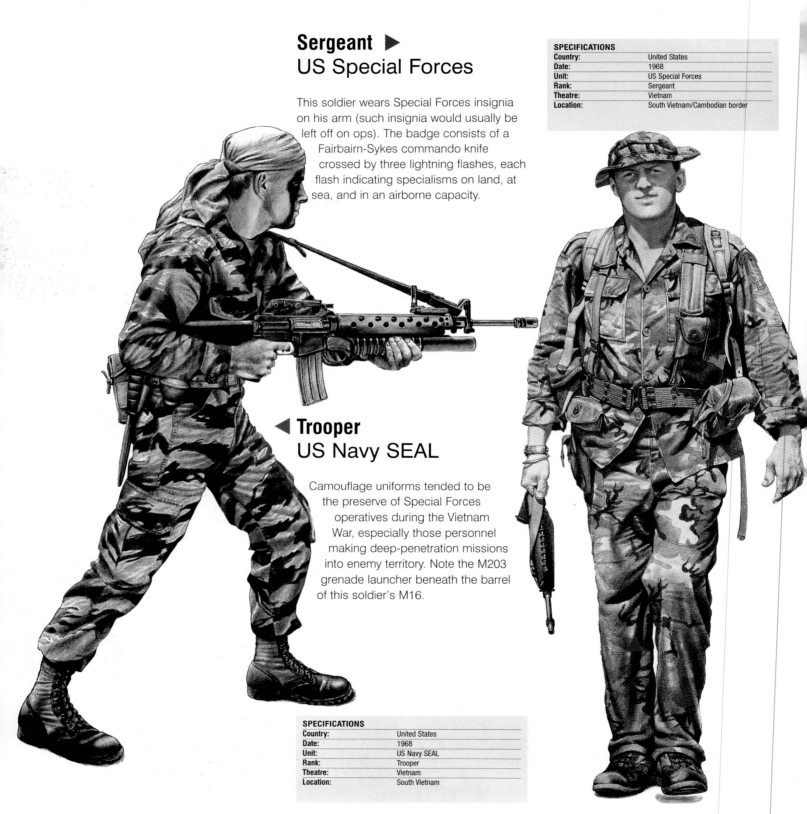

Sergeant ▶
US Special Forces

This soldier wears Special Forces insignia on his arm (such insignia would usually be left off on ops). The badge consists of a Fairbairn-Sykes commando knife crossed by three lightning flashes, each flash indicating specialisms on land, at sea, and in an airborne capacity.

SPECIFICATIONS	
Country:	United States
Date:	1968
Unit:	US Special Forces
Rank:	Sergeant
Theatre:	Vietnam
Location:	South Vietnam/Cambodian border

◀ Trooper
US Navy SEAL

Camouflage uniforms tended to be the preserve of Special Forces operatives during the Vietnam War, especially those personnel making deep-penetration missions into enemy territory. Note the M203 grenade launcher beneath the barrel of this soldier's M16.

SPECIFICATIONS	
Country:	United States
Date:	1968
Unit:	US Navy SEAL
Rank:	Trooper
Theatre:	Vietnam
Location:	South Vietnam

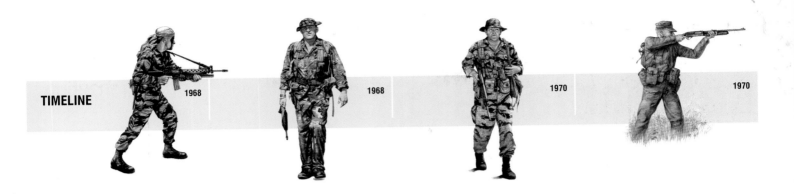

TIMELINE

1968

1968

1970

1970

◄ Trooper
Australian Army
Training Team Vietnam

This soldier, on a jungle patrol, wears the tiger-stripe pattern of camouflage, which became a virtual signature of Allied Special Forces during the war. His kit signifies the likelihood of combat – he carries a FN FAL rifle with two ammunition pouches on his belt, and M8 smoke grenades.

SPECIFICATIONS	
Country:	Australia
Date:	1970
Unit:	AATTV
Rank:	Trooper
Theatre:	Vietnam
Location:	South Vietnam

Marine ►
US Marine
Corps

Dressed in standard US Marine Corps olive-green fatigues, this marine is armed with a 12-gauge Remington Model 870 pump-action shotgun – an extremely reliable and powerful close-quarters firearm.

SPECIFICATIONS	
Country:	United States
Date:	1970
Unit:	US Marine Corps
Rank:	Marine
Theatre:	Vietnam
Location:	South Vietnam

Khmer Rouge Guerrilla, Cambodia 1975

The leadership and soldiers of Pol Pot's Khmer Rouge inflicted one of the worst genocides in 20th-century history within Cambodia, renamed Kampuchea after the Khmer Rouge takeover in 1975.

The Khmer Rouge used whatever weapons it could lay its hands on, including the US-made M79 'Blooper' grenade launcher. This single-shot, breech-loading gun fired a 40mm (1.57in) grenade to a distance of about 400m (1312ft), with a lethal kill radius of more than 5m (16ft).

Ex-French Army stocks of weapons were also heavily used in Southeast Asia. The MAT 49 was a 9mm Parabellum submachine gun carried by French forces in the Indochina War. It was a simple blowback weapon, firing at 600rpm.

Guerilla
Khmer Rouge

Being a guerrilla army, the Khmer Rouge had some diversity of dress and kit, yet there were essentially two patterns of recognizable 'uniform'. The first was a formal olive-green or dark brown military outfit sourced from the Khmer Rouge's main communist suppliers, China and North Vietnam. This soldier wears a Chinese Liberation Army cap, yet the rest of his appearance is perhaps more common of the Khmer Rouge. The jacket and trousers are civilian working clothes, following the Khmer Rouge's proletarian philosophy, while the neckscarf (often red and white) was Khmer Rouge identification. He is armed with a Type 56 assault rifle, with ammunition in 'Chi Com' (Chinese Communist) chest pouches.

SPECIFICATIONS	
Country:	Cambodia
Date:	1975
Unit:	Khmer Rouge
Rank:	Guerrilla
Theatre:	Southeast Asia
Location:	Cambodia

Indo–Pakistan Conflicts 1965–71

India and Pakistan have fought three major wars since Indian independence in 1947, costing hundreds of thousands of lives. On account of their colonial history, both sides brought recognizably British traditions to the battlefield.

◀ Lance-Corporal
Pakistani Army

This lance-corporal of the Pakistani Army wears the standard British Army 1940s and 1950s khaki tropical drill uniform, this being accompanied by British 1937-pattern webbing. It should be noted, however, that Soviet webbing was also worn by the Pakistani and Indian forces.

SPECIFICATIONS	
Country:	Pakistan
Date:	1965
Unit:	Pakistani Army
Rank:	Lance-Corporal
Theatre:	South Asia
Location:	Pakistan

Lance-Corporal ▶
Indian Army

The soldier here appears almost identical to Indian Army soldiers serving as British Empire forces during World War II. The light khaki shirt and battledress trousers are unadorned except for a single rank chevron on the sleeve. The webbing is British 1937-pattern with two utility/ammunition pouches.

SPECIFICATIONS	
Country:	India
Date:	1965
Unit:	Indian Army
Rank:	Lance-Corporal
Theatre:	South Asia
Location:	Kashmir

1965

1965

1971

1971

◀ Private
Pakistani Army

This soldier is wearing the US M1 steel helmet, but the webbing system is the British Army 1958-pattern. The uniform itself is the Pakistani khaki drill tunic and trousers, this being worn with a V-neck pullover in olive-green, which, despite its informal appearance, was a regular item of Pakistani Army uniform.

SPECIFICATIONS	
Country:	Pakistan
Date:	1971
Unit:	Pakistani Army
Rank:	Private
Theatre:	South Asia
Location:	West Pakistan

Guerrilla ▶
Bangladesh Liberation Army

The *Mukti Bahini* (Bangladesh Liberation Army) guerrilla here is powerfully armed with a German MG3 machine gun, an updated version of the MG42. His helmet is of British Army origin, but its lines are obscured by camouflage.

SPECIFICATIONS	
Country:	Bangladesh
Date:	1971
Unit:	Bangladesh Liberation Army
Rank:	Guerrilla
Theatre:	South Asia
Location:	East Pakistan

Indian Army, Paratrooper 1971

During India's invasion of East Pakistan in 1971, the Indian Army relied on its airborne forces to make rapid assaults and take the Pakistani forces by surprise. Occupation of the region was achieved in just 12 days.

The L1A1 was the British Army's version of the FN FAL rifle. It was little different from the original, but had its dimensions altered slightly to suit manufacture in imperial measurements. It would also only fire in semi-auto mode, not full-auto.

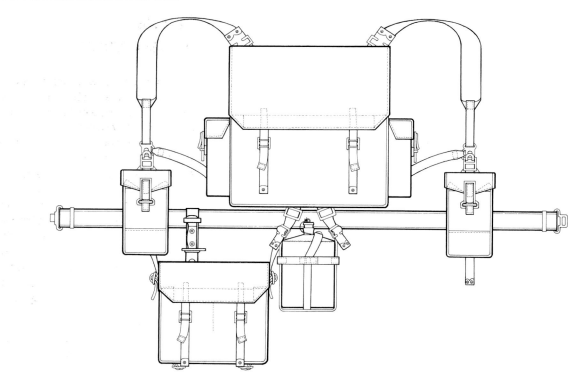

This Indian Army equipment is based on the British 1937-pattern webbing, albeit adapted for different kit and weapons. The two pouches on the belt are for ammunition, while hanging from the belt is a side pouch, water bottle and bayonet. The central backpack has two side pouches.

Private
Indian Army

This para has moved on from the khaki battledress of the 1960s, but the British influence remains, albeit in an updated form. He mostly wears British parachute clothing, including the Denison jump-smock in Disruptive Pattern Material (DPM); the smock features the white parachute and blue wings brevet on a khaki field. The helmet is also British para issue. Over the smock is the 1937-pattern webbing system, superseded by the 1958-pattern in the British Army but still a good system of load-carrying. The pouches hold 30-round magazines for the 7.62mm (0.3in) L1A1 rifle, here with its short knife bayonet fitted.

SPECIFICATIONS	
Country:	India
Date:	1971
Unit:	Indian Army
Rank:	Private
Theatre:	East Pakistan
Location:	Indo-Pakistani War

Peacekeeping Troops 1960–Present

Peacekeeping deployments increased dramatically in number with the creation of the United Nations (UN) in 1945. Africa, the Middle East and the Balkans have been the major destinations for peacekeeping forces.

◀ Private
Swedish Army (UN)

This infantryman's UN status is clearly indicated by the blue US M1-pattern helmet and the blue arm badge, both displaying the distinctive badge of the UN: white hemisphere and laurel leaves on a blue background. The only other insignia that this soldier wears is the crossed rifles of the Swedish infantry on the shoulder straps.

SPECIFICATIONS	
Country:	Sweden
Date:	1960
Unit:	Swedish Army (UN)
Rank:	Private
Theatre:	Africa
Location:	Congo

Warrant Officer ▶
Princess Patricia's Light Infantry

This soldier's weapon is the British Army's L1A1 Self-Loading Rifle, and his uniform is standard Canadian olive-drab. The webbing, however, is based on the US ALICE system, worn with two ammunition/utility pouches at the front.

SPECIFICATIONS	
Country:	Canada
Date:	1970s
Unit:	Princess Patricia's Light Infantry
Rank:	Warrant Officer
Theatre:	Europe
Location:	Cyprus

TIMELINE   1960   1970s   1982   2001

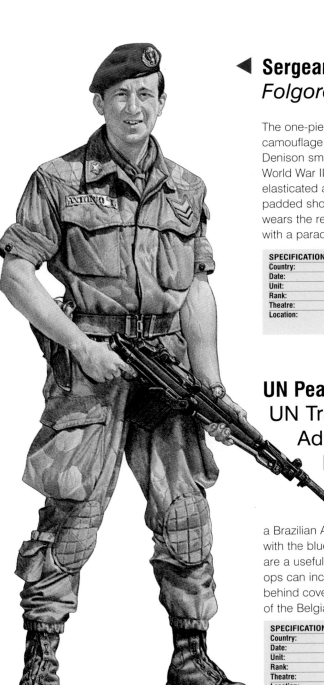

◀ Sergeant-Major
Folgore Brigade

The one-piece jump uniform here, in a camouflage similar to that of the British Denison smock, has its roots in Italian World War II para tunics. It features elasticated ankles and reinforced and padded shoulders and knees. This para wears the red beret of paras worldwide, with a parachute/laurel-leaf badge.

SPECIFICATIONS	
Country:	Italy
Date:	1982
Unit:	Folgore Brigade
Rank:	Sergeant-Major
Theatre:	Middle East
Location:	Lebanon

UN Peacekeeper ▶
UN Transitional Administration in East Timor

This Brazilian UN peacekeeper is wearing a Brazilian Army service camouflage uniform with the blue UN helmet. The kneepads are a useful piece of kit – peacekeeping ops can include lots of time spent kneeling behind cover. The rifle is a Brazilian version of the Belgian FN FAL.

SPECIFICATIONS	
Country:	Brazil
Date:	2001
Unit:	UNTAET
Rank:	UN Peacekeeper
Theatre:	East Asia
Location:	East Timor

Indonesian Marine, Borneo 1963

The Malayan 'Confrontation' in Borneo between 1963 and 1966 brought into conflict Indonesia – protesting against the formation of the Malaysian Federation – and British and Malaysian forces. The Marines were Indonesia's premier frontline troops.

Produced shortly after World War II, the vz52 was a Czech self-loading rifle chambered for 7.62 x 45mm (0.3 x 1.8in) M52 cartridges, although following the Soviet takeover of Czechoslovakia it was rechambered for the 7.62 x 39mm (0.3 x 1.5in) M1943 Soviet round.

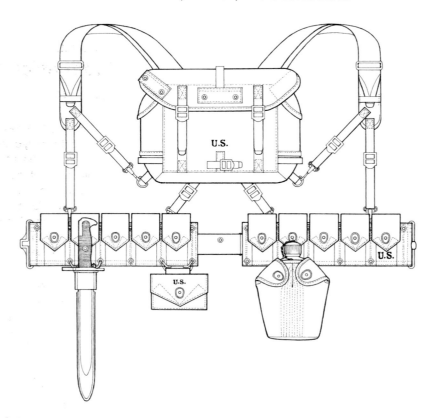

US kit and equipment was very common in Southeast Asia, such as the US paratrooper webbing seen here. It features 10 ammunition pouches on the belt, from which hang a bayonet, first-aid pack and water bottle. The main pack held rations and other items of equipment.

Marine
Indonesian Marine Corps

In dress, the Indonesian marines owed much to the long-standing US presence in the Pacific region, as can be seen in the uniform (but not the firearm) of this soldier. His steel helmet is the old US M1-pattern, covered in a dappled camouflage to match the rest of his uniform. This camouflage pattern – brown and olive-green patches on a light green base – was a US camouflage used during the Pacific campaign in World War II. His webbing, US airborne issue from the 1950s, includes the 10-pouch ammunition belt originally designed for the M1 Garand rifle. The Czech Vz52 rifle features a folding bayonet.

SPECIFICATIONS	
Country:	Indonesia
Date:	1963
Unit:	Indonesian Marine Corps
Rank:	Marine
Theatre:	Borneo
Location:	Indonesian Confrontation

Soviet–Afghan War 1979–89

The Soviet–Afghan War was a 10-year conflict that pitted the full might of the Soviet armed forces against the resilience and ingenuity of the *Mujahideen* warriors. Utlimately, the Soviets were defeated, suffering more than 70,000 casualties.

◀ Private
Afghan Army

The standard Afghan Army grey-drab combat uniform and soft-peaked cap provided scant protection from the severe Afghan weather. The webbing is of local manufacture, made from cheap leather, and the civilian belt has an inadvisably shiny gold buckle, which could be an aiming point for a sniper.

SPECIFICATIONS	
Country:	Afghanistan
Date:	1979
Unit:	Afghan Army
Rank:	Private
Theatre:	Central Asia
Location:	Afghanistan

Paratrooper ▶
Soviet Airborne Forces

This paratrooper is wearing a one-piece padded jumpsuit, though on the ground the standard infantry uniform would be worn. The leather head-protector seen here would have a helmet over it during jumps. Leather webbing supports a utility pouch (his left) and a 9mm (0.35in) APS pistol (his right).

SPECIFICATIONS	
Country:	Afghanistan
Date:	1979
Unit:	Soviet Airborne Forces
Rank:	Paratrooper
Theatre:	Central Asia
Location:	Afghanistan

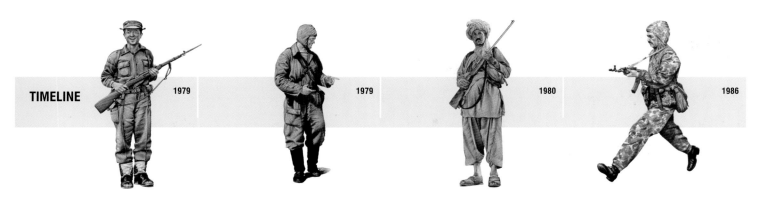

| TIMELINE | 1979 | 1979 | 1980 | 1986 |

◀ Guerrilla
Mujahideen

Ceremonial elements of dress here include the traditional headdress and the blue sash wrapped around the upper body. No webbing is worn, and all supplies are carried in the musette bag hung over one shoulder. The weapon is a civilian bolt-action hunting rifle.

SPECIFICATIONS	
Country:	Afghanistan
Date:	1980
Unit:	*Mujahideen*
Rank:	Guerrilla
Theatre:	Central Asia
Location:	Afghanistan

Sergeant ▶
Spetsnaz

This soldier has a hooded, one-piece leaf-pattern camouflage uniform of a type often worn by Soviet special forces. What are not typical are the calf-length high boots, based on patterns worn by soldiers in Imperial Russia. His weapon is the AKS-74, a 5.45mm (0.21in) version of the AK-47.

SPECIFICATIONS	
Country:	Afghanistan
Date:	1986
Unit:	Spetsnaz
Rank:	Sergeant
Theatre:	Central Asia
Location:	Afghanistan

Soviet Army, Sergeant-Major, Afghanistan 1980

Not all Soviet infantry were well dressed for the bitter winter climate of Afghanistan during the Soviet Union's occupation, and morale was extremely depressed. This sergeant-major, however, has good kit, and he is seen here on guard duty over traffic movements in west Afghanistan.

The Kraz-255B was a versatile Soviet truck manufactured from the 1960s. It had a powerful V8 diesel engine, and it included a type-pressure regulation system to improve mobility over difficult terrain. As well as providing logistics, it was adapted to various engineering roles.

The BMP-1 was one of the first of what are known as infantry fighting vehicles (IFVs). It was fully amphibious, could carry eight troops, and was armed with a 73mm (2.87in) cannon, a Sagger anti-tank missile and a 7.62mm (0.3in) coaxial machine gun.

Sergeant-Major
Motorized Rifle Battalion

The soldier's head is protected by the fur
ushanka, this having earflaps and the
communist Red Star centred on the fur front
flap. Over his khaki infantry uniform he
wears the standard Soviet-issue winter
greatcoat, grey-brown in colour and deeply
fly-fronted, without exposed buttons, to
protect against wind chill (essential in
Afghanistan's mountainous terrain). On his
belt he has a Makarov PM pistol (the
standard Soviet infantry pistol), an
ammunition pouch (right hip), a respirator
case and a bayonet for his AKM rifle, with
wire-cutting scabbard clearly visible.

SPECIFICATIONS	
Country:	Soviet Union
Date:	1980
Unit:	Motorized Rifle Battalion
Rank:	Sergeant-Major
Theatre:	Central Asia
Location:	Afghanistan

British Army, Falklands War 1982

On 2 April 1982, Argentine forces invaded the Falklands Islands, quickly overcoming the small British garrison. Within days, however, the British had assembled a task force of navy, army and air force units to retake the islands.

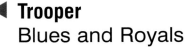

◀ Trooper
Blues and Royals

This tank crewman wears a plastic helmet fitted with communications equipment. Additional equipment is the pair of Avimo prismatic binoculars slung around his neck and a 9mm (0.35in)Sterling submachine gun.

SPECIFICATIONS	
Country:	Britain
Date:	1982
Unit:	Blues and Royals
Rank:	Trooper
Theatre:	South Atlantic
Location:	Falklands

Captain ▶
Royal Artillery

This captain is wearing 'Arctic windproof combat smock and trousers', to use its official nomenclature, in the 'RM' pattern (defined by its wire-stiffened hood). He has a pair of ski-march boots, to which further waterproofing is added via the gaiters.

SPECIFICATIONS	
Country:	Britain
Date:	1982
Unit:	Royal Artillery
Rank:	Captain
Theatre:	South Atlantic
Location:	Falklands

◄ Sergeant-Major
3rd Battalion, Parachute Regiment

The uniform here is the Arctic windproof combat smock and trousers, which essentially consisted of a hooded DPM jacket. This combat dress was issued to both 2 and 3 Para and also to 3 Commando Brigade RM.

SPECIFICATIONS	
Country:	Britain
Date:	1982
Unit:	3rd Battalion, Parachute Regiment
Rank:	Sergeant-Major
Theatre:	South Atlantic
Location:	Falklands

Gurkha ►
Gurkha Rifles

This Gurkha soldier wears a waterproof jacket over his DPM uniform, and he has the standard British Army 1958-pattern webbing system. The pouch at the front would contain magazines for the soldier's L1A1 self-loading rifle.

SPECIFICATIONS	
Country:	Britain
Date:	1982
Unit:	Gurkha Rifles
Rank:	Gurkha
Theatre:	South Atlantic
Location:	Falklands

British Army, Falklands War 1982

The British Army performed some heroic feats on the Falklands. At one point, for example, British paras and commandos marched 64km (40 miles) into battle with 50kg (100lb) of pack to each man.

▼ Radio Transmissions Operator
British Army

Efficient radio comms were essential, both to communicate between infantry units and the direct ground- and naval-based artillery fire. This soldier is wearing the bulky radio set on his back; as well as transmitting voice signals, it could also send out morse and other coded messages.

SPECIFICATIONS	
Country:	Britain
Date:	1982
Unit:	British Army
Rank:	Radio Transmissions Operator
Theatre:	South Atlantic
Location:	Falklands

Guardsman ▶
Scots Guards

This soldier of the Scots Guards wears a pair of quilted trousers, part of the British Army uniform designed for severe cold-weather conditions. The fingerless gloves allow him to retain good control of his rifle; note also the dressing taped to the stock of the gun for medical emergencies.

SPECIFICATIONS	
Country:	Britain
Date:	1982
Unit:	Scots Guards
Rank:	Guardsman
Theatre:	South Atlantic
Location:	Falklands

Engineer
Royal Engineers

The DPM camouflage jacket worn by this Royal Engineer featured four large pockets on the smock; the matching trousers had two 'bellows' pockets. The British Army Directly Moulded Sole (DMS) boot proved to be a poor performer in cold, wet weather.

SPECIFICATIONS	
Country:	Britain
Date:	1982
Unit:	Royal Engineers
Rank:	Engineer
Theatre:	South Atlantic
Location:	Falklands

Guardsman ▶
Welsh Guards

This Welsh Guards soldier is armed with the superb Belgian FN MAG, adapted for the British Army as the L7A2 General Purpose Machine Gun (GPMG). As its British name suggests, it could be used for a range of fire missions, from light support to sustained area fire.

SPECIFICATIONS	
Country:	Britain
Date:	1982
Unit:	Welsh Guards
Rank:	Guardsman
Theatre:	South Atlantic
Location:	Falklands

British Army, Falklands War 1982

Argentine forces surrendered on 14 June 1982, after one of the most efficient ground campaigns in British Army history. A total of 255 British servicemen had died to retake the islands, compared to more than 900 Argentine fatalities.

◁ Gunner
Royal Artillery

The 'Camo Dog Earflap' cap soon became an essential piece of uniform on the Falklands Islands, as the troops had to cope with sub-zero conditions. This soldier is a gunner with the Royal Artillery, part of a crew manning an 105mm (4.1in) L118 Light Gun howitzer.

SPECIFICATIONS	
Country:	Britain
Date:	1982
Unit:	Royal Artillery
Rank:	Gunner
Theatre:	South Atlantic
Location:	Falklands

Corporal ▶
Royal Military Police

In time-honoured tradition, this corporal of the Royal Military Police wears the 'MP' armband. He is armed with a handgun, the butt of the pistol attached to a lanyard that runs over the shoulder. Waterproof leggings and overboots provide protection against rain and snow.

SPECIFICATIONS	
Country:	Britain
Date:	1982
Unit:	Royal Military Police
Rank:	Corporal
Theatre:	South Atlantic
Location:	Falklands

Paratrooper
Parachute Regiment

The webbing of this British paratrooper has three pouches at the rear for rifle magazines. The standard British Army rifle at the time was the 7.62mm (0.3in) L1A1. Although it only fired in semi-auto mode, it had formidable take-down power.

SPECIFICATIONS	
Country:	Britain
Date:	1982
Unit:	Parachute Regiment
Rank:	Paratrooper
Theatre:	South Atlantic
Location:	Falklands

Soldier ▶
British Army

Two patterns of Disruptive Pattern Material (DPM) camouflage uniform were issued to the British Army in the 1960s. British soldiers like the man here went to war in the Falklands in the 1968 pattern. Two years after the conflict, a new pattern was issued, the 1984 pattern.

SPECIFICATIONS	
Country:	Britain
Date:	1982
Unit:	British Army
Rank:	Soldier
Theatre:	South Atlantic
Location:	Falklands

British Air Power, Falklands War 1982

Air power was critical to the British success in the Falklands War. Carrier-borne Harriers provided air defence and ground-attack duties, while helicopter crews performed rescue and logistics missions.

◀ Corporal
Army Air Corps

The soldier here is an Army Air Corps corporal, acting as a door gunner on a Gazelle helicopter. His uniform is fairly standard for the Falklands campaign. A windproof DPM smock is combined with a pair of lightweight OG nylon khaki trousers and insulated flying boots.

SPECIFICATIONS	
Country:	Britain
Date:	1982
Unit:	Army Air Corps
Rank:	Corporal
Theatre:	South Atlantic
Location:	Falklands

Helicopter Pilot ▶
British Army

Similarly dressed to the adjacent figure, this British Army helicopter pilot wears an inflatable life-jacket over his DPM jacket. A handgun is kept in a holster on his web belt, the weapon probably being something like a 9mm (0.35in) Browning Hi-Power.

SPECIFICATIONS	
Country:	Britain
Date:	1982
Unit:	British Army
Rank:	Helicopter Pilot
Theatre:	South Atlantic
Location:	Falklands

TIMELINE   1982   1982   1982   1982

◄ Squadron Leader
No. 1 Squadron RAF,
HMS *Hermes*

This RAF officer is seen in full flying gear. On the outside he wears an olive, one-piece flying overall that features clear plastic map pockets on the knees. Beneath is a Mk 10 immersion suit. He also wears the Mk 22 inflatable life-preserver.

SPECIFICATIONS	
Country:	Britain
Date:	1982
Unit:	No. 1 Squadron RAF, HMS *Hermes*
Rank:	Squadron Leader
Theatre:	South Atlantic
Location:	Falklands

Deck Crew ►
Royal Navy

As a member of naval deck crew for helicopter operations, this sailor wears a high-visibility waterproof uniform and a communications headset. Part of his responsibility would be to guide helicopters onto their landing pads.

SPECIFICATIONS	
Country:	Britain
Date:	1982
Unit:	Royal Navy
Rank:	Deck Crew
Theatre:	South Atlantic
Location:	Falklands

Argentine Buzo Tactico Commandos, Falklands 1982

The Argentine Marines' own special forces unit – the Buzo Tactico – played an active part in the Falklands War, particularly in the initial invasion and the capture of Port Stanley. Yet the rest of their war was inauspicious; the unit suffered significant casualties and was outperformed by British Army units.

The Sterling submachine gun was a 9mm (0.35in) Parabellum weapon that entered service with the British Army in 1953. It was a reliable and popular firearm, and its side-mounted 34-round magazine made it ideally suited to prone firing.

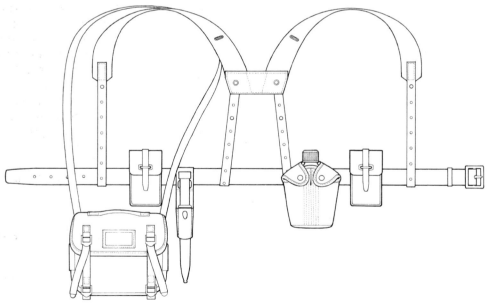

Here is a typical set of Argentine webbing. There are just two small ammunition pouches on the web belt, each capable of holding an additional magazine; the belt also features a water bottle and a bayonet frog. The canvas side pack would be for provisions.

Unknown rank
Buzo Tactico

Like all special forces units, the soldiers of the Buzo Tactico had the best uniforms and equipment of their nation, usually hand-selected by the soldiers themselves. Much of this trooper's uniform is not military at all – the quilted jacket and trousers are civilian mountaineering wear – though the woollen hat is traditionally worn by Argentine special forces as a signature item. The weapon is the British L34A1, a suppressed version of the Sterling submachine gun; magazines, stored in a leather pouch on the hip, are next to a 9mm (0.35in) Browning pistol.

SPECIFICATIONS	
Country:	Argentina
Date:	1982
Unit:	Buzo Tactico
Rank:	Unknown
Theatre:	South Atlantic
Location:	Falklands

British Special Forces, Falklands War 1982

British Special Forces performed a variety of combat and reconnaissance missions during the Falklands War, including an operation to retake South Georgia and a diversionary raid on Argentine positions at Goose Green.

◀ Trooper
22 SAS Regiment

Arranged around a 1958-pattern webbing belt, the equipment this soldier carries is restricted mainly to ammunition pouches and water bottles, though a kidney pouch at the back makes provision for carrying demolitions materials or various survival supplies.

SPECIFICATIONS	
Country:	Britain
Date:	1982
Unit:	22 SAS Regiment
Rank:	Trooper
Theatre:	South Atlantic
Location:	Falkland Islands

Marine ▶
Special Boat Service

This SBS soldier is heavily kitted out in an Arctic smock and trousers – both rendered in the DPM camouflage pattern – and wears a Bergen rucksack. Other features include civilian mountaineering boots and waterproof gaiters and a zip-neck Norwegian Army shirt.

SPECIFICATIONS	
Country:	Britain
Date:	1982
Unit:	Special Boat Service
Rank:	Marine
Theatre:	South Atlantic
Location:	Falkland Islands

◀ NCO
40 Commando, Royal Marines

The Royal Marine soldier here is armed with the 9mm (0.35in) L2A3 Sterling submachine gun, a sound weapon for close-quarters assault work. The Sterling's side-mounted magazine allowed the user to adopt a prone firing position when required.

SPECIFICATIONS	
Country:	Britain
Date:	1982
Unit:	40 Commando, Royal Marines
Rank:	NCO
Theatre:	South Atlantic
Location:	Falkland Islands

Marine ▶
Special Boat Service

The injured SBS soldier here is in full combat gear – generally the SBS wear standard Royal Marines uniforms. It is usually only possible to distinguish the SBS by the combination of parachute wings and a 'Swimmer-Canoeist' badge worn on the right shoulder and forearm.

SPECIFICATIONS	
Country:	Britain
Date:	1982
Unit:	Special Boat Service
Rank:	Marine
Theatre:	South Atlantic
Location:	Falkland Islands

Argentine Senior Sergeant, Marines, Falklands War 1982

During the Falklands War in 1980, the arctic conditions of the South Atlantic posed a challenge to both sides. Although standards of uniform wavered throughout the Argentine Army, this soldier has good clothing for the environment – the Argentine Marines tended to receive a higher quality of winter uniform than regular units.

The FN FAL Para version was designed to provide a more compact version of the standard rifle for special forces and airborne soldiers' use. It featured a folding metal skeleton stock and a shortened barrel.

The CETME was another extremely common firearm in Latin American armies. Developed by Spain, it was a gas-operated weapon firing (depending on model) a variety of rounds and calibres, including the standard 7.62 x 51mm (0.3 x 2in) NATO, and had a full-auto rate of fire of 600rpm.

Senior Sergeant
Argentine Marines

This marine wears a thermal parka jacket: padded, windproof and waterproof, with a deep hood capable of going over the helmet. The helmet is of US supply, as is the webbing and ammunition pouches on the belt (more ammunition is carried in the two bandoliers hung over the shoulders). As the US was a major supplier of military stock to Argentina, a US Army appearance is typical among its forces, but the blue and white patch above the red rank chevrons on the chest clearly defines nationality. The soldier carries eye goggles for protection against the weather.

SPECIFICATIONS	
Country:	Argentina
Date:	1982
Unit:	Argentine Marines
Rank:	Senior Sergeant
Theatre:	South Atlantic
Location:	Falklands

British Marine/Royal Navy Forces, Falklands War 1982

The Royal Marines distinguished themselves in the Falklands War, fighting in battles such as that at Goose Green and playing a key role in the retaking of the Falklands' capital, Port Stanley.

◀ **Marine**
Royal Marines

In contrast to the General-Purpose Machine Gun usually used by British forces as their light support weapon, this soldier carries the L4A2, a later version of the .303-calibre Bren converted to take the NATO 7.62mm (0.3in) round and SLR magazines.

SPECIFICATIONS	
Country:	Britain
Date:	1982
Unit:	Royal Marines
Rank:	Marine
Theatre:	South Atlantic
Location:	Falkland Islands

Marine ▶
45 Commando

Alongside the DPM uniform, other standard British Army features here include the 1958-pattern webbing, which would typically carry a 1958-pattern water-bottle carrier with 1944-pattern water bottle, three ammunition pouches, respirator and poncho roll.

SPECIFICATIONS	
Country:	Britain
Date:	1982
Unit:	45 Commando
Rank:	Marine
Theatre:	South Atlantic
Location:	Falkland Islands

TIMELINE 1982   1982   1982   1982

◄ Marine
Royal Marines

The uniform is the Arctic windproof combat smock and trousers rendered in Temperate Disruptive Pattern Material camouflage, the standard camouflage of the British Army. The smock had a large hood; when this included a wire stiffener, it was an 'RM pattern'; otherwise it was an 'SAS pattern'.

SPECIFICATIONS	
Country:	Britain
Date:	1982
Unit:	Royal Marines
Rank:	Marine
Theatre:	South Atlantic
Location:	Falkland Islands

Medic ►
Royal Navy

The role of this Royal Navy medic is prominently declared by the red cross displayed on the white overvest. He is otherwise wearing simple Navy-issue trousers and a jumper, plus protective clothing for his hands and face.

SPECIFICATIONS	
Country:	Britain
Date:	1982
Unit:	Royal Navy
Rank:	Medic
Theatre:	South Atlantic
Location:	Falkland Islands

Special Forces 1980s–90s

Post-1945 colonial conflicts and the Vietnam War established the importance of Special Forces units within modern armies. With the rise of international terrorism during the 1970s and 1980s, demand for their services was high.

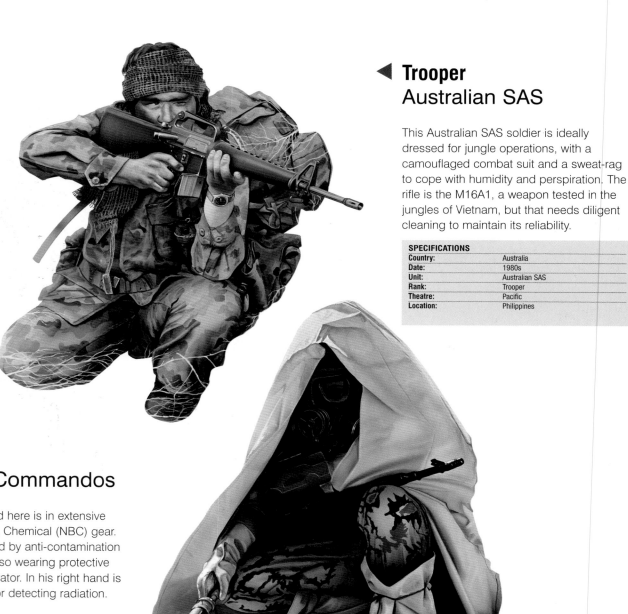

◀ Trooper
Australian SAS

This Australian SAS soldier is ideally dressed for jungle operations, with a camouflaged combat suit and a sweat-rag to cope with humidity and perspiration. The rifle is the M16A1, a weapon tested in the jungles of Vietnam, but that needs diligent cleaning to maintain its reliability.

SPECIFICATIONS	
Country:	Australia
Date:	1980s
Unit:	Australian SAS
Rank:	Trooper
Theatre:	Pacific
Location:	Philippines

Trooper ▶
As-Saiqa Commandos

The soldier pictured here is in extensive Nuclear, Biological, Chemical (NBC) gear. His feet are covered by anti-contamination covers and he is also wearing protective gloves and a respirator. In his right hand is a Geiger counter for detecting radiation.

SPECIFICATIONS	
Country:	Egypt
Date:	1980s
Unit:	As-Saiqa Commandos
Rank:	Trooper
Theatre:	Middle East
Location:	Egypt

TIMELINE | 1980s | 1980s | 1980s | 1990s

◀ Officer
GIGN

The *Groupe d'Intervention Gendarmerie Nationale* (GIGN) is France's foremost counter-terrorist unit, formed in 1974. This man is a GIGN sniper, armed with a 7.62mm (0.3in) Giat FR-F2. He wears thermal-imaging goggles for night-vision, featuring a built-in radio mike. Hanging from his belt is a fast-rope.

SPECIFICATIONS

Country:	France
Date:	1980s
Unit:	GIGN
Rank:	Officer
Theatre:	Europe
Location:	France

Officer ▶
Grenzschutzgruppe-9

The *Grenzschutzgruppe-9* (Border Guard Group 9; GSG-9) ranks as one of the best hostage-rescue and anti-terrorist units in the world. Here we see an operative in classic urban assault gear, with an airborne harness for fast-roping down to buildings.

SPECIFICATIONS

Country:	Germany
Date:	1990s
Unit:	*Grenzschutzgruppe-9*
Rank:	Officer
Theatre:	Europe
Location:	Germany

Special Forces 1980s–90s

Terrorist bombings, aircraft hijackings and assassinations plagued most European states between the 1970s and 1990s. For this reason, many Special Forces units created elite counter-terrorist sub-groups within their organizations.

◀ Officer
Nucleo Operativo Centrale

Protection for this officer comes from a kevlar flak jacket and visored helmet made from kevlar or ballistic nylon. All the officer's weaponry is Italian-produced: a Beretta Model 12S submachine gun and a Beretta Model 84 pistol.

SPECIFICATIONS	
Country:	Italy
Date:	1990s
Unit:	*Nucleo Operativo Centrale*
Rank:	Officer
Theatre:	Europe
Location:	Italy

Officer ▶
Grupo Especial de Operaciones

The *Grupo Especial de Operaciones* (Special Operations Group; GEO) was formed in the 1970s. The officer here wears a one-piece combat overall with minimal insignia, but a unit badge on the right sleeve.

SPECIFICATIONS	
Country:	Spain
Date:	1990s
Unit:	*Grupo Especial de Operaciones*
Rank:	Officer
Theatre:	Europe
Location:	Spain

1990s   1990s   1990s   1990s

◄ Sergeant
Spetsnaz, Russian Army

This soldier has a 5.45mm (0.21in) AKS-74 assault rifle, a high-velocity weapon fitted with a distinctive muzzle brake to stop climb during automatic fire. In his right hand is an AK-series bayonet/combat knife. Spetsnaz troopers wear a variety of uniforms, but camouflage patterns are most common.

SPECIFICATIONS	
Country:	Russia
Date:	1990s
Unit:	Spetsnaz, Russian Army
Rank:	Sergeant
Theatre:	Europe
Location:	Russia

Private ►
Spetsnaz, Russian Army

Spetsnaz is a contraction of the words *Spetsialnoye Nazhacheniye*, which are translated as 'special purpose'. This soldier, operating in Chechnya in the 1990s, has taped two AK magazines together for rapid reloading in combat.

SPECIFICATIONS	
Country:	Russia
Date:	1990s
Unit:	Spetsnaz, Russian Army
Rank:	Private
Theatre:	Central Asia
Location:	Chechnya

British/US Special Forces 1980s–90s

The breaking of the Iranian Embassy siege in London in 1980 cemented the international reputation of the British SAS, while US Special Forces also made their mark through operations in Latin America and the Middle East.

◄ **Trooper**
22 Special Air Service

This SAS trooper is dressed in a black, flame-resistant combat overall; his head is covered by an S6 respirator for breathing in rooms choked by CS gas, smoke and munitions fumes. Beneath his smock can be seen the Armourshield GPV 25 body armour with groin protector.

SPECIFICATIONS	
Country:	Britain
Date:	1980
Unit:	Special Air Service
Rank:	Trooper
Theatre:	Europe
Location:	London

Master Sergeant ▶
1st SFOD-D, US Army

This soldier from Special Forces Operational Detachment-Delta (SFOD-D) has loaded up his webbing system heavily with ammunition pouches. His main weapon is the M4 carbine, a shortened version of the M16A2 rifle popular with both Special Forces and regular US Army units.

SPECIFICATIONS	
Country:	United States
Date:	1993
Unit:	1st SFOD-D, US Army
Rank:	Master Sergeant
Theatre:	Africa
Location:	Somalia

TIMELINE 1980   1993   1990s   1990s

◀ Private
US Special Forces

Apart from his standard woodland-camouflage uniform, the only other clothing this soldier wears is a green bandana tied around his head to prevent sweat from dripping into his eyes. His weapon is the XM177 submachine gun, here fitted with the curved 30-round magazine.

Private ▲
US Special Forces

The soldier here is wearing a standard US Army woodland camouflage uniform with PASGT helmet and combat boots. The firearm is also the standard US issue: the 5.56mm (0.22in) M16A2. The gun is fitted with a blank-firing adapter, indicating that the soldier is on training.

SPECIFICATIONS	
Country:	United States
Date:	1990s
Unit:	US Special Forces
Rank:	Private
Theatre:	South America
Location:	Unknown

SPECIFICATIONS	
Country:	United States
Date:	1990s
Unit:	US Special Forces
Rank:	Private
Theatre:	United States
Location:	Unknown

SAS Counter-Revolutionary Warfare Wing Trooper 1980s

The SAS Counter-Revolutionary Warfare (CRW) wing was formed during the 1970s to combat the rapidly expanding threat of terrorism. It included a dedicated counter-terrorism unit, manned by specialists in hostage-rescue and urban assault missions.

The Browning High-Power Model 1935 pre-dated World War II, but its merits kept it in service with more than 50 countries into the 1980s. One of its strengths was a high magazine capacity – 13 rounds stacked in a double row.

The MP5 has become virtually the industry-standard submachine gun for special forces, hostage-rescue and SWAT-type law-enforcement teams worldwide. It fires from a closed bolt, making it very accurate, and on full-auto mode has formidable take-down power.

Trooper
Special Air Service

The three profiles of this figure give a good impression of the kit worn by SAS CRW operatives during the 1980s. The S6 respirator was a standard-issue British gas mask issued from the 1960s until 1986, and here the sides of the mask are enclosed by a hood, giving the SAS soldier complete anonymity. His uniform is a fire-retardant overall, over which he wears body armour (including a groin-protecting plate) and a fast-rope system for making rapid descents down building exteriors. The figure on the left has two stun grenades enclosed in pouches (right) and two magazine pouches for the Heckler & Koch MP5K submachine gun, seen carried by the centre figure. The man on the right also has a hammer for making forced entries through doors and windows.

SPECIFICATIONS	
Country:	Britain
Date:	1980
Unit:	Special Air Service
Rank:	Trooper
Theatre:	Europe
Location:	London

US Police and Internal Security 1970s–90s

The threat from terrorism and domestic unrest also had an impact on the police and security forces of the developed nations. Particularly in the United States, law-enforcement tactics and firepower became more militarized.

◄ Riot Control Officer
Washington DC Police

Here we see a US riot control officer of the 1970s, wearing his standard police uniform but also donning a respirator. The respirator is to protect him from the CS gas he is about to launch from his single-shot riot gun. Shells for the gun are held in the bag around his back.

SPECIFICATIONS	
Country:	United States
Date:	1970s
Unit:	Washington DC Police
Rank:	Riot Control Officer
Theatre:	United States
Location:	Washington

Officer ►
FBI

The Federal Bureau of Investigation (FBI) has been at the forefront of the militarization of police firepower. Here we see an FBI officer with a cut-down pump-action 12-gauge shotgun. With its handle removed and the barrel shortened, the gun is short enough to be concealed beneath a jacket.

SPECIFICATIONS	
Country:	United States
Date:	1970s
Unit:	FBI
Rank:	Officer
Theatre:	United States
Location:	Unknown

1970s   1970s   1970s   1990s

◄ Officer
SWAT

The Special Weapons and Tactics (SWAT) units were first established in the late 1960s, and they have become the primary force for dealing with high-risk security situations. This officer wears body armour, a visored helmet and carries a pump-action shotgun; the weapon would carry around eight shells in the underbarrel magazine.

SPECIFICATIONS	
Country:	United States
Date:	1970s
Unit:	SWAT
Rank:	Officer
Theatre:	United States
Location:	Unknown

Criminal ►
Bank Robber Team

A view of the enemy – here a bank robber, his features obscured by a stocking, points a sawn-off shotgun at bank staff. Sawing the barrel off a shotgun not only makes the weapon more concealable, it also increases the spread of shot at close ranges, enhancing the gun's lethality.

SPECIFICATIONS	
Country:	United States
Date:	1990s
Unit:	None
Rank:	Criminal
Theatre:	United States
Location:	Unknown

Security Police 1980s

Riot control became a critical duty of police forces worldwide in the turbulent 1980s. The range of coercive options available to the law-enforcement community ranged from CS gas and water cannon through to lethal firepower.

◀ Officer
Swiss Riot Police

This Swiss riot-control officer has a helmet fitted with full face and neck protection. He also carries a distinctive riot shield woven from wicker, of questionable utility. The officer's force option is in the form of a hardwood baton, typically used to strike at elbow and leg joints.

SPECIFICATIONS	
Country:	Switzerland
Date:	1981
Unit:	Swiss Riot Police
Rank:	Officer
Theatre:	Europe
Location:	Switzerland

Officer ▶
British Riot Police

This British officer is armed with the Federal Model 201-Z riot gun. A single-barrel (break-open action) weapon, it could fire both gas grenades and flares. The 37 x 122mm (1.5 x 4.8in) shells here are worn around the waist in a bandolier.

SPECIFICATIONS	
Country:	Britain
Date:	1985
Unit:	British Riot Police
Rank:	Officer
Theatre:	Europe
Location:	Britain

TIMELINE   1981   1985   1980s   1980s

◄ Officer
South African Police

This South African officer has no protective clothing, apart from his regular police cap. He does, however, have serious firepower in the form of his service handgun (worn on his hip in a holster) and a pump-action 12-gauge shotgun. For crowd-control duties, the shotgun would usually be loaded with bird shot.

SPECIFICATIONS	
Country:	South Africa
Date:	1980s
Unit:	South African Police
Rank:	Officer
Theatre:	South Africa
Location:	Johannesburg

NCO ►
British Army

In Northern Ireland during the 1980s, riot control was a regular duty of British Army soldiers. Here this NCO is wearing a flak jacket over his DPM uniform, and his lower legs are protected by leg guards. He is shown in the process of loading his Federal Model 201-Z riot gun.

SPECIFICATIONS	
Country:	Britain
Date:	1980s
Unit:	British Army
Rank:	NCO
Theatre:	Europe
Location:	Northern Ireland

European Infantry and Airborne 1980s–90s

Infantry and airborne forces of the late 20th century had to adapt to a battlefield transformed by the computerization of tactics and technology.

◀ Marine
Netherlands Marine Corp

This Dutch marine is wearing a traditional style of olive-green battledress, with ammunition pouches at the front for his 7.62mm (0.3in) FN FAL rifle. His helmet has been entirely obscured with foliage, and camouflage paint is applied to his face.

SPECIFICATIONS	
Country:	Netherlands
Date:	1980s
Unit:	Netherlands Marine Corp
Rank:	Marine
Theatre:	Europe
Location:	Netherlands

Private ▶
1st Airborne Division

The para here wears a two-piece jump uniform consisting of field-grey shirt and stone-grey trousers, with the colours of the German Federal Republic on his left tunic sleeve. The para helmet shape allows good hearing aboard a noisy aircraft and gives little for parachute lines to snag upon.

SPECIFICATIONS	
Country:	West Germany
Date:	1985
Unit:	1st Airborne Division
Rank:	Private
Theatre:	Europe
Location:	Germany

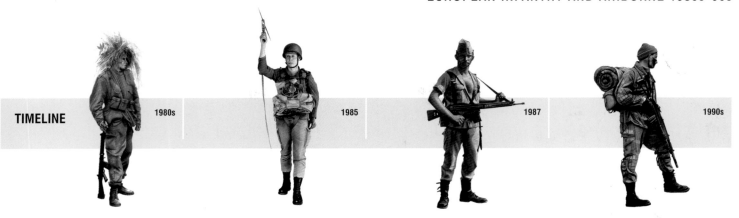

TIMELINE	1980s	1985	1987	1990s

◀ Legionnaire
Spanish Foreign Legion

This soldier wears Spanish Army fatigues, but Legion soldiers also don camouflage when necessary. He carries the 7.62mm (0.3in) CETME rifle; the 5.56mm (0.22in) NATO Model L version was adopted in the 1980s.

SPECIFICATIONS	
Country:	Spain
Date:	1987
Unit:	Spanish Foreign Legion
Rank:	Legionnaire
Theatre:	Atlantic
Location:	Canary Islands

Private ▶
Italian Alpini

This soldier is wearing the camouflage shirt and trousers worn by Alpini soldiers during the summer. It features reinforced elbow and knee sections for climbing, and tightly elasticated ankles, which are covered by a calf-high pair of rubber climbing boots.

SPECIFICATIONS	
Country:	Italy
Date:	1990s
Unit:	Italian Alpini
Rank:	Private
Theatre:	Europe
Location:	Northern Italy

European Infantry and Airborne 1980s–90s

The 1980s and 1990s were a colourful time for Europe's armed forces. Deployments varied from minor peacekeeping roles to major conflicts (in the 1990–91 Gulf War), while political and economic realities meant many structural changes across armies.

◄ Marine
San Marco Battalion

The San Marco Battalion forms a specialist sub-section of the Italian Marines. This soldier is in winter training in the mountainous regions of northern Italy, with a three-quarter-length ski jacket belted at the waist with an Italian-issue web belt. Beneath the jacket he is wearing the standard Italian Army camouflage combat uniform.

SPECIFICATIONS	
Country:	Italy
Date:	1990s
Unit:	San Marco Battalion
Rank:	Marine
Theatre:	Europe
Location:	Italy

NCO ►
Belgian Parachute Regiment

This Belgian para shares his appearance with many modern European armies. His uniform is in a Woodland pattern similar to British Army Disruptive Pattern Material (DPM), though in Belgium this pattern actually separates the paras from the rest of the army, who wear a plain olive-drab.

SPECIFICATIONS	
Country:	Belgium
Date:	1990s
Unit:	Belgian Parachute Regiment
Rank:	NCO
Theatre:	Europe
Location:	Belgium

TIMELINE

1990s   1990s   1990s   1990s

Corporal
French Foreign Legion

Except in parade dress, the French Foreign Legion have generally followed fairly spartan styles of uniform. What is constant is the infamous *kepi* hat. Two common types of service *kepi* prevail. This NCO gets to wear the *kepi noir*, a black-covered hat, while all lower ranks usually wear the *kepi blanc*, which has a white cover.

SPECIFICATIONS	
Country:	France
Date:	1990s
Unit:	French Foreign Legion
Rank:	Corporal
Theatre:	Europe
Location:	Corsica

Private ▶
Italian Folgore Brigade

Like most paratroopers around the world, the soldiers of the Folgore Brigade wear a maroon beret that displays their parachute wings, though this soldier has a standard parachute helmet. He is armed with the 7.62mm (0.3in) BM-59 rifle, with a folding para stock.

SPECIFICATIONS	
Country:	Italy
Date:	1990s
Unit:	Folgore Brigade
Rank:	Private
Theatre:	Europe
Location:	Italy

British Army 1980s

The 1980s brought significant changes to British Army uniform and equipment. Not least of these changes was the replacement of the time-proven L1A1 rifle with the 5.56mm (0.22in) SA80/L85A1 as the standard British Army rifle.

◀ Private
Intelligence Corps

This soldier is wearing the 1968-pattern Combat Dress rendered in the No. 8 Temperate Disruptive Pattern Material (DPM) camouflage, which was the British Army standard (DPM was introduced in 1972). He is also wearing the 1958-pattern webbing system and the green beret of the Intelligence Corps.

SPECIFICATIONS	
Country:	Britain
Date:	1980
Unit:	Intelligence Corps
Rank:	Private
Theatre:	Europe
Location:	Britain

Rifleman ▶
Gurkha Rifles

This Gurkha wears a 1984-pattern DPM uniform with 1958-pattern webbing (distinguished by the metal buckle). His firearm is the 5.56mm (0.22in) L86 Light Support Weapon, a heavy-barrelled version of the standard SA80 rifle used for delivering light covering fire.

SPECIFICATIONS	
Country:	Britain
Date:	1980s
Unit:	Gurkha Rifles
Rank:	Rifleman
Theatre:	Europe
Location:	Britain

TIMELINE   1980   1980s   1985   1985

◀ **Corporal**
Corps of Royal Engineers

This combat engineer has the Individual Weapon Sight (IWS) sniper sight fitted to his L1A1 rifle. True to the mid-1980s, he is wearing the 1984-pattern uniform or, as it was officially known, No.8 Dress Temperate Combat Uniform.

SPECIFICATIONS	
Country:	Britain
Date:	1985
Unit:	Corps of Royal Engineers
Rank:	Corporal
Theatre:	Europe
Location:	Britain

Paratrooper ▶
5th Airborne Brigade

The 5th Airborne Brigade was a post-Falklands War conversion of the 5th Infantry Brigade. This soldier is preparing to make a para drop; he is wearing both main and reserve parachutes, and grips his hefty Bergen rucksack. His uniform is 1984-pattern DPM.

SPECIFICATIONS	
Country:	Britain
Date:	1985
Unit:	5th Airborne Brigade
Rank:	Paratrooper
Theatre:	Europe
Location:	Britain

British Paratrooper, Northern Ireland 1980

A soldier pauses on the streets of Londonderry during a patrol in the early 1980s, a time when ambush and bomb detonations were everyday threats. Despite the hostility of nationalist organizations towards the Parachute Regiment, this soldier still proudly wears the famous red beret.

The British Army's L1A1 rifles were replaced by the radically different 5.56mm (0.22in) SA80 during the 1980s. The SA80 is a 'bullpup' design, in which the magazine sits behind the pistol grip to allow a full-length barrel in a shorter overall weapon.

The Humber 'Pig' was a common security vehicle used by British armed forces in Northern Ireland. It was lightly armoured and could be configured for riot-control duties with additional equipment such as barricade-removal devices.

Lance-Corporal
Parachute Regiment

This soldier is wearing a DPM camouflage shirt with a pair of olive-green fatigues and leather, ankle-high para boots. His webbing is the 1958-pattern, though the 1980s saw an updated webbing introduced as the new SA80 rifle began to be issued. For this patrol he carries only ammunition for his L1A1 rifle and water. The final, and essential, items of this soldier's kit are the kevlar body armour and the two-way radio with the microphone attached to the flak-jacket collar.

SPECIFICATIONS	
Country:	Britain
Date:	1980
Unit:	Parachute Regiment
Rank:	Lance-Corporal
Theatre:	Europe
Location:	Northern Ireland

British Army/Marines 1990s

The 1990s continued the trend of uniform and kit changes in the British armed forces. The layered-principle, lightweight Combat Soldier 95 (CS95) uniform replaced the previous DPM No. 8 and 9 Dress.

◀ Private
Parachute Regiment

Here we see a private of the Parachute Regiment dressed in the CS95 system. CS95 works on a layering principle, and provides a range of different clothing items: a T-shirt, a lightweight combat shirt; a Norwegian pattern roll-neck overshirt; camouflaged fleece jacket; ripstop, weatherproof combat jacket and a fully waterproof, Gore-Tex outer jacket.

SPECIFICATIONS	
Country:	Britain
Date:	1990s
Unit:	Parachute Regiment
Rank:	Private
Theatre:	Europe
Location:	Britain

Mountain Leader ▶
M&AW Cadre

The Mountain & Arctic Warfare Cadre (M&AW) is an elite unit within the Royal Marines. The Mountain Leader here is wearing a white, waterproof smock and trousers made from a breathable fabric, such as Gore-Tex, over a windproof uniform.

SPECIFICATIONS	
Country:	Britain
Date:	1990s
Unit:	M&AW Cadre
Rank:	Mountain Leader
Theatre:	Europe
Location:	Norway

◄ Coxswain
539 Assault Squadron, Royal Marines

Typical Arctic-waters uniform for this Royal Marine is a one-piece waterproof immersion suit with permanently attached rubberized boots. The Marine here also wears a life-jacket, to which a strobe light is fitted in case he goes into the water.

SPECIFICATIONS	
Country:	Britain
Date:	1990s
Unit:	539 Assault Squadron, Royal Marines
Rank:	Coxswain
Theatre:	Europe
Location:	Norway

Gunner ►
Royal Artillery

Part of the CS95 range is a redesigned boot. The boot's breathable liner allows air to reach the foot, while keeping the foot dry, and the shock-absorbing soles and a speed loop-lacing facility make the boot protective and convenient in one. Here the boots are worn with waterproof covers.

SPECIFICATIONS	
Country:	Britain
Date:	1990s
Unit:	Royal Artillery
Rank:	Gunner
Theatre:	Europe
Location:	Britain

British Army/Marines 1990s

Serious issues with the British Army's new SA80 rifle emerged during the 1980s and 1990s, with problems including frequent jamming and parts breaking off. The failures were cured in 2000 following a major overhaul of the weapon by the German Heckler & Koch company.

▼ Marine
Royal Marines

The Marine here has his partially camouflaged SA80 equipped with the large Common Weapon Sight (CWS), a Starlight sight that provides image intensification in low-light or night-time conditions. His boots are part of the Combat Soldier 95 (CS95) range of kit.

SPECIFICATIONS	
Country:	Britain
Date:	1990s
Unit:	Royal Marines
Rank:	Marine
Theatre:	Europe
Location:	Britain

Trooper ▶
22 SAS Regiment

The SAS soldier here is using a Burst Morse Radio handset, which records Morse Code messages then transmits them at high speed to avoid enemy detection. He is also wearing the 1990-pattern Personal Load-Carrying Equipment (PLCE), with quick-release buckles.

SPECIFICATIONS	
Country:	Britain
Date:	1990s
Unit:	22 SAS Regiment
Rank:	Trooper
Theatre:	Europe
Location:	Britain

◀ EOD Officer
Royal Engineers

This Explosive Ordnance Disposal (EOD) officer is dressed in full protective clothing, which basically consists of an Aramid fibre suit into which ceramic or steel blast plates are inserted to withstand shrapnel and pressure injuries. The helmet is the Galt EOD Mk 3, around which a neck brace is fitted to protect against blast whiplash.

SPECIFICATIONS	
Country:	Britain
Date:	1990s
Unit:	Royal Engineers
Rank:	EOD Officer
Theatre:	Europe
Location:	Britain

Private ▼
5th Airborne Brigade, Pathfinder Platoon

The Pathfinder Platoon specializes in rapid airborne deployment by parachute. Over a DPM camouflage and windproof jump suit, this soldier is wearing a Mk4 ramair controllable parachute with a PR3 reserve, and an Irvin Hitefinder altimeter.

SPECIFICATIONS	
Country:	Britain
Date:	1990s
Unit:	5th Airborne Brigade, Pathfinder Platoon
Rank:	Private
Theatre:	Europe
Location:	Britain

US Forces 1980s

Following the troubled Vietnam War period, the US armed forces substantially reinvented themselves during the 1980s, renewing their tactics and much of their kit.

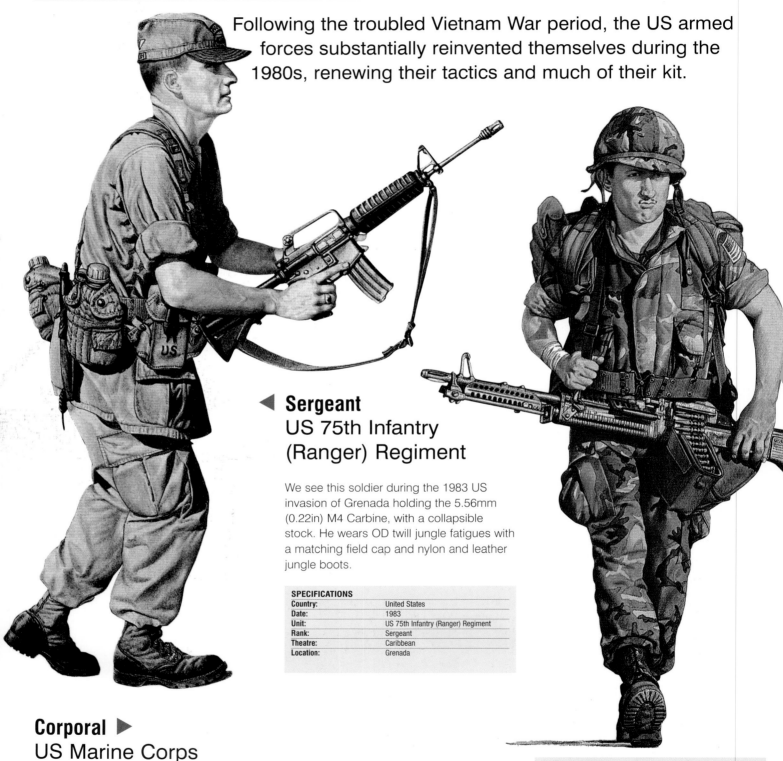

◀ Sergeant
US 75th Infantry (Ranger) Regiment

We see this soldier during the 1983 US invasion of Grenada holding the 5.56mm (0.22in) M4 Carbine, with a collapsible stock. He wears OD twill jungle fatigues with a matching field cap and nylon and leather jungle boots.

SPECIFICATIONS	
Country:	United States
Date:	1983
Unit:	US 75th Infantry (Ranger) Regiment
Rank:	Sergeant
Theatre:	Caribbean
Location:	Grenada

Corporal ▶
US Marine Corps

This corporal is wearing a new M81 Woodland camouflage uniform. Of older issue is the helmet, the steel M1. His webbing is the ALICE system – All-Purpose Lightweight Individual Carrying Equipment – which was introduced during the 1970s.

SPECIFICATIONS	
Country:	United States
Date:	1983
Unit:	US Marine Corps
Rank:	Corporal
Theatre:	Caribbean
Location:	Grenada

TIMELINE 1983   1983   1985   1980s

◄ Corporal
US Marine Corps

A Marine corporal shown here on parade in Quantico, the USMC headquarters, wears the Dress Blue B uniform that was donned mainly for ceremonial and official functions. The uniform's primary item is a dark blue tunic that has a stand collar and is trimmed in red, worn with a white belt.

SPECIFICATIONS	
Country:	United States
Date:	1985
Unit:	US Marine Corps
Rank:	Corporal
Theatre:	Caribbean
Location:	Grenada

Winter Warfare Soldier ►
US Army

This US Army soldier on arctic warfare training is wearing full white winter camouflage combat dress, including studded ice boots and face mask. The weapon is the M240 machine gun, a US version of the Belgian FN MAG.

SPECIFICATIONS	
Country:	United States
Date:	1980s
Unit:	US Army
Rank:	Unknown
Theatre:	North America
Location:	Alaska

425

F-117 Pilot, Balkans 2006

The Lockheed F-117 Nighthawk entered service in 1983, and was revolutionary in terms of aircraft design. Its angular shape and radar-absorbing materials give it a negligible radar signature, and it has the capability to deliver both conventional and nuclear ordnance loads.

The F-117 can carry a variety of ordnance in its internal bomb bays, including the BLU-109B low-level laser-guided bomb, GBU-10 and GBU-27 laser-guided bombs, and Raytheon AGM-65 Maverick and Raytheon AGM-88 HARM air-to-surface missiles. To increase its stealth, it does not use radar for navigation or target guidance, instead relying on infrared visual cameras and the Honeywell inertial navigation system.

Captain
US Air Force

This female captain in the US Air Force is the pilot on an F-117, and here wears modern flight gear for a mission over the Balkans in 2006. Over her olive-drab one-piece flight overall you can see a G-suit wrapped around her torso and legs; this inflates during high-G manoeuvres to prevent too much blood flowing into the lower half of the body. Under her arm is an HGU-55/P flight helmet, here with an MBU-12 oxygen mask fitted. The interior of the helmet is fully wired with communications systems.

SPECIFICATIONS	
Country:	United States
Date:	2006
Unit:	US Air Force
Rank:	Captain
Theatre:	Europe
Location:	Balkans

North American Peacetime Forces 1990s–Present

US and Canadian armed forces are today better equipped than at any point in their history. Weapons are more powerful and less prone to failure, and uniforms have been designed around advanced ergonomic principles.

◀ Private
US 82nd Airborne Division

Crowning this soldier is the standard US issue Personnel Armour System, Ground Troops (PASGT) helmet, a protective dome of kevlar. The PASGT equipment also includes a body-armour vest, worn under or over the blouse.

SPECIFICATIONS	
Country:	United States
Date:	1990s
Unit:	US 82nd Airborne Division
Rank:	Private
Theatre:	North America
Location:	United States

Marine ▶
US Marine Corps

The camouflage of this Marine's uniform is based on the M81 Woodland pattern, which was introduced in 1980. Here the main camouflage item is a smock with press-stud fastened front and a drawstring hood; he is without the PASGT 'Fritz' helmet that was worn by most US combat units in the 1990s.

SPECIFICATIONS	
Country:	United States
Date:	1990s
Unit:	US Marine Corps
Rank:	Private
Theatre:	North America
Location:	United States

1990s

1990s

c. 2000

c. 2000

◀ Private
101st Airborne Division

This US soldier of the 10st Airborne Division perfectly illustrates the anti-tank capabilities of modern US infantry through his M72 Light Anti-Tank Weapon (LAW rocket) system. The LAW fires a 66mm (2.6in) High-Explosive Anti-Tank (HEAT) warhead missile to a maximum range of 1000m (3280ft).

SPECIFICATIONS	
Country:	United States
Date:	c. 2000
Unit:	101st Airborne Division
Rank:	Private
Theatre:	North America
Location:	United States

Ranger ▶
75th Ranger Regiment

This soldier is wearing the US Army's Battle Dress Uniform (BDU), which was the standard temperate zone uniform from 1981 to 2005. The BDU camouflage not only replaced other camouflage types, but also the olive-drab service dress.

SPECIFICATIONS	
Country:	United States
Date:	c. 2000
Unit:	75th Ranger Regiment
Rank:	Ranger
Theatre:	North America
Location:	United States

Soldiers of the Iran–Iraq War 1980

The Iran–Iraq War (1980–88) cost more than a million lives for little strategic gain. The uniform and weaponry of the humble infantryman on both sides could be extremely basic, with both Soviet and Western supplies in use.

The G3 is one of the most widely distributed assault rifles in post-war history. Using a delayed-blowback system, the 7.62 x 51mm (0.3 x 2in) NATO rifle is reliable and powerful, although firing the rifle cartridge at full-auto is not conducive to accurate shooting.

The RPK is basically a standard AKM assault rifle but with a longer, heavier barrel and a bipod for delivering light support fire. The barrel is fixed, which means that the firing rate must be controlled carefully to avoid the barrel overheating. Any standard AK magazine will work in the RPK, but it can also take a 40-round box or 75-round drum.

Captain
Revolutionary Guard Corps

Corporal
Iraqi Army

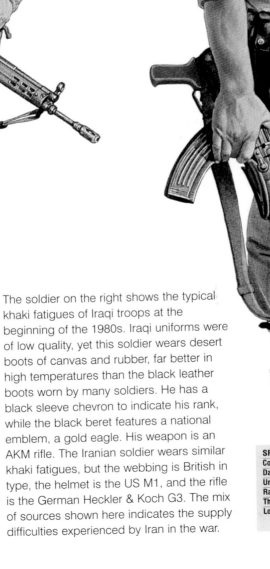

The soldier on the right shows the typical khaki fatigues of Iraqi troops at the beginning of the 1980s. Iraqi uniforms were of low quality, yet this soldier wears desert boots of canvas and rubber, far better in high temperatures than the black leather boots worn by many soldiers. He has a black sleeve chevron to indicate his rank, while the black beret features a national emblem, a gold eagle. His weapon is an AKM rifle. The Iranian soldier wears similar khaki fatigues, but the webbing is British in type, the helmet is the US M1, and the rifle is the German Heckler & Koch G3. The mix of sources shown here indicates the supply difficulties experienced by Iran in the war.

SPECIFICATIONS

Country:	Iran
Date:	1980
Unit:	Revolutionary Guard Corps
Rank:	Private
Theatre:	Middle East
Location:	Iran/Iraq border

SPECIFICATIONS

Country:	Iraq
Date:	1980
Unit:	Iraqi Army
Rank:	Corporal
Theatre:	Middle East
Location:	Shatt al-Arab waterway

Gulf War 1990–91

The Gulf War in 1990–91 pitted a US-led coalition force against the Iraqi Army of Saddam Hussein. As events proved, the poorly led and technologically inferior Iraqi Army was no match for modern Western forces.

◄ Private
2nd Marine Division

The pattern of uniform worn by this US infantryman is the Desert Battle Dress Uniform (DBDU), rendered in a six-colour camouflage and introduced into service in 1981. The webbing is the All-Purpose Lightweight Individual Carrying Equipment (ALICE), phased out in the later 1990s.

SPECIFICATIONS	
Country:	United States
Date:	1991
Unit:	2nd Marine Division
Rank:	Private
Theatre:	Middle East
Location:	Kuwait

Private ►
Iraqi Army,
Republican Guard

The maroon triangle on the sleeve, and his matching beret, mark this soldier out as a member of the Iraqi Army Republican Guard formation. Despite his supposedly elite status, he is dressed in little more than olive-drab fatigues.

SPECIFICATIONS	
Country:	Iraq
Date:	1991
Unit:	Iraqi Army, Republican Guard
Rank:	Private
Theatre:	Middle East
Location:	Iraq

TIMELINE

1991   1991   1991   1991

◀ Commander
7th Armoured Brigade, British Army

The basic desert camouflage of British soldiers during the Gulf War was the No. 5 Desert Combat Dress, dappled in various shades of brown. Supply shortages persisted even in the British Army, hence this commander's clashing DPM overvest.

SPECIFICATIONS	
Country:	Britain
Date:	1991
Unit:	7th Armoured Brigade, British Army
Rank:	Commander
Theatre:	Middle East
Location:	Iraq

Trooper ▶
22 SAS Regiment

The SAS tends to pick and choose its uniform depending on preference and utility, hence this trooper is wearing a mix of items. Head protection comes from a piece of camouflage netting, and he has a thick jumper in desert pattern. The webbing is the British Army's 1958 system.

SPECIFICATIONS	
Country:	Britain
Date:	1991
Unit:	22 SAS Regiment
Rank:	Trooper
Theatre:	Middle East
Location:	Iraq

War in Afghanistan and Iraq 2001–

What has been termed the 'Global War on Terror' since 2001 has been a mixed experience for US and coalition forces, with victory in conventional engagements but tactical problems in handling insurgencies in both Iraq and Afghanistan.

◄ Guerrilla Fighter
Taliban Militia

This Taliban militia fighter has appropriated a camouflage jacket, but such is the only recognizably military form of dress. He holds the ubiquitous AK assault rifle, millions of which were left in Afghanistan following the Afghan–Soviet War fought in the 1980s.

SPECIFICATIONS	
Country:	Afghanistan
Date:	2001
Unit:	Taliban
Rank:	Guerrilla Fighter
Theatre:	Central Asia
Location:	Afghanistan

Marine ►
1st US Marine Division (Recon)

This Recon Marine is wearing the Fighting Load Carrier Vest of the Modular Lightweight Load-Carrying Equipment (MOLLE) system. The MOLLE system enables the soldier to carry multiple pouches and combat items on a single garment.

SPECIFICATIONS	
Country:	United States
Date:	2003
Unit:	1st US Marine Division (Recon)
Rank:	Marine
Theatre:	Middle East
Location:	Iraq

2001   2003   2010   2010

◀ Private
10th Mountain Division

This soldier's uniform is rendered in the Universal Camouflage Pattern (UCP), a pattern designed to provide basic camouflage in urban, temperate woodland and desert environments. He carries his equipment on an Improved Outer Tactical Vest (IOTV) system.

SPECIFICATIONS	
Country:	United States
Date:	2010
Unit:	10th Mountain Division
Rank:	Private
Theatre:	Central Asia
Location:	Afghanistan

Corporal ▼
4th Rifles, British Army

Here we see a British Army sniper in Afghanistan, a member of the 4th Rifles mechanized infantry regiment. Body armour, helmet cover and uniform are in a desert camouflage pattern. He is armed with the Accuracy International L115A3 sniper rifle, an 8.5mm (0.33in) rifle with an effective range out past 1000m (3280ft).

SPECIFICATIONS	
Country:	Britain
Date:	2010
Unit:	4th Rifles, British Army
Rank:	Corporal
Theatre:	Central Asia
Location:	Afghanistan

EOD Operator, Iraq 2009

Explosive Ordnance Disposal (EOD) is one of the most dangerous and respected jobs in the modern armed forces. In Iraq and Afghanistan, improvised explosive devices (IEDs) have become the principal weapon of the insurgents, and EOD officers must pit their wits against the ingenuity of the bomb-makers.

The use of IEDs has led to clothing and vehicles being specifically designed to protect against these destructive devices. The Mastiff PPV is the British variant of the basic Cougar armoured fighting vehicle built by Force Protection Inc. Acquired by both the British and US Armies, the Cougar is designed specifically to safeguard against mines and improvised explosive devices.

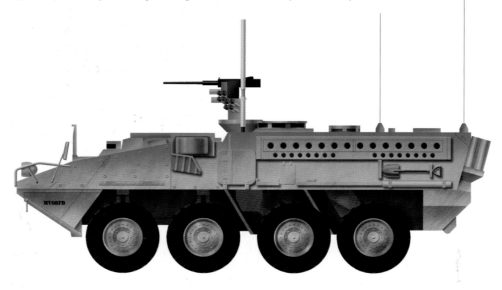

The eight-wheeled Stryker armoured fighting vehicle entered service with the US Army in 2002 and carries up to nine soldiers. Its mobility and protection have been instrumental during operations in Iraq.

EOD Officer
US Army

This EOD officer is clad in a full-body kevlar suit, into which ballistic panels are inserted for blast and fragmentation protection. The suit also includes a cool-air system to keep the temperature inside at manageable levels. The helmet is designed to withstand shrapnel striking it at the speed of a rifle bullet, and it incorporates both microphone and speakers plus a forced air ventilation system. (The control for the comms set is on the officer's wrist.) To protect the soldier's head in case of a detonation, the collar of the suit extends up around the base of the helmet. Protective gloves are worn, but many EOD officers work without these to improve their hand dexterity.

SPECIFICATIONS	
Country:	United States
Date:	2009
Unit:	US Army
Rank:	EOD Officer
Theatre:	Middle East
Location:	Iraq

Glossary

Aiguillette Ornamental plaited cords, fitted with metal tags at the end, worn around the shoulder. They are usually seen on the uniforms of officers.

ALICE Abbreviation of 'All-Purpose Lightweight Individual Carrying Equipment', a US Army system of load-carrying adopted in the 1970s.

Anklet A buttoned or buckled sleeve fitted around the ankle, to provide extra waterproofing or protection at the join between boot and trousers.

Arm of service A phrase used to denote which part of the armed forces a soldier belongs to, e.g. artillery, air force, marines.

Assault rifle A rifle capable of firing semi- or full-auto but which is chambered for an 'intermediate' cartridge designed for efficiency over short–medium ranges.

Bandolier A fabric or leather cartridge belt, typically worn around the waist or diagonally across the chest.

Battledress The uniform typically issued for combat, as opposed to barrack or ceremonial duties (although in practical terms, a battledress can fit many roles).

Bayonet A knife, dagger, sword, or spike-shaped weapon designed to fit in, on, over or underneath the muzzle of a rifle, musket or similar weapon, effectively turning the gun into a spear.

Bearskin A tall, thick hat made from bearskin, typically worn by soldiers of guards and grenadier regiments.

Breeches An item of clothing covering the body from the waist down, with separate coverings for each leg, usually stopping just below the knee, though in some cases reaching to the ankles.

Carbine A shortened form of rifle, intended for use by horse-mounted troops, those operating from within vehicles or light infantry/airborne troops.

Chevron (rank) A system of denoting rank (typically NCO ranks) through angled stripes worn on the sleeve.

Cockade A rosette worn on a uniform headdress, which usually represents national colours.

Collar tabs A patch of material fitted to the collar, and bearing insignia relating to a soldier's unit, rank etc.

Comb On some helmets, a vertically standing plate of metal running longitudinally along the crest of a helmet.

Cuirass A piece of armour, formed of a single or multiple pieces of metal or other rigid material, which covers the front of the wearer's person.

Cutlass A short, broad sabre or slashing sword. The preferred weapon and utility slicing implement of sailors.

Czapka The traditional cap of Polish cavalry, also seen worn by other Eastern European and some Western European cavalry troops.

Dog tags Metal tags bearing the soldier's identity, worn around the neck for identification purposes should the soldier be killed in combat.

Dolman A short and highly ornamental jacket or tunic worn by hussar cavalry; the chest is decorated with lacework and looping.

DPM Disruptive Pattern Material, a specific pattern of camouflage developed for and adopted by the British Army (and many other armies) from the 1960s.

EOD Abbreviation of Explosive Ordnance Disposal.

Epaulettes A cloth pad or strap worn on the shoulder of a tunic; in military use an epaulette is used to display a variety of information, including rank and unit.

Fatigues Clothing issued to be worn by military personnel when they are performing manual work or similar non-combat duties.

Field cap A soft form of headdress worn by soldiers on active service in place of a helmet.

Flintlock Pistol General term for any firearm based on the flintlock mechanism

Flying jacket A heavy, well-insulated jacket worn by pilots and other air crew to protect them from the freezing temperatures inside unheated aircraft at high altitudes.

Frog A device used to attach a sword or a bayonet to a belt.

Gaiters Covers for the ankles and lower legs, typically consisting of a sleeve of material that buttons or laces into place. Gaiters provide additional waterproofing and protect the legs from the terrain and surrounding foliage.

Gorget A crescent-shaped metal plate worn around the neck on a chain, and displaying the title of a certain office or duty.

GPMG Abbreviation of General-Purpose Machine Gun.

Greatcoat A large coat, made from a waterproofed wool, that entered into military use during the 19th century as a form of outer poor-weather clothing.

Insignia In military use, any system of symbol or marking that is used to denote authority, unit, formation, arm-of-service or similar organizational belonging.

Kepi A visored cap featuring a strong, cylindrical crown with a flat top, most commonly associated with the French Foreign Legion.

Khaki drill A type of uniform fabric used by the British armed forces from the beginning of the 20th century, and primarily applied to create tropical uniforms.

Lanyard In terms of uniforms, a lanyard is a cord worn around the neck and use to suspend items such as whistles, binoculars and pistols.

Mail A system of armour made by forming interconnected metal links into a flexible item of protective clothing.

Musket A smoothbore shoulder gun used from the late 16th through the 18th century.

MOLLE Abbreviation of 'Modular Lightweight Load-Carrying Equipment', a system of carrying personal equipment introduced into the US armed forces in the late 1990s.

NCO Non-commissioned officer.

Pea-coat A heavy woollen outer coat worn by naval personnel; pea-coats are generally double-breasted with large lapels and deep pockets.

Pelisse A long cloak or outer robe, usually of fur or with a fur lining.

Piping A fabric edging applied to the seams or edges of a garment; in military uniforms, the piping is often coloured to denote a particular arm of service or formation.

Puggree An Indian term for a turban.

Puttees Long fabric wrappings worn around the ankle and the lower leg, to protect those parts from the terrain.

Sahariana A light, comfortable khaki drill jacket designed (by the Italians) for tropical and desert use.

Service Dress The variety of uniform designed for wear on official duties but not on active service or in combat.

Shako A tall cylindrical military hat with a short visor; it generally features extensive ornamentation such as a metal regimental plate and a plume of animal hair, feathers or similar material.

Shelter-quarter An item of German WWII kit known as the Zeltbahn; it was a large section of waterproof fabric that could be worn as an improvised raincoat or buttoned together with other shelter-quarters to form tents or shelters.

Shoulder boards A flat cloth sleeve worn on a shoulder strap. The sleeve displays information about associations such as formation, arm of service or rank.

Side cap A simple soft cap, without a visor or brim, that can be folded up conveniently when removed. It is generally seen in garrison or ceremonial duties.

Slides Another name for shoulder boards.

SMLE Short-Magazine Lee Enfield (rifle).

Square rig A term applied to the familiar style of dress worn by naval ratings, which included, in navy blue or black, bell-bottomed trousers, pull-on tunic with coloured collar, coloured T-shirt and cylindrical cap.

Stand-and-fall collar A collar that rise up against the wearer's neck but folds back down again at the top.

Stand collar A collar that stands straight up against the wearer's neck (compare with 'stand-and-fall collar').

Walking-out dress An order of military uniform worn by personnel who are not on duty.

Webbing A strong fabric used to create load-carrying systems for military personnel; it largely replaced leather in this role.

Whites A white uniform worn by navies for tropical or, sometimes, ceremonial dress.

Index

Page numbers in *italics* refer to illustrations.

44

Picture Credits